The Unfinished Search for Common Ground

The Unfinished Search for Common Ground

Reimagining Howard Thurman's Life and Work

WALTER EARL FLUKER, EDITOR

ORBIS BOOKS
Maryknoll, New York 10545

Founded in 1970, Orbis Books endeavors to publish works that enlighten the mind, nourish the spirit, and challenge the conscience. The publishing arm of the Maryknoll Fathers and Brothers, Orbis seeks to explore the global dimensions of the Christian faith and mission, to invite dialogue with diverse cultures and religious traditions, and to serve the cause of reconciliation and peace. The books published reflect the views of their authors and do not represent the official position of the Maryknoll Society. To learn more about Maryknoll and Orbis Books, please visit our website at www.orbisbooks.com.

Copyright © 2023 by Walter Earl Fluker

Published by Orbis Books, Box 302, Maryknoll, NY 10545-0302.

All rights reserved.

No part of this publication may be reproduced or transmitted in any form or by any means, electronic or mechanical, including photocopying, recording, or any information storage or retrieval system, without prior permission in writing from the publisher.

Queries regarding rights and permissions should be addressed to: Orbis Books, P.O. Box 302, Maryknoll, NY 10545-0302.

Manufactured in the United States of America

Library of Congress Cataloging-in-Publication Data

Names: Fluker, Walter E., 1951– editor.
Title: The unfinished search for common ground : reimagining Howard Thurman's life and work / Walter Earl Fluker, editor.
Description: Maryknoll, New York : Orbis Books, [2023] | Includes bibliographical references and index. | Summary: "Howard Thurman scholars explore the life and work of the twentieth century Black theologian and spiritual writer"— Provided by publisher.
Identifiers: LCCN 2022051183 (print) | LCCN 2022051184 (ebook) | ISBN 9781626985117 (trade paperback) | ISBN 9781608339730 (epub)
Subjects: LCSH: Thurman, Howard, 1900-1981.
Classification: LCC BX6495.T53 U54 2023 (print) | LCC BX6495.T53 (ebook) | DDC 280/.4092—dc23/eng/20230117
LC record available at https://lccn.loc.gov/2022051183
LC ebook record available at https://lccn.loc.gov/2022051184

For Reverend Dr. James Earl Massey (1930–2018)
"How beautiful on the mountains are the feet of the messenger who
brings good news, the good news of peace and salvation" Isaiah 52:7 (NLT 2007)

Quiet counselor, wise guide, and disciplined literatus,
you leave a well-trodden path for the young runners who are coming!

Contents

Abbreviations ix

Howard Thurman: A Brief Chronology xi

Preface xiii
    The Long and Winding Road—
    Thirtieth Anniversary of the Howard Thurman Papers Project
        Walter Earl Fluker

Introduction 1
    The Unfinished Search for Common Ground
        Walter Earl Fluker

Part One

The Inner Life and World-Mindedness:
Spirituality and Social Transformation

1. Prophetic Vision and Its Radical Consequences 21
    Luther E. Smith Jr.

2. "I Can See It. Now, How to Say It?"
    Hearing the Aesthetic Dimension of Howard Thurman, the Interpreter 30
    Shively T. J. Smith

3. The Unfinished Search from Head to Heart:
    Howard Thurman's Crossroad Pedagogy 40
    Gregory C. Ellison II

4. From Prodigals to Good Samaritans:
    One Path to Common Ground in Howard Thurman's Life and Thought 50
    David B. Gowler

Part Two

Apostles of Sensitivity:
Ecclesial and Nonecclesial Communities and Interfaith Practices

5. Eccentric Apostles Leading from the Growing Edge 69
    Barbara Brown Taylor

6. Creating Little Islands of Goodwill and Fellowship in a Sea of Hatred 81
   Amanda K. Brown

7. Reimagining Howard Thurman's Use of Negro Spirituals and Hymnody 94
   W. James Abbington Jr.

8. Apostles of Sensitiveness:
   The Buddha Crown and Howard Thurman's Growing Edge 112
   Lobsang Tenzin Negi

9. Interreligious Hospitality:
   Howard Thurman and Zalman Schachter-Shalomi 124
   Or N. Rose

Part Three

America in Search of a Soul: Democratic Life and Practices

10. We Are Not Afraid: Howard Thurman and the Casting Out of Fear. 139
    Peter Eisenstadt

11. Howard Thurman, Democratic Life,
    and the Unfinished Search for Common Ground 157
    Paul Harvey

12. Free-Mindedness, Love, and Hope:
    Three Virtues for a Better Democratic Future 171
    Anthony Sean Neal

13. Howard Thurman: Strange Forms of Freedom 180
    Kipton Jensen

14. Creating and Cultivating Democratic Spaces:
    Reflections on Howard Thurman and Democracy 199
    Walter Earl Fluker

Acknowledgments and Editorial Note 221

About the Contributors 223

Index 229

Abbreviations

HT Howard Thurman

HTC Howard Thurman Collection, Howard Gotlieb Archival Research Center, Boston University, Boston, MA

PHWT Walter Earl Fluker, ed., *The Papers of Howard Washington Thurman*, volumes 1–5 (Columbia: University of South Carolina Press, 2009–19)

PITTS The Howard Thurman Digital Archive, Pitts Theology Library, Candler School of Theology, Emory University, Atlanta, GA

SCG Howard Thurman, *The Search for Common Ground: An Inquiry into the Basis of Man's Experience of Community* (Richmond, IN: Friends United Press, 1971, 1986)

SF Howard Thurman, *A Strange Freedom: The Best of Howard Thurman on Religious Experience and Public Life*, ed. Walter E. Fluker and Catherine Tumber (Boston: Beacon Press, 1998)

WHAH Howard Thurman, *With Head and Heart: The Autobiography of Howard Thurman* (New York: Harcourt Brace Jovanovich, 1979)

Howard Thurman: A Brief Chronology

1899	Born in Florida on November 19, raised in Daytona
1915–1919	Attends Florida Baptist Academy/Florida Normal and Industrial School in Jacksonville/St. Augustine
1919–1923	Attends Morehouse College, Atlanta
1923–1926	Attends Rochester Theological Seminary (Rochester, NY)
1926	Marries Katie Kelley; minister of Mount Zion Baptist Church, Oberlin, OH
1927	Daughter Olive is born
1928	Professor of religion, Morehouse and Spelman Colleges
1930	Katie Kelley dies
1932	Marries Sue Bailey; campus minister and professor of religion, Howard University
1935–1936	Chair of Negro Delegation on Pilgrimage of Friendship to South Asia
1944	Becomes co-pastor of Fellowship Church in San Francisco, pioneering interracial church
1949	Publishes *Jesus and the Disinherited*
1953	Becomes dean of chapel and professor of spiritual resources and disciplines at Boston University
1963	Travels to Africa, teaches at Ibadan University in Nigeria
1965	Retires from Boston University, returns to San Francisco, directs activity of Howard Thurman Education Trust
1971	Publishes *The Search for Common Ground*
1979	Publishes *With Head and Heart: The Autobiography of Howard Thurman*
1981	Dies on April 10

Preface

THE LONG AND WINDING ROAD

*Thirtieth Anniversary of the
Howard Thurman Papers Project*

Walter Earl Fluker

Silvia Glick, the former managing editor of the Howard Thurman Papers Project (HTPP), calls my journey with this work "the long and winding road."[1] "The long and winding road," and many fellow-travelers who accompanied me, have produced eight volumes thus far of Howard Thurman's writings, correspondence, speeches, lectures, and sermons, spanning sixty years of his life and work, including a digital edition: The Papers of Howard Washington Thurman (PHWT). PHWT has served as a critical resource for two biographies, an audio learning course, two film documentaries, dissertations, and numerous books, articles, and essays that continue to serve as reminders of Thurman's powerful legacy.[2] None of these would have been possible without the generous financial

---

[1] Silva P. Glick, "The Long and Winding Road: An Interview with Walter Earl Fluker," *Scholarly Editing: The Annual of the Association for Documentary Editing* 39, ed. Noelle Baker and Kathryn Tomasek (April 11, 2022).

[2] HT, SF; in PHWT, "My People Need Me, June 1918–March 1936," vol. 1 (2009); "Christian, Who Calls Me Christian?" April 1936–August 1943, vol. 2 (2012); "The Bold Adventure," September 1943–May 1949, vol. 3 (2015); "The Soundless Passion of a Single Mind," June 1949–December 1962, vol. 4 (2017); "The Wider Ministry," January 1963–April 1981, vol. 5; *Walking with God: The Sermon Series of Howard Thurman,* ed. Peter Eisenstadt and Walter Earl Fluker, *Moral Struggle and the Prophets*, vol. 1 (2020); *The Way of the Mystics*, vol. 2 (2021); *Democracy and the Soul of America*, vol. 3 (2022) (all Maryknoll, NY: Orbis Books). The fourth and final volume is in preparation. For biographies, see Paul Harvey, *Howard Thurman and the Disinherited: A Religious Biography* (Grand Rapids: Eerdmans, 2020); and Peter Eisenstadt, *Against the Hounds of Hell: A Life of Howard Thurman* (Charlottesville: University of Virginia Press, 2021). See also Quinton Dixie and Peter Eisenstadt, *Visions of a Better World* (Boston: Beacon Press, 2011); Amanda Brown, *The Fellowship Church: Howard Thurman and the Twentieth-Century Religious Left* (New York: Oxford University Press, 2021); Gary J. Dorrien, *The Making of American Liberal Theology: Idealism,*

and material support from the following contributors: the Lilly Endowment, the Louisville Institute, the Henry Luce Foundation, the Pew Charitable Trusts, the National Historical Publications and Records Commission, the National Endowment for the Humanities, Boston University Center for the Humanities, the Andrew W. Mellon Foundation, and a timely gift from the family of Virginia Scardigli, a close associate of Howard Thurman and secretary of the Fellowship Church.

I have shared in several places my journey with Thurman, beginning with my introduction to his meditations while serving as a chaplain's assistant in the US Army from 1971 to 1973.[3] One of my most memorable personal experiences with the wise old master was during my senior year at Garrett-Evangelical Theological Seminary. The school held a Howard Thurman Convocation in May 1979, hosted by its Church and Black Experience Program, and I, the fortunate student chaperone, was assigned to pick up our esteemed guest of honor at the airport and deliver him to his hotel. Instead, we spent the entire afternoon discussing *my* plans for the future. After that brief time together, Thurman and I exchanged letters regularly—I, always asking questions that he never quite answered—and he, smiling gently through his written words.

That last year in seminary was the hardest: I had to decide whether to pursue a PhD in religion or go another way. In the midst of this agonizing ordeal, I wrote a long letter to Thurman outlining my deepest fears and desires related to vocation. After what seemed a millennium, he replied in a two-page handwritten letter nearly impossible to decipher with doodles and tiny etchings in the margins. He suggested that my problem with choice was not for lack of opportu-

---

Realism, and Modernity, 1900–1950 (Louisville, KY: Westminster John Knox Press, 2003); Gregory C. Ellison II, ed., *Anchored in the Current: The Eternal Wisdom of Howard Thurman in a Changing World* (Louisville, KY: Westminster John Knox Press, 2020); and Larry Perry II, "The Undiscovered Thurman: The Early Howard Thurman and the Religious Left's Unfinished Business of Race Relations," PhD dissertation, University of Virginia, 2016, as examples of the emerging scholarship among scholars, activists, and practitioners interested in Thurman's relevancy for these times. For downloadable audio, see Liza Rankow, producer, *The Living Wisdom of Howard Thurman: A Visionary for Our Time*, Sounds True Audio Learning Course (Boulder, CO: Sounds True, 2010), https://www.soundstrue.com/products/the-living-wisdom-of-howard-thurman. The two film documentaries for which HTPP provided support are *Backs against the Wall: The Howard Thurman Story* (dir. Martin Doblmeier, 2019) and *The Psalm of Howard Thurman* (dir. Arleigh Prelow, in production), https://www.howardthurmanfilm.com/arleigh-prelow.

[3] Walter Earl Fluker, ed., "Biographical Essay," in PHWT, vol. 1; Walter Earl Fluker, "The Inward Sea: Mapping Interior Landmarks for Leaders," in *Anchored in the Current: The Eternal Wisdom of Howard Thurman in a Changing World*, ed. Gregory C. Ellison (Louisville, KY: Westminster John Knox Press, 2020); "Walter Fluker, Education Maker," *The History-Makers*, 2018, https://www.thehistorymakers.org/biography/walter-fluker.

nity but the converse, rather, I had many options. In his inimitable prose, laying out the choices with which I was struggling, and finally suggesting that whatever decision I made, "You must wait and listen for the sound of the genuine that is within you. When you hear it, that will be your voice and that will be the Voice of God." Over the years, many windswept days and trysting moments of the soul have visited me. These experiences were veritable crucibles of leadership where I had to decide whether to go forward with the work, leave it for another time, or release it to another set of hands more competent than mine; but that sound of the genuine held me and the various configurations of personnel steady and reinvigorated for the journey ahead.

Following *the sound*,[4] I chose in 1980 to enroll in the PhD program in social ethics at Boston University. Little did I know then that only one and a half years later, Thurman would pass on and his wife, Sue Bailey Thurman, would donate a large portion of his papers to BU. Eight years after that, I completed my dissertation, "A Comparative Analysis of the Ideal of Community in the Thought of Howard Thurman and Martin Luther King Jr."[5] and began a pastoral and teaching career that led me from St. John's Congregational Church in Springfield, Massachusetts, to Dillard University as dean of the chapel and assistant professor of religion, where I preached every Sunday in the Lawless Memorial Chapel that was dedicated by Thurman in 1955. In 1987, I was appointed an assistant professor of Christian ethics at Vanderbilt Divinity School, where I taught a regular seminar on Thurman and hosted the conference titled "America in Search of a Soul," a major convocation of scholars who studied the works of Thurman.

Through the generosity of Vanderbilt and the Mellon Faculty Fellowship, from 1989 to 1990 I spent an early sabbatical at Harvard College and the W. E. B. DuBois Institute for African and African American Research with the intention of returning to my earlier research on Thurman and King. My plans were altered, however, when I met James Melvin Washington, professor of church history at Union Theological Seminary, who encouraged me to apply for a grant to the Lilly Endowment to publish a few essays and sermons from the Thurman corpus. I continue to be amazed by the fated steps of those who have simple intentions. Little did I know then that our initial research would identify a universe of documents estimated at approximately fifty-eight thousand items

---

[4] For a conversation on Thurman's "sound of the genuine" and calling with Luther Smith, Gregory Ellison, and Walter Earl Fluker, see "Candler Black Excellence: Conversation on Howard Thurman," digital archive interview, Candler School of Theology, Emory University, October 25, 2021, https://candler.emory.edu/about/candler-black-excellence.html.

[5] The dissertation was published as Walter E. Fluker, *They Looked for a City: A Comparative Analysis of the Ideal of Community in the Thought of Howard Thurman and Martin Luther King Jr.* (Lanham, MD: University Press of America, 1989).

(111 linear feet) of correspondence, sermons, unpublished writings, and speeches of Thurman's vast documentary record. Jacqui Burton, religion program director of the Lilly Endowment, responded positively to my proposal, and in the fall of 1992 the Howard Thurman Papers Project was born.

During that year, I accepted a new academic post as Martin Luther King Jr. Memorial Professor of Theology and dean of black church studies at Colgate Rochester Divinity School (CRDS), where two projects were birthed. One was based on African American religious and moral traditions: The National Resource Center for the Development of Ethical Leadership from the Black Church Tradition, which was sponsored by a generous grant from the W. K. Kellogg Foundation; and the second, the Howard Thurman Papers Project. CRDS was the ideal place for launching these projects, serving as the seminary alma mater of Howard Thurman, '26 and Martin Luther King Jr. '51, and then home to the American Baptist Historical Society. The work performed by faculty, colleagues, researchers, students, and staff provided the necessary ingredients for the formation of the research and writing that would develop over the following years on Thurman, King, and ethical leadership.

I extend my special thanks to the late President James H. Evans for his support and patience during the early stages of HTPP and its many challenges and uncertain future. I am forever grateful to Catherine Tumber, who was completing a dissertation at the University of Rochester under historian and social critic Christopher Lasch, who joined me as associate editor and assistant director. Later assistant editors Peter Eisenstadt and Quinton Dixie, a student of James Washington, and a host of researchers and staff, most notably Michael Sauter and Candice Price, were hired as we began the work of collecting, assembling, selecting, transcribing, proofreading and annotating documents that would serve as the early database for what is now PHWT.

My dear friend and mentor, Luther E. Smith, has served as senior editorial consultant for the project since its inception. I shall never be able to express how important his generous scholarly labor and gentle and affirming personal grace guided me and the team over the years. This volume is a testament to his friendship and commitment to "the unfinished search for common ground." Two other very important intellectuals and historians provided counsel and assistance in these early stages of HTPP: Clayborne Carson, editor of the Martin Luther King Jr. Papers at Stanford University, and the inimitable Vincent Harding, the late Thurman aficionado and gallant warrior of the Black freedom struggle. Among others were members of the HTPP Advisory Board: the Thurman Family (Sue Bailey Thurman, Anne Spencer Thurman, Olive Thurman Wong, Anton Wong, and Suzanne Chiarenza), Marvin Chandler, Edward Kaplan, Mozella

G. Mitchell, Lerone Bennett, Otis Moss Jr., Peter J. Paris, Albert Raboteau, and Leslie S. Rowland.

Many others inspired and supported our work, but space does not allow for extensive commentary. Most memorable is the late James Earl Massey, who, until his death in 2018, would call regularly and inquire about the work and, most importantly, the state of my soul. This volume is dedicated to his memory.

In the spring of 1997, President Walter E. Massey extended an invitation to me to serve as a consultant and later as the first executive director of the Leadership Center at Morehouse College (renamed the Andrew Young Center for Global Leadership). I was also appointed as professor of religion and philosophy and later as the Coca-Cola Professor of Leadership Studies at that venerable institution. Morehouse was the undergraduate alma mater of both Thurman '23 and King '48.[6] While at Morehouse for nearly thirteen years, we completed both the physical building that housed the Leadership Center and the Howard Thurman Papers Project. I also taught courses on Thurman and King as the work of Thurman and ethical leadership reached national and global communities in Africa, Europe, and Asia. At the Leadership Center, their legacies served as critical resources in the development of curricular-driven strategies linking spirituality and ethics for the preparation of leaders at local, national, and international levels.

The HTPP editorial staff at Morehouse included many talented editors, researchers, and project assistants, among them JoAnn Lahmon and Martha Wiggins, who assisted in the transition from CRDS to Morehouse College and restructured the strategic processes of the project in its new home. Others followed, including Kai Issa Jackson, managing editor; Quinton Dixie and Peter Eisenstadt, now associate editors; and Luther E. Smith, continuing in his role as senior consulting editor. Consulting editors also included Alton P. Pollard, Clarissa Myrick-Harris, Alma Jean Billingslea, Laura-Eve Moss, and Carolyn Denard. Project assistants Paula Birth, Jamison Collier, and researchers LeRhonda Manigault, Josiah Robinson, Reginald Williams, Lauren Frazier, Jacqueline Forbes, Carey Gifford, Marquis Hwang, Yantee Neufville, and Warren Watson;

---

[6] The Center for Nonviolent Social Change, on historic Auburn Avenue next to the Ebenezer Baptist Church, houses the second-largest collection of King's papers and Morehouse College is home to King's personal library, correspondence from 1955 to 1961, and over eighty thousand items acquired through the auspices of then Mayor Shirley Franklin and her predecessor, Ambassador Andrew Young. In spring 2007 Morehouse College purchased the civil rights leader's personal library, correspondence from 1955 to 1961, and other precious artifacts, which are now at the Robert W. Woodruff Library at Atlanta University under the watch of Dr. Vicki Crawford of Morehouse College. I was privileged to serve as the first director of that collection.

Morehouse research assistants Malcolm Gossett, Brandon Jackson, and Nathaniel Johnson; and staff members Geri Oladuwa, LaKetha Hudson, J. Alisa James, Joyce Sheffield, Ruby Williams and scores of unnamed researchers and students were committed to the vision of HTPP that prepared the way for PHWT.

Interestingly, Thurman's and King's remains are both in Atlanta. Thurman's ashes are entombed in a huge obelisk erected in his honor at Morehouse College, and King's remains are at the MLK Center for Nonviolent Social Change. On the plaza of Morehouse College's Martin Luther King, Jr. International Chapel are two monuments, a towering obelisk dedicated to the memory of Howard and Sue Bailey Thurman and a huge statue of Martin Luther King Jr. pointing to the future. During my first year on the Morehouse campus, I stood one morning between these two monuments and realized my work had come full circle—from San Francisco to Boston University to Colgate Rochester and back to Morehouse, where it all began.

I was prepared to settle in at Morehouse and perhaps find a pastorate or expand my work in ethical leadership, but the ghosts of King and Thurman led me to the office of the newly appointed dean of the School of Theology (STH) during the summer of 2009, where I met with Mary Elizabeth Moore. When she announced that the Martin Luther King Jr. Chair was open, I felt again the polite urgings from *the sound*. Returning to the place of origins of my research and scholarship was fantastical, mystical, extraordinary, and fated. It was as if I had completed another spiral in a circular journey—a coming home. To be named the Martin Luther King Jr. Chair at my alma mater was to be initiated into a long line of pioneers who had prepared the way: Preston N. Williams, Gayraud Wilmore, John Henderson Cartwright, Praithia Hall Wynn, Chai-sik Chung, and Dale Andrews. I counted it a blessing to return to the place where I studied under Professor John Henderson Cartwright and where my academic career was launched. I would also have access to the largest collections of Martin Luther King Jr. and Howard Thurman material at the Howard Gotlieb Archival Research Center under the leadership of Bonavita Paladino and her wonderful staff: Sean Noble, Ryan Hendrickson, Laura Russo, Margaret Goosetray, and Charles Niles.

It was an experience of wonderment to be in a space where these titans of the spiritual and moral struggle for the soul of America had studied, taught, preached, and nurtured a dream that King called "the beloved community" and Thurman called "the search for common ground." I sought to be faithful to their visions of courage, justice, and compassion in my teaching, research, and writings. I am so grateful for the students, faculty colleagues at STH and throughout the university, the alumni/ae, the administration, and the staff who supported my work, which I hope has brought honor to its great tradition of learning, virtue, and piety. I miss those precious relationships, but I continue to find ways to be a part of the great company and cloud of witnesses that bear the mantle of "The School of the Prophets."

While contemplating retirement from Boston University, I received an invitation from Dean Jan Love to serve as the Alonzo L. McDonald Family Chair on the Life and Teachings of Jesus and Their Impact on Culture at Candler School of Theology at Emory University in Atlanta during 2018 and 2019. Later, I was invited to join the Candler faculty as the Dean's Professor of Spirituality, Ethics and Leadership. Candler is not a stranger to Howard Thurman, being home to Thurman scholars Luther E. Smith and Gregory Ellison II. Mozella Mitchell completed her dissertation there, later published as *The Spiritual Dynamics of Howard Thurman's Theology*. Candler is also home to The Howard Thurman Digital Archive at Pitts Theology Library that highlights materials related to Thurman's life, particularly audio recordings of his sermons, speeches, lectures, and interviews. Candler was an appropriate site for the 2022 conference "The Unfinished Search for Common Ground," where most of the essays in this volume were first presented.

Last but never least, I owe everything to my lifelong companion and spouse, Sharon Watson Fluker, goddaughter to Sue Bailey and Howard Thurman. Thurman speaks for me in an autographed copy of *Jesus and the Disinherited* for "Michelle" as she is fondly called: "To the apple of my eyes."

Introduction

THE UNFINISHED SEARCH FOR COMMON GROUND

Walter Earl Fluker

"In quietness and confidence shall be your strength."
Long before I was born God was at work.
Creating life, nature and the world of men and things.
The worlds were ideas in the mind of God
That have been realizing themselves through the ages.
God is not through with creation—
God is not through with me.

—Howard Thurman[1]

An "unfinished search" is a linguistic conundrum. To search implies that something is "unfinished," incomplete," or "ongoing." So why pin this tautological error to Thurman's "search for common ground"? First, the search for common ground is a rather general, hackneyed label for all things that need a shared linguistic repository in situations where there are conflicts of interests, opinions, and aggressions that require some premise from which to proceed in rational argumentation (e.g., political compromises, contested social issues, or even in the more grave and weightier contexts of negotiation and diplomacy among nations). One might say, for instance, that the United States' and China's search for peaceful coexistence or common ground is unfinished. In this sense, the process of seeking common ground is pragmatic, transactional (quid pro quo), and temporary because the proposed solutions and treatises that ensue are products of the tenuous interplay of power where the grounds of compromise are always

---

[1] HT, "Quietness and Confidence," in *Deep Is the Hunger: Meditations for Apostles of Sensitiveness* (New York: Harper and Brothers, 1951), 211.

shifting and therefore need deliberation, adaptation, revision, and reimagining. I am using the "unfinished search for common ground" in Howard Thurman partly in this sense. Thurman was not a stranger to conflict and aggression. In fact, he believed that "No understanding of the significance of community can escape the place and significance of aggression."[2] Therefore, he argued that those committed to the actualization of community must acknowledge the role of conflict as an essential element in the creation of a just and loving society. For this reason, he believed that democracy, at its best, is a squabble, a contentious exchange of ideas, opinions, values, and practices within the context of civil relations because "this is the kind of world that is grounded in creativity; that is essentially dynamic; that potentials are an important part of any present consideration or predicament."[3]

Thurman's teaching and ministerial positions as professor, pastor, and university chaplain, and his later work with the Howard Thurman Educational Trust Fund served as spiritual and intellectual laboratories in which his vision of community could be tested, revised, and reimagined.[4] Yet his creative search for common ground went beyond utilitarian calculi, measurable outcomes, and efficiency that mock the fall of modernity in neoliberal projects where *winners take all*.[5] With the rise of religious activism in the nation's highest court and the rampant rage and violence incited by Christian nationalism, Thurman's religious search for "democratic space," especially at this moment in the history of this nation and the globe, should be given equal par with social, political, and global contestations that seek common ground because the potential consequences of failing to do so could be devastating.[6]

I am also interested in "common ground" qua Thurman, as a religious or spiritual quest for knowledge of Presence, integrity, freedom, responsibility, love,

---

[2] HT, SCG, 90; HT, "Mysticism and Ethics," *Journal of Religious Thought* 27, no. 2 (Summer Supplement): 23.

[3] HT, "A Faith to Live By: Democracy and the Individual 1," Fellowship Church, October 19, 1952, in HT, *Democracy and the Soul of America*, ed. Peter Eisenstadt and Walter Earl Fluker (Maryknoll, NY: Orbis Books, 2022), 74–82.

[4] SCG is a philosophical exposition of the nature of community where he interrogates the basis and sources of community and seeks an understanding of its meaning within the context of the struggles between the civil rights movement and the rise of Black nationalism. See also his "Convocation Address," Pittsburgh Theological Seminary, November 1971, in *Perspectives, A Journal of Pittsburgh Theological Seminary* 13, no. 2 (Spring 1972), https://archive.org/stream/perspective19721973pitt/perspective19721973pitt_djvu.txt; and HT, "Community and the Will of God," Mendenhall Lecture, DePauw University, February 1961 (a series of unpublished lectures), HTC, Box 8, Folder 7:6a.

[5] Anand Giridharadas, *Winners Take All: The Elite Charade of Changing the World* (New York: Knopf, 2018).

[6] See my essay in the present volume titled "Creating and Cultivating Democratic Spaces: Reflections on Howard Thurman and Democracy."

and imagination.⁷ Thurman's vision of common ground is profoundly religious and metaphysical. On the one hand, it is incomplete, *arriving* but never quite finished. Yet he believed, paradoxically, that there was an end, a *telos*, an omega point in which common ground would be fulfilled in time and history. He often quoted the prophet Isaiah, that finally, "The earth will be full of the knowledge of the LORD as the waters cover the sea."⁸ Luther Smith, in his excellent essay published in this volume, writes, "Thurman does not pretend to be a seer who knows if this will occur soon or in one thousand or ten thousand years. But he does believe in a time of finality. We may argue with him about this common ground conclusion. I certainly do. From my personal experiences with him, I believe Howard Thurman would welcome the debate."⁹

In this introduction, I join Smith, Thurman, and others in this debate. I believe that Thurman's search for common ground is unfinished and that however we resolve the apparent contradictions or paradoxes, we are nonetheless summoned by him to continue the search that he has bequeathed to us in his voluminous writings, sermons, and public addresses. Our work is not to accept at face value his claims of "common ground" as an essentialist project that is embedded in modernistic language and paradigms that he also struggled to reimagine for his time.¹⁰ I refer here to the ways in which the misappropriation of common ground can be a foil for the ways in which the democratic ideal of "the radical egalitarian hypothesis" has masqueraded—and continues to masquerade—as a shape-shifting national imaginary of a nonracial, colorblind society while the economic, political, and social situations of the poor of all colors and creeds progressively deteriorate.¹¹ Therefore our task is, in some respects, a harder and more complex challenge to seek new and fresh meanings

---

⁷ Walter Earl Fluker, "The Inward Sea: Mapping Interior Landmarks for Leaders," in *Anchored in the Current: The Eternal Wisdom of Howard Thurman in a Changing World*, ed. Gregory C. Ellison (Louisville, KY: Westminster John Knox Press, 2020), 55–70.

⁸ Isaiah 9:11, New American Standard Bible.

⁹ Luther E. Smith, "Prophetic Vision and Its Radical Consequences," in this volume.

¹⁰ Victor Anderson, *Beyond Ontological Blackness: An Essay on African-American Religious and Cultural Criticism* (New York: Continuum, 1995), 38–50, 80–81, and 159; see also Victor Anderson, *Creative Exchange: A Constructive Theology of African American Religious Experience* (Minneapolis: Fortress Press, 2008), chapter 4, "The Smell of Life: A Pragmatic Theology of Religious Experience," esp. 113–15. I have suggested in another place that we might experiment with Thurman's modernistic liberal language of common ground as a call to *congregate, conjure,* and *conspire* in *commons. Commons* is a reereading of HT's common ground that can be reconfigured and translated into *common loyalties and commitments to justice and peace*. Walter Earl Fluker, *The Ground Has Shifted: The Black Church in Post-Racial America* (New York: New York University Press, 2016), 85–96.

¹¹ For a more fully developed argument along these lines, see Fluker, *The Ground Has Shifted*.

from his magnificent architectonic of common ground. As he often quoted from Hermann Hagedorn, "We died, but you who live must do a harder thing than dying is, for you must think and ghosts shall drive you on."[12]

Thurman's Unfinished Search

A key theme in Thurman was his intensely personal understanding of community, in which he saw himself as both subject and object in a parabolic journey toward community.[13] Thurman reflects in his autobiography on a "watershed moment" at an informal retreat in 1925 in Pawling, New York, where he encountered the South African writer Olive Schreiner for the first time. George "Shorty" Collins read her allegory of "The Hunter,"[14] a searcher after truth, who while hunting for wild fowl caught a glimpse of a reflection in a lake of an elusive, "vast white bird, with silver wings outstretched, sailing in the everlasting blue." The hunter was so struck by this reflection that he spent the rest of his life searching for another glimpse of her. After traveling through numerous mountains and valleys of "beliefs, immortality, realism, sensuality, negation and the dark night of the soul," his white hair, feeble frame, and shrunken face revealed the torturous paths and incredible sacrifices made in his quest for one more glimpse of this beautiful creature. Schreiner writes, "The old, thin hands cut the stones ill and jaggedly, for the fingers were stiff and bent. The beauty and the strength of the man was gone." In his last breath, the Hunter cries out,

> "I have sought," he said, "for long years I have laboured; but I have not found her. I have not rested, I have not repined, and I have not seen her; now my strength is gone. Where I lie down worn-out others will stand, young and fresh. By the steps that I have cut they will climb; by the stairs that I have built they will mount. They will never know the name of the man who made them. At the clumsy work they will laugh; when the stones roll, they will curse me. But they will mount, and on my work; they will climb, and by my stair! They will find her, and through me! And no man liveth to himself and no man dieth to himself.... My soul

---

[12] A favorite quote of HT's, which he used in a variety of settings. See Hermann Hagedorn (1882–1964), "The Boy in Armor," in *Ladders through the Blue: A Book of Lyrics* (Garden City, NY: Doubleday, 1925), 59–61.

[13] Mozella Gordon Mitchell, *Spiritual Dynamics of Howard Thurman's Theology* (Bristol, IN: Wyndham Hall Press, 1985), 51.

[14] Olive Schreiner, "The Hunter," in *A Track to the Water's Edge: The Olive Schreiner Reader*, ed. HT (New York: Harper and Row, 1973), 84–95. George "Shorty" Collins was a lifelong friend and colleague of HT's. See HT, PHWT 1:lix.

hears their glad step coming," he said; "and they shall mount! they shall mount!" He raised his shrivelled hand to his eyes.

Then slowly from the white sky above, through the still air, came something falling, falling, falling. Softly it fluttered down and dropped on to the breast of the dying man. He felt it with his hands. It was a feather. *He died holding it.*

Thurman's personal quest for truth, "the search for common ground," is mirrored in this allegory, but it is not his search alone. His religious search for common ground was *unfinished* because it was rooted in the spiraling dance of the God of Life who is always on "the hunt," always seeking actualization within and beyond the time-space continuum of nature, people, and things.[15] Thurman's biography—from his earliest explorations of the sense of Presence while hunting in the lonely woods, caressing the mystery and comfort of dark Florida nights, fishing in the Halifax River and meditating under his old oak tree, to his lifelong quest to create and sustain religious and democratic spaces where individuals and collectives might share common consciousness—was part of a *double-search*.[16] Those high moments of resolve and the possibilities inherent in this double-search were fraught with the ambiguities and contingencies of history and time—never quite arriving but always yearning for completion, wholeness, and harmony. His experiments at Rankin Chapel at Howard University, Fellowship Church in San Francisco, and Marsh Chapel at Boston University are examples of the attendant challenges of achieving common ground through religious experience in the institutional settings of churches and universities. Each of these sites of ecclesial and nonecclesial practices had its "fresh starts, its false starts, its rising and its falling."[17] Yet for him they were signals of what is at stake in the mystic's quest for knowledge of and union with God, and illustrations of his firm hope that common ground would come to pass "somewhere, sometime, someplace—even on earth."[18]

---

[15] HT uses the metaphor of a hawk circling in a hunt from the poet Robinson Jeffers in the opening paragraph of SCG. The poet asks, "Why does God hunt in circles? Has he lost something? Is it possible—himself? In the darkness between the stars did he lose himself and become godless, and seeks—himself?" Robinson Jeffers, "The Inhumanist," stanza I (Stanford University Press, 1991), 256. Quoted in HT, SCG, 1.

[16] See Fluker, "Creating and Sustaining Democratic Spaces"; HT, *The Creative Encounter: An Interpretation of Religion and the Social Witness* (Richmond, IN: Friends United Press, 1972), 39; Rufus Jones, *The Double Search* (Philadelphia: J. C. Winston Co., 1904), 6.

[17] HT, "America in Search of a Soul," January 20, 1976, University of Redlands, Redlands, California, in SF, 265–72. Also in HT, *Democracy and the Soul of America*, 114–124.

[18] HT, "Mysticism and Social Change," February 13–16, 1939, Eden Theological

Before his death on April 10, 1981, Thurman was still in pursuit of his early investigations of the larger question of particularity and universality and how these were related to his own personal quest to "find God" in authentic religious experience.[19] Finding God, for Thurman, speaks to the dynamic interplay between infinity and finitude, and his personal acknowledgment during his last days that there is a "nonspatial and nontemporal dimension of my personality that has to do with life and is not bound by death,"[20] because the contradictions of life are not final.

There are two events in his last days where he speaks openly of his unfinished search for God. One was at the Interdenominational Theological Center (ITC) in Atlanta, Georgia, in 1978, where I was in attendance.[21] In his distinct and mesmerizing cadence, he spoke about the mystery of life and death and the "double-search, the hunt" for his elusive God. He indicated that he had questions for God that were unanswered. In language reminiscent of the epigraph in his autobiography, "Always we are on the outside of our story, always we are beggars who seek entrance to the kingdom of our dwelling place."[22] In his last dramatic sentences, after a long, silent, waiting moment with his hands folding and unfolding in prayer-fashion, trying to grasp the elusive meaning that haunted him, he exclaimed to his breathless audience, "I shall find Him—how long I do not know—but I shall find Him somewhere under the old oak tree."[23]

Seminary, St. Louis, Missouri, in PHWT 2:190; see also Olive Schreiner, "The Dawn of Civilization," *The Nation and the Athenaeum*, March 26, 1921, 912–14.

[19] HT, "Finding God" (1927), in PHWT 1:110–14; HT, "The Perils of Immature Piety" (1925), in PHWT 1:47–51.

[20] Peter Eisenstadt, *Against the Hounds of Hell: A Life of Howard Thurman* (Charlottesville: University of Virginia Press, 2021), 390; HT, "'Concluding Chapter' Head and Heart" (unpublished draft), HTC, Box 4, Folder 1–4.

[21] The author has not been able to locate the proceedings of this conference that took place in fall 1978. The conference organizer was the late Reverend Dr. Ndugu G. B. T'Ofori-Atta (aka George B. Thomas), Professor Emeritus of Persons, Society and Culture at ITC and a devotee of Howard Thurman. The conference included an array of speakers, including Vincent Harding.

[22] "Always we are on the outside of our story, always we are beggars who seek entrance to the kingdom of our dwelling place. When we are admitted, the price that is exacted of us is the sealing of our lips. And this is the strangest of all the paradoxes of the human adventure: we live inside all experience, but we are permitted to bear witness only to the outside. Such is the riddle of life and the story of the passing of our days." HT, WHAH, 270.

[23] See Shively T. J. Smith's essay in this volume, where she examines Thurman's interpretive quest and raises the critical issue of imagination as an aesthetic vehicle into Thurman's own passionate and personal hermeneutical imagining as "a conundrum of interpretation and articulation that ... we miss if we do not ask, 'How does Thurman search for common ground?'"

The other occasion was the recording of an audio during his hospitalization at Mt. Zion Hospital in San Francisco in the spring of 1981.[24] I was privileged to listen to the tape along with Reverend Marvin Chandler, former pastor of the Fellowship Church and former executive director of the Howard Thurman Educational Fund, and Thurman's daughter, Anne Spencer Thurman. According to them, Thurman, who was suffering from the debilitating effects of cancer, respiratory deterioration, and a ruptured appendix, went into crisis and they thought he had died. They sat at his bedside mourning his passing when suddenly Thurman awakened and returned from what he called "the fight that I was having with death."[25] Startled, but with prescience of mind, they asked him to share what he experienced and then recorded his response. Thurman indicated that he was traveling through the universe in search of God, and that he had two questions that he wanted to ask: "Why is there black and white?" and "Why is there male and female?" During this encounter, Thurman declared to the Creator of Life and existence, "I am going to follow you through the ends of existence until you give me an answer to these questions."[26]

This was not the only occasion where these questions for God were raised. American author and philosopher Sam Keen reports that in an intimate meeting with Thurman two weeks before his death, he asked similar questions: "Why was I born a black man and you a white man? What in the universal way of things required me to be the particular person that I am?" Then Thurman whispered to Keen, "Why should the ultimate secret of my life be kept from me?"[27]

His beloved companion, Sue Bailey Thurman, commented in several places on the "psychic trauma" of Thurman's inward struggle with particularity and universality that lasted until his final days. She says that during his aforementioned hospital stay, "he stayed the hand of death while he encountered 'the particular man' and the 'universal man' within himself and wrestled them to earth, until he won the consent of both—to Life, to Death, and Back to Life."[28]

---

[24] I was fortunate to read a transcript of his reflections on this experience prepared by Joyce Sloane, librarian of the HT Trust. "Howard Thurman's Last Reflections: Howard Thurman Talking to Joyce Sloane about His Hospital Experience, April 3, 1981." Unpublished.

[25] "I did not know what death was about and I wanted to know who or what was responsible.... And I was determined to bird dog it throughout all the universe." Ibid.

[26] Ibid.

[27] Eisenstadt, *Against the Hounds of Hell*, 390–91. See also Sam Keen, "Memorial Tribute," in *Debate and Understanding*, "Simmering on the Calm Presence and Profound Wisdom of Howard Thurman" (special issue), ed. Ricardo A. Millet and Conley H. Hughes (Spring 1982): 90.

[28] Sue Bailey Thurman, "Epilogue," in "Simmering on the Calm Presence and Profound Wisdom of Howard Thurman," 91.

Revisiting Thurman's Common Ground

Thurman's use of "common ground" proceeds from his theological and philosophical conceptualization of "community" and his personal wrestling with the moral demands of religious experience. Beyond its utilitarian functionality, Thurman saw common ground as a transcendent ideal that calls us to seek wholeness, integration, and harmony within our private lives and in public discourse and practice. He believed that all life is interrelated and involved in goal-seeking, and therefore, in each manifestation of life, there is the potential for it to realize its proper form, or to come to itself; but in coming to itself, it shares in the ongoing cycle of life, death, and rebirth. Life itself is always *unfinished*. This, for him, is the dynamic character of the interrelatedness and interdependence inherent in all living things, at microscopic levels of existence, and in human society—never quite arriving but always giving way to "the growing edge"—the new, that which is not yet, but is becoming.[29]

For Thurman, life's "capacity to begin again" is a theological supposition that the mind of God realizes itself in time.[30] The origin and goal of community, therefore, is in the mind of God, which is coming to Godself in time—and perhaps even God is revealing Godself *to* Godself in myriad time and space variations that yearn for wholeness, integration, and harmony.[31] But for Thurman, this process is not a thing or merely an idea; it is profoundly personal. "When I refer to God, I am not talking about a thing, I am not talking about an object: I am talking about a Presence." Thurman's God is not only the creator of life but is the source of the "living stuff" of existence out of which every living thing is fashioned, and exists outside of its particular manifestations, so that "God bottoms existence—bottoms it—bottoms it!" It is through "disciplines of the spirit" (he names these disciplines at various places as detachment, commitment, prayer, growth, suffering, and reconciliation) that a fluid area of awareness of Presence emerges for the individual, so that experiences of union in divine and human encounter occur in episodic "for instances" of newness, openness, and vitality. These occasions for coming home to oneself and discovering that God is also part of "the *borning* process"—that is, God is longing to become "self-conscious" like a spring that "spills over in time and space, therefore when the Godhead which is at the core of me spills over in my time-space relationships, at least I can say that wherever such a person is there the

---

[29] See Barbara Brown Taylor's essay in this volume.

[30] Nimi Wariboko, *The Pentecostal Principle: Ethical Methodology in New Spirit*, Pentecostal Manifestos (Grand Rapids: Eerdmans, 2012), 1, 48–50.

[31] See HT, "Mysticism and Social Change: God as Presence," July 12, 1978, Pacific School of Religion, in *Walking with God: The Sermon Series of Howard Thurman: The Way of the Mystics,* ed. Peter E. Eisenstadt and Walter Earl Fluker (Maryknoll, NY: Orbis Books, 2021), 121–40.

kingdom of God is at hand." Thurman admits that when he uses the formal names of "Creator" and "God," he is aware of the anthropomorphic description of deity and its inherent limitations and paradoxes. He chooses this language because he feels it is impossible to think of action or agency as abstraction and that the mind can only make sense of this complexity by using symbols.[32]

This religious dimension of community is fundamental for all his theological and ethical claims. The nature of the problem of community is rooted in the relationship of the individual to social existence. While the primacy of the individual is a major concern for Thurman, his ultimate vision is of a harmonious human society. Life, in this sense, is a dynamic, ongoing project. God is at work in creation in a manner akin to an artist shaping and reshaping their masterpiece. God is not finished with creation, and consequently, God is not finished with the human story, which is ever unfolding and coming to itself in time and history. Similarly, personality is an unfinished project involving the individual in relation to God in a concerted endeavor of free and responsible acts that issue forth in human and nonhuman flourishing rooted in "common consciousness." Common consciousness is the unique, essential element that human beings share with all of life in its varied and manifold expressions. It is the veritable creative presence of the Spirit of God that moves undisguised and uninhibited beneath all the complex and intricate stories that mark conscious existence. It finds its residence in human consciousness through cultivated disciplines that allow for the development of habits and practices that make moral life possible. At the heart of these disciplines, and the aim of the human quest, is the experience of love.[33] This understanding of "common consciousness" is fundamental to Thurman's understanding of religious experience and the role of imagination.[34]

---

[32] Ibid. See also HT, SCG, 5–6. He is comfortable in using a variety of symbols or names to point to what is always behind human thought and comprehension. "You may say truth; you may say the supreme good. I don't care. That is not my affair. But to me it is God." HT, "The Meaning of Loyalty III: The State," May 20, 1951, in *Democracy and the Soul of America*, 32. Thurman's use of "borning" is a reference to Meister Eckhart's idea of the *eternal birth*. See *The Complete Mystical Works of Meister Eckhart: Sermons and Treatises*, vol. 1, trans. and ed. Maurice O'C. Walshe (New York: Crossroad, 2008), Sermon 1, 29–38; HT, "Meister Eckhart," in *The Way of the Mystics*, 82–90; HT, "Men Who Walked with God: The Great Hunger," in *Walking with God*, 93–101; and HT, *Jesus and the Disinherited* (Boston: Beacon Press, 1996).

[33] "Common consciousness" refers to the affinity between human consciousness and other forms of conscious existence evident in nature. For Thurman, the theme of the kinship of all living things extends even into the realm of communication between animals, plants, and human beings. He reasons that if life is one, then there ought to be a sense of unity at all levels of existence. Since life in any form cannot be fundamentally alien to life, then more than two forms may share the same moment in time without resistance and without threat. See HT, "Convocation Address," Pittsburgh Theological Seminary, and SG, 57.

[34] Walter E. Fluker, *They Looked for a City: A Comparative Analysis of the Ideal of*

Religious Experience and the Moral Imagination

For Thurman, imagination is related to "spirit."[35] But spirit is not disassociated from the body—in fact, the search begins *with* the body. The body is the individual's unique dwelling place and "home," and every person "lives under the necessity for being at home in their own house."[36] He suggests that the "mind *as* mind" evolved from the body as part of the unfolding process of potential resident in life, and that mind as such is the basis for the evolution of "spirit." The imagination as "mind-evolved spirit" continued the same inherent quest for community that is resident in nature and the body.[37] When an individual consciously seeks community, therefore, he or she will discover "what he is seeking deliberately is but the logic of meaning that has gone into his creation."[38]

Thurman often spoke of this experience as "listening for the sound of the genuine." "There is something within each of us," says Thurman, "which waits and listens for the sound of the genuine within oneself and within the other."[39] This something, this undifferentiated level of being, is the seat of common consciousness. The sound of the genuine involves imagination. For Thurman, imagination is a constituent part of being, and it becomes a veritable *angelos* when persons put themselves in another's place. Imagination, in this sense, is the agency through which empathy is realized. Through imagination, the individual is enabled to reach the other at the core of their being, at the seat of "common consciousness." This occurs when one person becomes for the other what is needed and when the need is most urgently and acutely felt.[40] In doing so, the other is addressed at a

---

Community in the Thought of Howard Thurman and Martin Luther King Jr. (Lanham, MD: University Press of America, 1989). See the discussion of love as ethical principle in the actualization of community in chapter 3.

[35] Luther Smith captures this idea of "spirit" as the "breath of God" in creation, providing value and meaning to existence. He writes, "Realizing and expressing itself in the material world, the work of the spirit is historical and political. It is the source for the definition of the individual, and the individual in relationship to the collective. As it discerns self, it discerns God and what it means to be a creature of God.... Spirituality is a way of life committed to understanding the nature and urgings of the spirit; the life organizes all its desires, energies, and resources so that they might be dominated by the spirit. Spirituality brings a harmony to living consistent with the peace and will of God." Luther E. Smith, *The Mystic as Prophet* (Richmond, IN: Friends United Press, 2007), 12.

[36] HT, *Deep Is the Hunger*, 195; HT, *The Luminous Darkness: A Personal Interpretation of the Anatomy of Segregation and the Ground of Hope* (1965; repr., Richmond, IN: Friends United Press, 1989), 101.

[37] HT, Mendenhall Lecture, "Community and the Will of God," February 1961, 1, HTC.

[38] HT, SCG, 34.

[39] HT, "The Sound of the Genuine: Baccalaureate Address, Spelman College, May 4, 1980," *Spelman Messenger* 96, no. 4 (Summer 1980).

[40] HT, *The Inward Journey* (New York: Harper and Row, 1961); paperback ed. (Rich-

place beyond all that is blameworthy or praiseworthy. This, according to Thurman, is the experience of love: when a person is addressed at the centermost place of personality, experiencing wholeness and harmony within and with the other:

> I see you where you are striving and struggling and in light of the highest possibility of your personality, I deal with you there. My religious faith is insistent that this can be done only out of a life of devotion. I must cultivate the inner spiritual resources of my life to such a point that I can bring you to my sanctuary before his presence, until, at last, I do not know you from myself.[41]

The Unfinished Search and Moral Imagination in Public Life

Thurman's unfinished "search for common ground" between diverse groups finds creative resonance at this critical impasse of American and world history.[42] With increasing tensions of race, class, gender, sexuality, and the concomitant need to carve a fresh and critical approach to the often violent usages of religious discourse as warrants for moral action, Thurman's gentle wisdom and clear analytic provides a resource for a religiously inspired public ethic that does not fall prey to parochialism and the politics of division. He often suggested that "A parochial religious experience cannot sustain a universal ethic."[43] In fact, part of

---

mond, IN: Friends United Press, 1971), 121, 130, 133, 139–55; HT, *Mysticism and the Experience of Love* (Wallingford, PA: Pendle Hill Pamphlet 115, 1961), 21.

[41] HT, *The Growing Edge* (New York: Harper and Row, 1956); paperback ed. (Richmond, IN: Friends United Press, 1974), 27–28.

[42] Darrell J. Fasching, "Holy Man for the Coming Millennium," in *The Human Search: Howard Thurman and the Quest for Freedom: Proceedings of the Second Annual Thurman Convocation*, Martin Luther King Jr. Memorial Studies in Religion, Culture and Social Development, Volume 2, Mozella G. Mitchell, ed. (New York: Peter Lang, 1992), 191–203; Jan Corbett, "Howard Thurman: A Theologian for Our Times," *American Baptist Quarterly*, December 1979, 9–12; Lerone Bennett, "Howard Thurman: Twentieth Century Holy Man," *Ebony*, February 1978, 68–70, 72, 76, 84–85; John D. Mangram, "Jesus Christ in Howard Thurman's Thought," in *Common Ground: Essays in Honor of Howard Thurman on the Occasion of His Seventy-Fifth Birthday, November 18, 1975*, ed. Samuel Lucius Gandy (Washington, DC: Hoffman Press, 1975), 65; J. Deotis Roberts, "The American Negro's Contribution to Religious Thought," in *The Negro Impact on Western Civilization*, ed. John Slabey Roucek and Thomas Kiernan (New York: Philosophical Library, 1970), 87. See also Martin Marty, "Mysticism and the Religious Quest for Freedom," in *God and Human Freedom*, ed. Henry J. Young (Richmond, IN: Friends United Press, 1983).

[43] Walter Earl Fluker, "Leaders Who Have Shaped U.S. Religious Dialogue: Howard Thurman: Intercultural and Interreligious Leader," in *Religious Leadership: A Reference Handbook*, vol. 2, ed. Sharon Henderson Callahan (Thousand Oaks, CA: Sage, 2013), 574.

Thurman's broad appeal is that while he is properly located within the African American Christian tradition, he is not in the least limited to it. Nor is Thurman's theology limited to Christian categories per se. Instead, he believed that

> The things that are true in any religious experience are to be found in that religious experience precisely because they are true; they are not true simply because they are found in that religious experience.... Around any road, at any turning, a man may come upon the burning bush and hear the Voice saying, "Take off your shoes because the place where you are now standing is a holy place, even though you did not know it before."[44]

Therefore, his perspective provides a broad basis for interreligious dialogue and illustrates the profundity of his ministry with respect to social justice, ecclesial and nonecclesial spaces, and the American democratic experiment.[45]

At stake in the search for common ground is the place of personal and private identity. Thurman was highly critical of the spurious distinction between knowledge and values that erodes personal identity and severely impairs public discourse. He consistently warned of the danger of promoting a parochial view of knowledge at the expense of the private life of the individual. The obfuscation of individuality was, for him, a key problematic of the epistemic validation of claims to authority and meaning in a pluralistic culture. The quest for authority in the public sphere was at once a quest for personal assurance and security that are provided for the individual through religious experience, but not a narrow vision of religious interpretation that restricted the freedom of choice toward unsavory political ends that impede human and nonhuman flourishing.[46]

For Thurman, the normative character of speech and action should be guided by what one experiences at the innermost place of oneself and in community with others. Consequently, the ethical life is not informed exclusively on autonomous nor heteronomous bases, but by a religious core that is the private domain of the individual. Yet this private domain is neither exclusive nor ahistorical but rooted in a relational ethic that finds its validation in public speech and action anchored in freedom and equality. This perspective was important for Thurman because he

---

[44] HT, WHAH, 120.

[45] See essays by Geshi Lobsang Tenzin Negi and Or N. Rose in this volume.

[46] "Individuality" for Thurman is not be to confused with the Western notion of "individualism," which portrays the person as a discrete entity, unrelated to community; individuality rather is a profound dimension of human development and personality. See "Mysticism and Social Change," where he insists that the mystic "discovers that he is a person and a personality in a profound sense can only be achieved in a milieu of human relations. Personality is something more than mere individuality—it is a fulfillment of the logic of individuality in community." PHWT 2:213; and HT, *The Creative Encounter*, 30–31.

believed that the ultimate sanction of the moral life is personal integrity born of the need to be in harmony within the self as a basis for public interaction and engagement. For him, civic participation that is not guided by a coherent and meaningful personal existence generates social practices that conspire against the harmonic possibilities of public life. Central to his understanding of civic virtue is the integrity and moral inviolability of the individual that ultimately rest upon a transcendent reference.[47] Transcendence, however, is not narrowly defined in deontological terms, but is relational and inherent in the very being and practices of the moral agent. Therefore, religious experience allows for the discovery of a transcendent reference within the moral self that is at once the ground and guarantor of the very processes of life that seek community. And personal knowing, in the quest for moral authority, is indispensable to creative public engagement amid the discordant voices that speak about the future of American democratic culture.

Even more is at stake for Thurman. The ground of the private life that floats the individual's quest for wholeness rests upon a fierce and unrelenting loyalty to truth (integrity, sincerity), which is inviolate.[48] Therefore, the individual must always return to the very source of one's loyalty to the truth, which for Thurman is the will of God manifesting itself in time and history. In the political contestations between loyalty to the state and loyalty to the truth, the individual is morally bound to the demands of truth, which for Thurman is at once transcendent and embodied in the integrity of the will. Therefore, in the search for common ground, especially in situations where the rise of unbridled nationalism is evident, it is incumbent that one's loyalty to God serve as the final word, even at the risk of death. This is a persistent theme in Thurman's writings and sermons that finds even greater resonance as we witness the growing tide of fascism and violence in the United States and around the globe. In a sermon titled "The Meaning of Loyalty III: The State," he said,

> This means that as long as an individual can be rooted and easily committed to the kind of nationalism about which I have been thinking, and make that nationalism vehicular or expressive of this major, dominant loyalty which ultimately gives to the individual the basis of her own self-estimate and self-respect, there is no conflict, in my judgment, between that kind of patriotism and a recognition of a transcendent cause. But it is contingent, you see, upon the will-ing [in text], the self-conscious yielding of the devotion and personality. And that is why I can understand and appreciate the provisions that are made in our

---

[47] HT, "A Faith to Live By #7: Democracy and the Individual, II," sermon, Fellowship Church, October 26, 1952; in HT, *Democracy and the Soul of America*, 88–89.
[48] Ibid.

constitution for loyalty to the country, to the state. That seems to me to have a very creative logic in it that is fundamental to the very genius of the experience of group belonging. It is inherent in the whole process of sharing the common life. I can understand that. But I cannot understand at all in terms of the meaning either of loyalty or of religious experience anything beyond that formal insistence that men declare themselves in terms of the registering of their ultimate loyalty, non-competitive loyalty to a state. That I cannot understand.[49]

This imaginative quest for community within and without finds its fulfillment in the experience of love. Love, for Thurman, is the experience through which one passes when she or he is able to deal with another human being at a point in that person beyond all good and evil. Likewise, to *be loved* is to have the sense of being dealt with in oneself at a point beyond all good and evil. Love is intrinsic interest in the other; it goes beyond abstract generalizations and expresses itself *in concreto*. Love and reason are not opposed, for Thurman, but the head and the heart must work together in the actualization of community. Love transcends and fulfills justice. Included in the experience of love is the role of the imagination, which allows the individual to identify with the other at the centermost place of their being. Finally, through the exposure of oneself to the other (including the enemy) with all its attendant risks, love issues forth in radical nonviolence the creative power that reconciles and restores community.

Saddling Our Dreams

There are inherent dangers in this imaginative quest for common ground. For Thurman, imagination can become a "self-absorbing" drama when one fails to traverse "a thin line" between undisciplined subjectivism and *megalothymia*.[50]

---

[49] HT, "The Meaning of Loyalty III: The State," May 20, 1951, in HT, *Democracy and the Soul of America*, 29–30.

[50] Geshi Lobsang Tenzin Negi comments on the danger of "self-absorption" and that "Thurman and His Holiness The Dalai Lama have anticipated what current research is demonstrating: that excessive self-focus is exacerbating many of our modern problems including the alarming rates of loneliness, depression, burnout, and self-harm, as well as the prevalence of social conflict, injustice, and ecological destruction." See his essay printed in this volume, "Apostles of Sensitiveness: The Buddha Crown and Howard Thurman's Growing Edge." For HT, the undisciplined imagination leads to an unbalanced inwardness and the shirking of responsibility for one's society and its problems. HT, "Mysticism and Social Action," in *Lawrence Lectures on Religion & Society, 1977–1978* (Berkeley, CA: First Unitarian Church of Berkeley, 1978), 18. See also "Introduction," HT, *Democracy and the Soul of America*. Mega-

Thurman is acutely aware of the danger of subjectivism and privatization of meaning implied in the emphasis on the development of inner consciousness. He tries to guard against this tendency by accentuating the need for external empirical verification of what one experiences in his inner life. He contends, "The real questions at issue here are, how may a man know he is not being deceived? Is there any way by which he may know beyond doubt, and therefore with verification, that what he experiences is authentic and genuine?"[51] Rational coherence between the inner experience of self and the external world is the methodology employed to test for self-deception. He argues that "whatever seems to deny a fundamental structure of orderliness upon which rationality seems to depend cannot be countenanced."[52]

In 1964, Elizabeth Yates published the first biography of Howard Thurman, titled *Howard Thurman: Portrait of a Practical Dreamer*.[53] Her depiction of him as a "practical dreamer" spoke to the ways that Thurman tended to concentrate less on formal systematic presentations of ideas, calling listeners and readers instead to seek their own religious experience and respond to their contexts with integrity and imagination. For Thurman, this was no casual enterprise, because it demanded a "moral struggle" filled with a sense of the tragic, angst, and frustration, "the consequence of individuals finding their dreams and visions of a good society thwarted because of forces outside of their control and internal inhibitions that restrict the private will."[54] He was insistent that we must "saddle our dreams before we ride them."

> It is the nature of dreams to run riot, never to wish to contain themselves within limitations that are fixed. Sometimes they seem to be the cry of the heart for the boundless and the unexplored ... yet, our dreams must be saddled by the hard facts of our world before we ride them off among the stars. Thus, they become for us the bearers of the new possi-

---

lothymia refers to "the inordinate need for recognition and respect, the need to stand out as a symbol of prowess and power, to demand by height what one lacks in depth, to wrest from the other what one thinks is absent in oneself, and to find security in the obsequiousness of the other." Walter Earl Fluker, *Ethical Leadership: The Quest for Character, Civility and Community* (Minneapolis: Fortress Press, 2009), 105; Francis Fukuyama, *The End of History and the Last Man* (New York: Free Press, 1992), 141–339; and David Brooks, "All Politics Is Thymotic," *New York Times*, March 19, 2006.

[51] HT, *Creative Encounter*, 57.
[52] Ibid., 57–58.
[53] Elizabeth Yates, *Howard Thurman: Portrait of a Practical Dreamer* (New York: John Day Company, 1964).
[54] "Introduction," *Moral Struggle and the Prophets*, Walking with God: The Howard Thurman Sermon Series, vol. 1 (Maryknoll, NY: Orbis Books, 2020).

bility, the enlarged horizon, the great hope. Even as they romp among the stars they come back to their place in our lives, bringing with them the radiance of the far heights, the lofty regions, and giving to all our days the lift and the magic of stars.[55]

Reimagining the Search for Common Ground

So it is for our troubled and fragile times. Thurman's life and work are an invitation to a new generation of dreamers and activists who dare to continue the search for common ground amid the challenges and threats that confront us in the third decade of this century. We must inquire within our own contemporary contexts and seek responses that proceed from "the sound of the genuine" within us. This challenge before us involves reimagining Thurman's work and legacy at this critical impasse in democratic life and practices and to forge new "tools of the spirit" that enable us to not only imagine new possibilities for democratic space. But we must also seek practices that ensure that our speech and actions are always rooted in the vitality of life and spirit.

What might a reimagined search for common ground look, sound, smell, and feel like? It will certainly bear some affinity to the biblical narrative from which Thurman drew his own imaginative and creative public language. There is a common consciousness, common space, and common ground of meeting the other whose face bears the distinct representation of the Divine, realizing that necessary to see the other is to see your God; to hear the sound of the genuine in the other, however strange and dissonant, is to hear the melody of the divine.

For a public discourse that marks this suggestion from Thurman it will be necessary to return to another place long-forgotten in the discordant melodies of postmodernity and to hear afresh as it were for the first time—the sound of the genuine in the perplexing sirens of the public sphere: complex and obtuse sounds that beg for answers to the pressing moral issues of our day. Can we hear beyond the often conflicting demands of religion, race, class, sexuality, and gender, the voice of an other who calls us to attention to the place of common consciousness and public imagination? Thurman was not sure, yet he remained hopeful (not sentimental) that even if human beings destroy themselves through their own devices, the creator of life is infinitely more resourceful and creative than any expression of life. He agreed with Arnold Toynbee that "if we are so foolish to destroy our entire civilization and our own lives, then the creator of life could very easily make an ideal culture out of the ant."[56]

---

[55] HT, "Saddle Your Dreams," in SF, 297–98.
[56] HT, *Deep Is the Hunger*, 38.

The truth that the religious experience and moral imagination will supply to the prevalent public debates is not specific, utilitarian answers couched in legal and political diatribes—important but ultimately inadequate, as we are witnessing in our contemporary battles around gun violence, abortion rights, sexual orientations, and the natural environment. Rather Thurman's imaginative search for common ground calls for a fresh and vibrant articulation of hope in human agency to reinvent itself for this time, with answers that proceed from the encounter with a truth that moves at levels unrestrained by religious formulae and political dogma—that imagines a future with the other where peace will cover the earth as the waters cover the sea, where the child will play at the hole of the adder, and nations will beat the swords and weapons into plowshares and pruning hooks. Shall we—are we able to—put ourselves in that space? To be in the place when the Sound, like a mighty and rushing wind, fills the room and we hear in our own language the many voices that herald the New Age?[57]

> *God is not through with creation—*
> *God is not through with us....*

If so, the essays in this volume provide us with windows through which we may peer into and eavesdrop on creative conversations taking place regarding this twentieth-century prophetic voice.

---

[57] Fluker, "Leaders Who Have Shaped U.S. Religious Dialogue," 577.

Part One

The Inner Life and World-Mindedness

Spirituality and Social Transformation

1

Prophetic Vision and
Its Radical Consequences

Luther E. Smith Jr.

The Vision of Common Ground

The Search for Common Ground was Howard Thurman's last published book before writing his autobiography. Although this is a later publication in Thurman's publishing career, his "search" was lifelong. He writes, "From my childhood I have been on the scent of the tie that binds life at a level so deep that the final privacy of the individual would be reinforced rather than threatened."[1] Eight years before *The Search for Common Ground,* in *Disciplines of the Spirit*, he states,

> The literal fact of the underlying unity of life seems to be established beyond doubt. It manifests itself in the basic structural patterns of nature and provides the precious clue to the investigation and interpretation of the external world.... If life has been fashioned out of a fundamental unity and ground, and if it has developed within such a structure, then it is not to be wondered at that the interest in and concern for wholeness should be part of the conscious intent of life, more basic than any particular conscious tendency toward fragmentation. Every expression of life is trying to experience itself. For a form of life to experience itself it must actualize its own potential. In so doing it experiences in miniature the fundamental unity out of which it comes.[2]

Thurman's religious experiences arise from his times in nature, relationships with individuals, worship, reading sacred Scripture, and prayer. All these contexts are candidates for common ground experiences that give rise to compelling visions of beloved community. Common ground, for Thurman, is both an

---

[1] HT, SCG, xi.
[2] HT, *Disciplines of the Spirit* (New York: Harper & Row, 1963), 104.

experience of arrival *and* an experience to be pursued. Throughout his writing and speaking about this "common ground," he uses the terms "wholeness," "harmony," "oneness," and "unity." His religious experiences convinced him that "the human spirit is exposed to the kind of experience that is capable of providing an ultimate clue to all levels of reality, to all the dimensions of time, and to all aspects of faith and the manifestations therein."[3] Another way to describe the content of Thurman's prophetic vision of common ground is his intense awareness of God's loving presence and God's intent for our lives. He experiences God's desire for us to embrace our oneness through compassion and care for one another.

I believe that one reason Howard Thurman was influential and celebrated during his lifetime, and has continued to inspire so many since his death, is that he identifies a compelling truth about pursuing personal meaning and the necessity for beloved community. As we recognize this truth in our religious traditions, or the dramas of history, or our personal experiences, it speaks to "the hunger of our hearts." Thurman's prophetic vision of common ground is experienced *by us* as a vision *for us*. We endorse the vision. We trust the prophet's experience and authority. We can envision how common ground is our reality and our destiny.

Confronting Prophetic Messages

Even as Thurman's prophetic vision and witness continue to inspire personal and social transformation, I believe his common ground vision is susceptible to being distorted to diminish its radical significance. Prophets are often celebrated as their calls to action are ignored. Prophets' words are quoted within others' speeches that interpret prophets as guardians for the status quo. Domesticating a prophet's message is the effort to domesticate the prophet. We see this occur as politicians, media personalities, and reactionary individuals call Dr. Martin Luther King Jr.'s name and quote from his speeches to argue that he would be appalled at protests and legal efforts that inveigh against racial disparities and racial injustice. The "taming" of Martin Luther King Jr. is in fact a pervasive effort to control the meaning of his "dream," and to barricade justice from "rolling down like mighty waters and righteousness like an ever-flowing stream."

Howard Thurman's vision of common ground is no less susceptible to being stripped of its radical meaning for our lives. A major stripping of the vision is to characterize common ground as being focused only on our similarities and ignoring our differences—especially differences that are the basis of conflicts and injustice

---

[3] HT, *The Creative Encounter: An Interpretation of Religion and the Social Witness* (New York: Harper & Brothers, 1954), 30.

in our history. Therefore, it's crucial that we give ourselves to understanding Thurman's vision, his interpretation of it, and its consequences. All the while, we will need to be aware of our own discomfort with the radical consequences that could lead us to kidnap Thurman as a hostage within our comfort zones.

To be clear, I am not using the word "radical" to indicate inconsiderate reactions to cultural norms. My working definition for "radical" is "of or relating to the root of something." The word is often used when people who challenge conventional ideas and behaviors in society seem to be *pulling up accepted standards by their roots*. Radicals are then seen as destroyers of the status quo. Another meaning of radical is *getting back to the roots*. Here the effort is to make the society see how it has veered far from the fundamental principles and behaviors that nourish its identity of excellence. This image of a radical, as one who insists on returning to sacrosanct traditions, also threatens the status quo. Thurman's prophetic vision insists that we pull up by their roots understandings of self, community, and religion that violate what God has dreamed for us. And that we get back to the roots of self, community, and religion that are nurtured in common ground.

Regarding the self, Thurman considers it to be a vast landscape inviting endless exploration. The self is of ultimate worth. It not only has personal meaning, it discerns meaning for community as it interacts with life. Thurman is so adamant about the capacity of ourselves to enact their sense of ultimate meaning in life, he insists that we have no excuses in honoring who God has called us to be. We have agency in all circumstances. We may not have all the options we desire, but choice and initiative are available. Although we are influenced by dire and nurturing experiences, they do not predetermine how we enact our true selves in life. Consequently, we are responsible for our lives.

I have heard critics of Thurman's most celebrated book, *Jesus and the Disinherited*, complain that his insistence that the disinherited counter the oppression of their enemies with love is to place upon the disinherited the burden of transforming racism. The critics argue that this shifts the burden from the oppressor to the oppressed, and that it releases the oppressors from taking the lead in addressing evil. Thurman's insistence that the disinherited embrace the power to love enemies, however, has nothing to do with relieving the burden and responsibility of oppressors. He is affirming the capacity of every person, even the most beleaguered, to assert their God-given power for creative transformation. This is an empowering message for the disinherited. They can follow the way of Jesus without the intervention of the privileged or the changed behavior of oppressors. Failing to see this, from Thurman's perspective, is to restrict the disinherited to reactive behaviors and increased dependence on their oppressors. Stressing that people take the initiative with their enemies also relates to forgiveness. One does not have to wait for a confession or an apology or changes in behavior. Waiting for these outcomes keeps the initiative for healing with the enemy. An individual has the agency to be freed from bitterness and the mire of hatred by choosing to forgive—even if the process of forgiveness requires considerable effort and time.

The ultimate value of all selves, and the necessity to nurture them, aligns with Thurman's prophetic vision of common ground. The nurturing comes from family, personal relationships, community, and religion. However, rooted in communities and religions are ideas and behaviors that contradict common ground principles of respect, compassion, growth, and justice. The "radical action" of pulling up these roots is required. And radical action is required to affirm and nurture the roots that welcome and respect diversity, energize compassion through love, embrace growth even when it threatens long-standing convictions, and flood the land with the beauty of justice.

Thurman's prophetic vision involves each of us taking responsibility for the communities in which we rely for a vital life. The self is not only responsible for its vitality, but also for the climate of community. Thurman addressed deadly realities of society and affirmed movements that honored what God dreams for us to become for one another. Remember, prophets are not considered dangerous to the status quo if they only announce the need for justice and righteousness throughout the land. Just about everyone will nod agreement to a *general* proclamation for justice and righteousness. It's when a prophet is *specific* about an injustice and immorality that the prophet faces anger and suspicion. Thurman was specific when he spoke and wrote about the pervasiveness of racism in the church and society. An example of "radical consequences," to address the evil of racism, is a 1966 essay where he argued that racial segregation exists because one race has the ability to exert "raw power" over the lives of a different race. Thurman concludes that for dismantling segregation "to be meaningful and effective [it] has to involve revolution, social upheaval."[4] Proclaiming the need for "revolution" and "social upheaval" evokes fear and anger not only in beneficiaries of the status quo but also in a general population that interprets such actions as chaos. Thurman was pulling up deeply rooted racism.

Another example of the prophet being specific about individuals taking responsibility for their communities is his 1962 sermon, "The Quest for Peace and Responsibility," where Thurman declares the need for every American to carry the burden of the United States having used atomic bombs on the people of

---

[4] HT, "Desegregation, Integration, and the Beloved Community," in *Benjamin E. Mays: His Life, Contributions, and Legacy*, ed. Samuel DuBois Cook (Franklin, TN: Providence House, 2009), 197–207. Quoted in PHWT 5:148–49.

Japan. I quote a lengthy passage of the sermon because it illustrates his prophetic speaking to a congregation, radio audience, and country that will be disturbed by what he has to say about the soul of the nation and our responsibility for it:

> For Americans ... there must be a felt sense of collective guilt and responsibility for initiating, in the modern world, complete violence by atomic bombs.... That whatever finally is said about the fateful historic moment in which Harry Truman was functioning relevantly, the fact remains that on behalf of us all, he acted.
>
> And the guilt, whether he feels it or not, cannot be isolated in these strange and deranged stirrings of that hapless colonel who dropped the bomb, but the guilt is ours, and it has to be felt and sensed and realized. And there is no escape.... There must, as a part of this, be an effort to try to see if, at the level where we operate, we can enter into another kind of moral revolution. A revolution that will undertake to re-establish the moral values by which we have been tutored and in which we have been nurtured, which moral values had to be violated when we took the fateful step.... We have not felt as a people that men and women and children, who were not involved professionally in carrying out the armed will of a nation, should be included. We have not felt that little children should be killed, and women, and those non-participators in the active military will.... And now suddenly we find ourselves breaking with that whole assumption in our past by participating in an act that included everybody—men, women, children, those who are armed, those who are not armed. And this means a radical rupture in the collective psyche of the American people. And this has to be redeemed in some way.⁵

Thurman is wise enough to know this is a gut-wrenching message that will provoke anger, resentment, hostility, and dismissal, as well as doubts about his patriotism. The United States' use of nuclear weapons in World War II is often justified as having saved countless American lives that would have been lost in ongoing conventional warfare. This rationale assuages the doubts and guilt that many feel when the horrors from the nuclear bombs are depicted. However, Thurman emphasizes an outcome that continues to be morally costly and life threatening for the world. For the sake of each person understanding one's personal and collective responsibility, for the sake of the soul of the nation, for the sake of the world coming to its senses about the power to annihilate, he

---

⁵ HT, "Quests of the Human Spirit, Part 10: The Quest for Peace (continued)," May 13, 1962, PITTS.

speaks this discomfiting message. His message is a radical consequence from his prophetic vision of the violation of common ground.

His witness to the transformation of the self and the transformation of community has radical consequences for the self and community. As we recognize the significance of these transformations to honoring common ground, we must remember that the source for Thurman's vision of common ground is religious experience. He is deeply rooted in religion. He committed himself to nurturing religion's roots that enable the self and community to flourish. And he pulled up religion's roots that strangle the growth of self and community. Additionally, he pulled up roots that stunted the growth of religion. The transformation of religion is a radical consequence of his prophetic vision.

His own sense of identity is as a disciple of Jesus. On one of my visits with Dr. Thurman, I asked him to talk about his Christology. I had heard many clergy conclude that he did not have a Christology, but that he embraced a "Jesusology." So I wanted to know his own way of characterizing the meaning of Jesus to his Christian faith. He responded, "Jesus was my friend." In his autobiography, Thurman writes,

> I prayed to God, I talked to Jesus. He was a companion. There was no felt need in my spirit to explain this companionship. There never has been.... It was Jesus with whom I talked as I sat under my oak tree fingering the bruises and scars of my childhood. Such was the pre-theological ground for me when both life and time spread out before me.[6]

To comprehend how Thurman understands the personal transformation that occurs from this kind of fellowship with Jesus, we read in his book *The Creative Encounter*, "Slowly his mind becomes my mind, and then the amazing discovery that the mind that is more and more in me is the mind that was more and more in him. The mind that was in him becomes more and more clearly to me the mind that is God."[7] Thurman's own sense of identity, as one who enacts radical consequences, is evident from his characterization of the Jesus he has come to know:

> And do you wonder why we have a so-called Christian civilization that doesn't bother with Jesus? He's the most dangerous, the most dangerous figure on the horizon of modern man. And if we seek to reproduce in ourselves the religion which he experienced, we shall destroy our civilization, and there shall be not one stone left on the other. So, what do we do? We pray to him instead. That's easier. We

---

[6] HT, WHAH, 266.
[7] HT, *The Creative Encounter*, 83.

just walk by as they do once a year in the Soviet Union, I'm told, on Lenin's birthday, pass before his bier and pay tribute. Because this is a dangerous man.[8]

Thurman understands himself to be a follower of a "dangerous man," a radical, one who pulls up roots, who transforms despite public outrage and the reality of crucifixion.

Citing the titles of his books, we perceive how Howard Thurman, as a companion of Jesus, gave himself to exploring and interpreting their companionship. He felt the bond with Jesus as he perceived the relationship of "Jesus and the disinherited." He knew that Jesus's life was guided by "the inward journey," and like Jesus he opened his heart to be on a journey that involved uncertainties, joys, frustrations, discoveries, and questions—a journey taken "with head and heart," "disciplines of the spirit," "centering moments," and "creative encounters" in response to the "deep hunger" of the self.

As a Christian, a companion of Jesus, Thurman gave himself to prophetic pronouncements against racism, pronouncements that involved indicting those who claimed to be followers of Jesus yet who accepted segregation and discrimination. He was committed to love as the difficult and necessary way of life with friends, strangers, and enemies. He taught that the power of nonviolence is a means of love that enables opponents to experience common ground. He established and led a congregation that pursued the inward journey, opened their minds and hearts to truth from various religions and philosophies, and demonstrated how a church could become a common ground with people of diverse faiths, races, ethnicities, and cultures.

His religious roots fed his sense of identity, purpose, radical discipleship, and beloved community. I heard him suggest that religion may be the only hope for community. This idea was also mentioned in a sermon where he speculated that experiencing common ground—that has overcome social and political adversities—will depend upon "one faith." He says, "And by one faith I do not mean one creed, one doctrine, one dogma, one church—I don't mean that—but one faith, one pulse beat that is so fontal, that is so basic to all of the movement of life that it is capable of feeding all the little heartbeats and recognized as such."[9] A radical consequence from his vision of common ground is the transformation of religion so that it can be the means "to ground and sustain a neighborhood the size of a planet."[10] Thurman gave himself to this transformative mission.

---

[8] HT, "Parables of Jesus, Part 6: Commitment," October 21, 1951, PITTS.
[9] HT, "Men Who've Walked with God: Brahman Mystics," April 26, 1953, PITTS.
[10] Ibid.

Our Prophetic Opportunities

Who joins him in this transformative work? As devotees of faith traditions, do we believe we should engage in creatively transforming our religions? Is the vision of common ground compelling for reimagining how we are called by God to be radical? As we all know, people who have given their lives to transforming religion are fortunate to only be ostracized, because history is replete with examples of such prophets being condemned to torture and an array of options for execution. Whether having just left Egypt for the promised land or having just left home with our children impatient in the back seat on a long cross-country drive to see family, the question arises, "Are we there yet?" And if we are not about to arrive, "How much longer will it be?" These same questions are asked about experiencing common ground. They indicate our eagerness to arrive. The questions can also indicate our ambivalence about common ground being worth whatever effort it takes to get there.

Thurman experienced common ground in his religious experiences, and he experienced common ground in interpersonal and communal relationships. As such, yes experiences of common ground are available and near. Sometimes the experiences come from arduous planning and work, and sometimes we are surprised to find ourselves in the midst of common ground experiences that were not foreseen.

Then there is the question, spoken or unspoken, that abides even with those inspired by the vision: will we ever arrive on common ground and know the search, the journey, to be over? Many ask the question because they hold images of common ground as a time and place of relief from the painful struggles that enabled arrival at common ground. Images of common ground where relationships are sealed by respect and compassion carry the assumption or hope that the ordeals from getting to common ground are confined to the past. Common ground is not, however, a conflict-free time and place. Discerning what is true has never had consensus. Common ground is a place of vision—and interpretation, debate, persuasion, contention, frustration, loss, grief, and forgiveness. The diversity that inspires us also challenges us to address our conflicts with others. Most precious for sustaining the community is having a reservoir of trust that is drawn upon when misunderstandings persist.

Thurman's experiences of common ground have eternal significance for him even when what was celebrated no longer exists—except in memories. The experiences are cherished and reassuring as his search for common ground continues. Thurman knows that even the most inspiring and long-lasting experiences of common ground are tenuous. Still, he envisions a time when common ground will come into being and remain, because he believes "the contradictions of life are not final." What aligns with God's love will prevail. Thurman does not pretend to be a seer who knows if this will occur soon or in one thousand or ten thousand years, but he does believe in a time of finality. We may argue with him about this common ground conclusion. I certainly do. But from my personal experiences with him, I believe he would welcome the debate.

Either way, what is required of us now is to live into the prophetic vision of common ground and to embrace its radical consequences. To repeat Thurman's conviction that each of us has the responsibility and the ability to fulfill our prophetic calling: we have no valid excuses to withdraw from committing ourselves to the realization of common ground. None!

We live in a time when many people speak of being in despair over the political divides, the retreat from advances in dismantling racism, mass incarceration, the increased fascination with fascism, the assault on democratic institutions, environmental crises, international wars, and constant news about the world falling apart. They conclude that now is a time with realities more overwhelming than any generation has faced. This conclusion can raise doubts, therefore, about Thurman's relevance to our contemporary challenges.

Every generation has its distinctive and new challenges, but are we living in the worst of times? Really? We must remember that Thurman lived during a time when he knew personally Black people who had been enslaved; a period when the gains from Reconstruction were reversed and Jim Crow laws established, the First World War, a flu pandemic that killed tens of millions, years of typhoid fever and polio as constant health threats, outbreaks of violence against Black communities that resulted in mass murders and total destruction from White mobs, the Great Depression, pervasive lynching of Black people, World War II and Japanese internment camps in California, nuclear war, the vilification and pursuit of Communists as traitors, the Korean War, the civil rights movement and the assassination of its leaders, the Vietnam War, riots in cities that led to fears that the very fabric of the United States was irreparably torn, and incessant poverty.

We dare not insult our ancestors by exclaiming that we are incapable of enacting the prophetic vision of beloved community because we live in the worst of times. We cannot even use the complexity of our lives as an excuse. Every generation has dealt with the complexity from abundance or the complexity of living day to day with scarcity. This is our time to give ourselves to the search for common ground and its radical consequences. We have the advantage of engaging our opportunities for common ground with the prophetic guidance of Thurman and others. This is our time. Thurman often quoted the following from Hermann Hagedorn's "Lines from an Unknown Soldier": "We died, but you who live must do a harder thing than dying is, for you must think and ghosts shall drive you on." On our pursuit of common ground, may our lives welcome their company.

2

"I Can See It. Now, How to Say It?"

*Hearing the Aesthetic Dimension of
Howard Thurman, the Interpreter*

Shively T. J. Smith

Readers of Howard Washington Thurman encounter his thought patterns and essential beliefs in his many writings. Thurman describes his "lifelong working paper" as a quest for "the scent of the tie that binds life" at a deeply personal level.[1] Having embarked on earlier iterations of his "pursuit for community" in *Jesus and the Disinherited* (1949) and *Footprints of a Dream* (1959), Thurman provides the fullest articulation of his endeavor in *The Search for Common Ground* (1971) with the concluding statement "… that community cannot feed for long on itself; it can only flourish where always the boundaries are giving way to the coming of others from beyond them—unknown and undiscovered brothers."[2] Community, for Thurman, was not just transgressive, but expansive. Threaded throughout his writings is a vision of human relations that crosses borders and destroys contrived social boundaries, yet he did not draft his position paper solely through an iterative literary process. To learn from him today we can do more than study his books, sermons, essays, and correspondences from the twentieth century. We can *listen* to his searching practice unfold.[3]

He was not just a spiritual writer who penned reflections on the discovery of God, self, and community. He was an orator. Skilled in the arts of preaching and lecturing, he wrote and verbalized his proclamations, prayers, and inquiries. Thurman spoke with the vocal range of a tenor that was sonorous and musical.

---

[1] HT, SCG, xiii.
[2] Ibid., 104.
[3] Two university-based archives offer virtual listening rooms featuring both Howard and Sue Bailey's library of recordings. See the Howard Thurman and Sue Bailey Thurman Collections at Boston University (HTC) and the Howard Thurman Digital Archive at Emory University (PITTS).

Much like how the trumpet master Miles Davis took his listeners on an odyssey through sound, Thurman's oratorical mastery played jazz with images that invite listeners to embark on a journey. He often started his sermons and lectures at an even tone seasoned with a slight and playful, dry humor. His pitch caught hearers' attention and drew them into an unfolding exposition that roused the spirit and the mind. Thurman's voice lulled a listener into a still attentiveness, easing listeners into a space of introspection and wonder. To *hear* him engage matters of head and heart is to experience a spiritual genius drafting a working paper in social intervention and human relations.[4] According to Thurman, an individual's life working paper is constituted by "a creative synthesis" of what she is in all her parts and how she "reacts to the living process."[5] Thurman records his reactions to the process of life and death in spoken and written forms. For example, he blends spirituality, imagination, and thoughtfulness in one of his most famous collections of contemplative poems and prayers, *Meditations of the Heart* (1953).[6] The collection begins with a reflection, "The Inward Sea," which personifies the divine in the form of an angel standing guard at an altar. The meditation guides readers through a tour of the inner self through a description of an Edenic setting:

> There is in every person an inward sea, and in that sea there is an island and on that island there is an altar and standing guard before that altar is the "angel with the flaming sword." Nothing can get by that angel to be placed upon that altar unless it has the mark of your inner authority. Nothing passes "the angel with the flaming sword" to be placed upon your altar unless it be a part of "the fluid area of your consent." This is your crucial link with the Eternal.[7]

His literary verse casts vivid images of a vast and watery horizon from which emerges a single land mass unique to each person. He portrays individuals as independent property owners of private islands. In so doing, the book's opening metaphor of a sea island centers the reader's self as text. The island of oneself is the site from which she interprets what is essential to the living process. Reading the meditation creates space to envision new proximities of consent and to reflect on fields of human accord and discord. The image of an altar, a guardian angel, and a sword of fire captures a reader's imagination, and it invites her to pause in a space of introspective possibility. She wonders, *What if?*

---

[4] HT characterizes his personal story as one of head and heart in the title of his autobiography: HT, WHAH.

[5] HT, *Jesus and the Disinherited* (1949; repr., Boston: Beacon Press, 1996), 100.

[6] HT, *Meditations of the Heart* (1953; repr., Boston: Beacon Press, 1981).

[7] HT, "The Inward Sea," in ibid., 15.

In addition to writing about the inner sea and island of consent, Thurman recites it to listening audiences. While it can be read off a page, one can hear Thurman spin the metaphorical tale in his own voice from a recording. In the audio collection titled *The Living Wisdom of Howard Thurman*, he begins a sermon by reciting a modified form of the meditation. Thurman's oral performance stirs the heart and mind through voice control that emphasizes words like "every person," "sea," and "the connecting link with the Eternal." His cadences flow at an elegant andante pace that modulate with each melodic line. His listeners are held in stasis. After narrating the island of inner consent and its accoutrements, he unpacks its significance in the rest of the sermon. Personal agency fashions human particularity, but Thurman insists it also cultivates human "belonging" and duty to each other. Captivated by his voice, listeners participate in the enactment of what authentic common ground must *feel* like, at least when the experience is conducted by Thurman's genuine sound. Assured the conductor knows where to lead, his listeners take the journey confident that each rhetorical move is intentional and measured—until the moment the stutter occurs.

Approximately seven minutes into the sermon, we hear Thurman grapple playfully with the limitations of language. Having asked his congregation the question "What are you for?" Thurman struggles to explain why it is important to incorporate such personal inquiries into the living process. As we listen, we are enthralled in Thurman's every word, and yet words begin to fail him in his spiritual and moral probing. He resists spinning a rhetoric of declaration and prescription and performs a speech act in wonderment and discovery. It is as if he pulls back the veil and provides his audience a glimpse into his human dilemma. Even Thurman struggles with frustrations born from the limitations of human comprehension. From the same conductor who exuded certainty about the journey, listeners experience his moment of uncertainty, reticence, and revision.

Frustrated by the distance between what he sees and can articulate, Thurman signals his struggle by saying, *"Gee, how to say this? I can see it. Now, how to say it? Let me see if I can say it."* Thurman is searching for something more than eloquent words. He expresses a conundrum of interpretation and the difficulty of communicating the full range of existence: "Given the fact of life, there is much which has to do with interpretations of its meanings, its point and even its validity."[8] His search for common ground involves the hermeneutical task of stretching language to communicate patterns of living and relating beyond conventional forms. Although difficult—even frustrating—Thurman strives to foment new objects of collective human vision through wordplay.

---

[8] HT, "The Negro Spiritual Speaks of Life and Death," in *Deep River and The Negro Spiritual Speaks of Life and Death* (Richmond, IN: Friends United Press, 1975), 25.

Thurman's Verbal Aesthetic Play

"I can see it. Now, how to say it?" This statement is an experiential source funding Thurman's theological vision of community. His aesthetic draws meaning at the intersection between multiple forms of knowing: lived human experience; religious encounter; cycles of nature and the earth; and inner human moments of peace, grief, turmoil, and hope. Thurman even resourced the quizzical and awkward silences that his listening audiences produced. In this way, he drew on the fullness of human existence as inroads for imagining new forms of human kinship.

In a 1949 sermon preached at the Fellowship Church for All Peoples in San Francisco, he addressed the importance of the "aesthetic sense" for bridging gaps in human kinship.

> Now, dimension is an aesthetic sense. The experience of unity in the presence of God, of the oneness of God, puts a scent in my nostrils that sends me, in all of the things that I do, trying to express it. In my work, in my relationships with people on the street, I look with new eyes on those with reference to whom, when I was imprisoned in my little narrow self, I had no experience of oneness. The fears that I had, that kept eating away at the basis of social security, are now removed, because I have let down my guards in an effort to move creatively into an understanding of other people and let them move creatively into an understanding of me. And in that moment of shuttling, they become a part of me forever.[9]

Thurman tests the boundaries of language through his nonverbal pauses and extemporaneous statements. His public speech experiments evince his creative pursuit for community like the worship experiments he staged as dean of Rankin Chapel at Howard University and Marsh Chapel at Boston University. Similar to when he introduced dance in university chapel services in the 1930s and 1950s, Thurman risked losing credibility with his congregations and audiences as he searched for precise words through inquisitory silences.[10]

Listening to him, we encounter Thurman's aesthetic playfulness, which is constituted by more than merely the content of his sermons and lectures. The aesthetic quality of the inner life, for Thurman, is sensory rich. It evokes the full

---

[9] I am grateful to Walter Earl Fluker, who shared this quotation with me from a lecture he gave on October 23, 2018, for the Alonzo L. McDonald Lecture titled "Walking with God: Preparation, Presence and Practice." The original source for the quotation is HT's sermon titled "The Commitment," March 1949, at the Fellowship Church for All Peoples in San Francisco, California. Also see PHWT 3:309–10.

[10] HT, WHAH, 92.

range of human bodily experiences defined by hearing, seeing, feeling, tasting, and touching. His speech acts connote an "aesthetic consciousness" that Hans-Georg Gadamer identifies as a work of art that "has its true being in the fact that it becomes an experience changing the person experiencing it."[11] Yet Thurman is not changed alone. As he wrestles with how to express his inner life publicly, his listeners and viewers are "swept up" to belong more fully to the world they share. His pregnant pauses and surprising verbal asides, coupled with the effects they have on listeners, find affinity with Gadamer's descriptions about the interplay between a work of art and "the world of real existence." Together they produce generative settings for meaning-making (interpretation) for both artist and audience alike.[12]

Thurman's oral performance captures the difficulty of articulating the "yet unrealized" experience. Characterized by arbitrary breaks and searching questions, younger generations of "Thurmanites" cannot "read themselves into" his verbal aesthetic. Thurman's verbal wrestling is absent in his literary explorations. Much of his writings—even in his more philosophical deliberations such as *The Creative Encounter*—communicate rhetorical intention and clarity of thought. But to listen to Thurman is to realize that his intuitive path is not direct, linear, or clear. Thurman searches in the darkly lit gaps created between prophetic sight and prophetic utterance. When he verbalizes his struggle out loud by saying, "I can see it. Now how to say it?" we hear his prophetic craft at work.

Thurman's asides are productive interruptions. They disrupt his expository flow and awaken hearers from the malaise that sets in when one listens to any preacher for an extended time. Through his oratorical departures, he awakens audiences to something different—namely, the disquieting nature of Thurman's dithering over an idea as opposed to his decisiveness. He fills pauses with forms of the question "How to say it?" These are not homiletical digressions. Nor are they instances in the intellectual tendency to lose one's train of thought. Each verbal tangent reveals something about his prophetic insistence that the search for common ground is relentless and stretching. Those asides establish Thurman as an exemplar of "the prophet's burden," which entails the responsibility "to language" in public. (And, yes, I am turning language into a verb here.) It is a part of prophetic utterance and the burden of prophetic action "to see the unseen." He tussles with the limitations of language to capture what he sees outside the realm of words and grammar, reaching for images to support his prophetic communication.

---

[11] Hans-Georg Gadamer, *Truth and Method*, 2nd ed., trans. Joel Weinsheimer and Donald G. Marshall (London: Bloomsbury Academic, 2013), 107.
[12] Ibid., 135.

For example, in 1962, Thurman met with the Federation of Indigenous Chiefs of Saskatchewan to share ideas about their respective social struggles and commitments. For both parties, their intercultural proximity and exchange qualified as a new experience. Neither the chiefs nor Thurman had shared before this kind of intercultural space and collaboration. In addition to inexperience, Thurman and his conversation partners faced a challenge in communication although they opted, nonetheless, to meet and nurture conversation and comradery. Only one of the Indigenous leaders spoke fluent English, and Thurman did not speak Cree at all. To bridge the communication gap, Thurman deployed images as their common tongue. "I found from the outset that it was necessary for me to use as many *images* as possible in my conversation, the pictorial being more easily communicated than the conceptual and abstract. Once I got the drift, our discussion moved rather quickly into areas of mutual concern."[13] He resourced their shared visual world to facilitate understanding and connection across difference. His aesthetic of pausing to observe what he sees as a tool for advancing common agendas for freedom, equality, and unity persists in both his spoken and written communications.

Thurman, however, did not merely use images as literary forms. He constructs his metaphorical hermeneutics in service to the spoken word first—especially the rhetorical action of preaching. "Though I have published these and other books, my craft remains the spoken word. Even when I am writing, I hear the sound of the word as it goes on the page. If the sound does not please me, I am reluctant to write the word."[14] The sound of words and the images they conjured guided Thurman's measured selection. This sound-based approach to his written and spoken word is not evident in the final forms of his writings, but we can hear him involved in the process through his recordings.

Sources Funding Thurman's Verbal Aesthetic

Anytime one talks about the process of interpretation and how meaning-making occurs—be it within the field of biblical interpretation or the average person's unconscious habit of answering the question "What does this mean?"—sources are used to make things comprehensible. For Thurman, the sources for understanding religious experience and cultivating human fellowship that is intercultural and socially transgressive do not exist solely in texts, archeology, or language. His search for common ground utilized images generated from the "stuff of life." It included human journeys of life and death, moments of happiness

---

[13] HT, WHAH, 243 (italics added).
[14] Ibid., 228.

and seasons of sorrow, the springs of hope and the deflation that comes with disappointment. According to Thurman, "There are also those ideals that seem to be created out of the stubborn realities, in the midst of which men work and live. They belong essentially to the stuff of life, the very raw materials of experience. They are never separate from what a man knows to be the character of his daily living."[15] As an interpreter, he gleaned images from the routines of daily life in conversation with the thought world of biblical writings and other religious discourses. For example, the simple common experience of walking through the unlocked door of one's home because someone remembered to leave it ajar is an image Thurman provides in relationship to biblical stories of resurrection (John 11:25–26; Luke 24) in his meditation titled "The Glad Surprise."[16] Thurman's prophetic burden to verbalize what he saw unearthed the range of human patterns of life that either lock or unlock "the idiom" of God in people, individually and corporately.

His metaphors are broadly conceptual and visually oriented. His oratorical aesthetic occurred as an interplay between connection and communication. At times, his metaphors attempt to shift the thinking of his audiences. Sometimes they fasten their original thoughts in place to broaden their ethical field and social responsibility. Still other times, Thurman's metaphors shatter conventional thought worlds by changing perspectival angles and breaking fallow ground for new viewpoints to emerge. In the hands and on the tongue of Thurman, metaphors create opportunities for novel extensions, redirection, disorientation, and disruption.

Word pictures serve a cognitive function for Thurman, structuring knowledge and meaning in new ways. Sallie McFague calls this function of metaphor an "indirection," while contemporary metaphor research calls it "cross-domain mapping in the conceptual system."[17] Thurman uses metaphors to map knowledge about one concept, person, place, or thing onto knowledge about another.

> "To the extent that we know ourselves, our world, and our God, that knowledge is profoundly relational and, hence, interdependent, relative, situational, and limited. The implication for models of God is obvious: we must use the relationships nearest and dearest to us as metaphors of that which finally cannot be named. Aware that we exist only in rela-

---

[15] HT, "Two Kinds of Ideals," in *Meditations of the Heart,* 35 (italics added).
[16] HT, "The Glad Surprise," in *Meditations of the Heart*, 108.
[17] George Lakoff, "The Contemporary Theory of Metaphor," in *Metaphor and Thought: Second Edition*, ed. Andrew Ortony (New York: Cambridge University Press, 1993), 202–3. Also see George Lakoff and Mark Johnson, *Metaphors We Live By* (Chicago: University of Chicago Press, 2003).

tionship and aware therefore that all our language about God is but metaphors of experiences of relating to God, we are free to use many models of God. Aware, however, that the relationship with God cannot be named, we are prohibited from absolutizing any models of God."[18]

Before Sallie McFague wrote *Metaphorical Theology* in the 1980s, Thurman had already created a repository of forays into metaphorical hermeneutics through his books and public sermons and lectures. Thurman masterfully deployed metaphors to equip readers and hearers with a way of understanding and envisioning one familiar thing in terms of something else. As McFague states, "To be a human being is to interpret, to think of 'this' as 'that,' to make judgments concerning similarity and difference, to think metaphorically."[19] Word pictures are signposts, signaling toward what ultimately defies absolute conception. Thurman used metaphors as vehicles to interpret human strivings toward belonging and particularity. No one image satisfied his many excursions. He, therefore, possessed parking lots full of metaphorical vehicles; listening to him, we can hear him strolling his lots of possibility.

It is the responsibility of every human being to assume the prophetic role of an interpreter who sees and struggles to say what he sees. In the opening sentences of his Ingersoll Lecture titled "The Negro Spiritual Speaks of Life and Death," Thurman defines interpretation as the essential task of all human beings:

> The mystery of life and death persists despite the exhaustless and exhaustive treatment it has been given in song and story, philosophy, and science, in art and religion. The human spirit is so involved in the endless cycle of birth, of living and dying, that in some sense each man [person] is an authority, a key interpreter of the meaning of the totality of the experience. The testimony of the individual, then, is always fresh if he is able to make himself articulate to his fellows.[20]

The prophetic burden for Thurman's vision of common ground is discerning "the scent of the tie that binds life" together. He pinpoints the construction site of the self as more than a general location between life and death. He wrestles with how to speak of the many moments in the birth of the self as well as the multiple forms of its death. In this way, common ground is a wall-less and boundaryless space where particularities coexist. "Belonging" is the fundamental tie

---

[18] Sallie McFague, *Metaphorical Theology: Models of God in Religious Language* (Minneapolis: Fortress Press, 1982), 194.
[19] Ibid., 65.
[20] HT, *Deep River and The Negro Spiritual Speaks of Life and Death* (Richmond, IN: Friends United Press, 1975), 11.

that binds humans together. He assigns the quality of human relationship as the responsibility of those on the journey of personal self-exploration who are also utterly committed to the journey of community. It is an unending exercise in corporate, interpretive practice and a relentless undertaking to create "belonging" for the full range of human experiences.

To this end, Thurman resources the mundane visual landscapes of our daily routines, nature, worship, and fellowship to fund the visions he expressed in his polished writings. Something that frustrated his head, heart, and tongue was the challenge to verbalize the unarticulated because it was always that: a challenge. Thurman concludes *The Search for Common Ground* by urging readers to interpret their current experiences in terms of other people, moments, and community formations:

> Let us now go forth to save the land of our birth from the plague that first drove us into the "will to quarantine" and to separate ourselves behind self-imposed walls. For this is why we were born: Men, all men belong to each other, and he who shuts himself away diminishes himself, and he who shuts another way from him destroys himself. And all the people said *Amen*.[21]

It is at that "Amen" where I imagine Thurman still working on his final statement about the necessity of common ground. I suspect if we listen, we might hear him saying once again, *"I can see it? Now, how to say it?"*

Conclusion

A rich repository of word pictures and metaphors contribute to the aesthetic quality of Thurman's interpretation of life, religious experience, and sacred texts like the Christian Bible and Torah.[22] He writes words that enable his readers to "see something"—often for the first time. When one focuses solely on his literary archive, it is easy to miss the richness of his verbal play, which he intentionally collected for posterity's sake. In his 1971 autobiography, Thurman reflects on the global proliferation and influence of his recordings:

> At the time of this writing more than five hundred people scattered all over the United States and Canada regularly contribute to the work of the Trust. In a few short years scholarships have been established in

---

[21] HT, SCG, 104.

[22] My research addresses HT's hermeneutical processes and traces his interpretive wordplay. See my digital humanities exhibit titled *Images of Interpretation* at www.images-ofinterpretation.com.

eighteen colleges, seminars conducted at Trust headquarters all through the year, and listening rooms based on the extensive collection of tape recordings sent from San Francisco have been located in many parts of the United States and in seventeen foreign countries, the latest of these, South Africa.[23]

He assigned equal importance to his recordings and writings. His literal sound and the genuine struggles captured in his oral presentations highlight the aesthetic dimension of his search. Thurman endeavored to forge new human proximities that transgressed cultural and religious boundaries. Such aspirations sparked public and disruptive moments of pause, uncertainty, reflection, and revision.

For Thurman to *say something*, he needed to *see something*. Sometimes that sight was clear, and he was able to convey it with ease. Other times, he saw something off in the distance that not even he could articulate effectively. Nonetheless, he persisted in the endeavor to interpret out loud for others to see. Thurman's recorded voice was his investment in communities he was addressing in the moment and for generations born after his lifetime. The concluding sentences in his autobiography make his commitment plain: "I take my stand for the future and for the generations who follow over the bridges we already have crossed. It is here that the meaning of the hunger of the heart is unified. The Head and the Heart at last inseparable; they are lost in wonder in the One."[24]

According to Thurman's spoken and written words, the human endeavor for communion with self, God, creation, and other human beings necessitates transcending current social realities of separation, polarization, stigmatization, and distance. Current generations need only access the range of Thurman media to wade in an interpretive aesthetic constituted by the full orb of human sensory experiences. If we listen to his recordings long enough, Thurman, the interpreter, guides a new generation in word and speech with his museful statement: *"I can see It. Now, how to say it?"* His past invitation to see something becomes a refracting lens for current Thurman listeners to do and say something now.

---

[23] HT, WHAH, 262.
[24] Ibid., 269.

3

The Unfinished Search from Head to Heart

Howard Thurman's Crossroad Pedagogy

Gregory C. Ellison II

It felt as if she could see my soul, yet it was such an odd feeling. We were the only two seated on the back pew of a rickety old church on the side of the road in rural Georgia. I attended the evening service to support my college peers on their annual spring gospel choir tour, but the gray-haired saint on our shared pew did not clap or sway to the music. She just peered through me. Several minutes later, she broke the silence with a wry smile and this odd pearl of wisdom, "Baby, if you don't want to get old … die young." I furled my brow in confused gratitude. She commenced her silent stare through another gospel song or two. Then the sagacious elder pierced the silence and etched these words in the inner chambers of my heart, "Son, the longest journey you will take in life is the trip from your head to your heart." My eyes widened as the weight of her words landed in me. Before I could request her name and offer proper thanks, she quietly gathered her purse and tipped out the back door in the middle of the choir's song.

Since that evening in the rural church, I have worked to meld theory and practice, and live out the theology I profess. Admittedly, on the thoroughfare from head to heart, I have encountered complex scenarios that left me questioning how best to proceed. I give thanks for elders, mentors, and unlikely teachers who serve as guides in these moments of deep discernment. Like many fellow sojourners, Howard Thurman has come as a teacher when I found myself at life-defining crossroads. Maybe you have stood at similar intersections. When I was uncertain if I should move forward with boldness or sit in contemplation, Thurman would come. When I was reckoning with deep aloneness while surrounded by many, Thurman was there. When I was hearing the whispers of the ancestors and the cries of those not yet born, he stood nearby.

For half my life, Thurman has served as a teacher, a guide. In these years, I have perceived a pedagogical method of how he instructs me when I stand at life-defining crossroads. Perhaps this method will be of service to you at your next critical juncture on the unfinished search. There are three components to this crossroad pedagogy, yet they rarely unfold in chronological order. First, Thurman captures my imagination with a *creative tension*. Second, Thurman leads me on what Luther Smith calls a "quest with *questions*."[1] Third, Thurman challenges me to make a *commitment*. Below I outline three decisive moments in my journey when Thurman's crossroad pedagogy offered guidance at critical junctures.

Beyond a Vocation of Negation

On the first week of August 2015, scores of old friends, colleagues, and mentors flocked to the Show-Me State. Together they gathered in Ferguson, Missouri, to honor Michael Brown's life, protest police brutality, and call America to reckon with its history of systemic racism. From my home in Atlanta, I followed on social media play by play, step by step as my kinfolk staged teach-ins and marched in protest and remembrance along with the young and fearless leaders spearheading the Black Lives Matter movement. All the while, I sat comfortably in my home office writing my second book.

At my desk, I stared into the computer screen, glimpsed a silhouette of my reflection, and pondered, *Do I see myself in the ways that the world sees me?* In the eyes of casual observers, I present as a young, confident, and finely dressed tenure-track professor with an ability to care through teaching, preaching, and advocacy. With eyes affixed on news out of Ferguson, I grew more conflicted with that external perception and who I actually believed myself to be. Creative tensions around vocational identity swirled within. Then "the picture" emerged atop my social media feed and triggered a frenzy of internal questions that thrust me into an existential tailspin.

On that Monday afternoon, I digitally followed the footsteps of three hundred protesters marching from Christ Church Cathedral to Missouri's Thomas F. Eagleton Federal US Courthouse. Around 1:30 pm, nearly a quarter of those chanting protesters crossed the barricade surrounding the courthouse. Face to face with police in bulletproof vests, the unarmed protesters interlocked their arms and as a human chain readied themselves for conflict. Detainment was

---

[1] Gregory C. Ellison II, ed., *Anchored in the Current: Discovering Howard Thurman as Educator, Activist, Guide, and Prophet* (Louisville, KY: Westminster John Knox Press, 2020), 173–76.

expected. However, "the picture" of this scene in Ferguson told a unique story of my vocational life.

In "the picture," my graduate school teacher Dr. Cornel West, my prayer partner Reverend Dr. Starsky Wilson, and my little sister Rahiel Tesfamariam stood arm in arm before vested officers. As Facebook commentators "liked" the picture and pronounced their opinions, feelings of guilt, hypocrisy, and vocational unrest consumed me. My self-understanding as a scholar, minister, and activist came into question: *Where am I? Why am I here? Why am I not there? Who am I?* Hours upon hours, day after day, I gazed at "the picture," and in the wake of the destruction one question remained: *Who am I not?*

From one angle, "the picture" spoke a thousand words about my educational formation, my ministerial calling, and my identity as an activist. Yet from another angle, it debunked my self-understanding as a public intellectual, a prophetic minister, and an activist on the front lines. Confronted by the creative tensions of the picture, a litany of vocational questions challenged my purpose and my call.

> *What good is a behind-the-scenes public intellectual?* I am not Cornel West, bell hooks, or James Baldwin. I am not. I am not. I am not.
>
> *How can I be a prophetic preacher without a pulpit to proclaim?* I am not Starsky Wilson, Martin Luther King Jr., or Traci Blackmon. I am not. I am not.
>
> *Can I call myself an activist, if I rarely find a picket line?* I am not Rahiel Tesfamariam, Stokely Carmichael, or Darnell Moore. I am not.[2]

Standing at the crossroads of creative tensions, I recognized that for over a decade I defined my vocational identity through negation: by who I was not. Seeking a more affirmative frame to structure my vocational confusion, I was drawn to the echoing timbre of Thurman's baritone voice in a meditation titled "What Do I Want, Really?" After introducing the title query Thurman poses a litany of questions that seized the totality of my being:

> What is it that is the fundamental thing that I am after with my life? What is the meaning of all of the activities, the strivings, and the struggles? What after all is my point? Am I really concerned, ultimately, about providing some windbreak against the world around me? Am I really concerned about the accumulation of economic power which would give to me a sense of quiet security and tranquility . . . ? Is this

---

[2] Gregory C. Ellison II, *Fearless Dialogues: A New Movement for Justice* (Louisville, KY: Westminster John Knox Press, 2017), 123–29.

the be all and end all of my striving? Or is it for something else, perhaps for fame, for a certain kind of honor so that my name or memory will be preserved ...? Is this the thing that I'm after? What is it that I really want? What is that [that] is capable of making me bring to bear upon a single end or focus or purpose all of the resources of my life—my thinking, my dreaming, my struggling—so that in the fulfillment of myself this thing will follow? ... What is it that I really want? What is it that I am trying to find, to become, to get hold of?[3]

For months on end these questions rumbled within. All the while, I gazed at "the picture," worked to untangle my vocation of negation, and sought to unfurl the mystery behind what it was I really wanted. Then, on a trip across the vast openness and seemingly brown desolation of the Mojave Desert, I beheld an oasis of color strewn across the evening sky. Against the backdrop of this dry and barren landscape, this wellspring of color precipitated a vocational epiphany that flooded my consciousness: *I am an artist. I see beauty in places where others see death. I am an artist. I see hope in people where others see despair. I am an artist who does not sing, paint, or draw. I create spaces for unlikely partners to have hard, heartfelt conversations with themselves and others. I am an artist when I teach, preach, counsel, or write. I am an artist in classrooms and boardrooms, while standing in pulpits and on street corners. I am an artist.* Since that dusty eve in California's Mojave, I have owned my vocational lot as artist. It is what I really want for my life, and to this, I commit. *Now to you, beloved, I ask ... what do you want, really?*

A Single Respiration

The final breath escaped his lungs in the dawning hours of March 5, 2018. My beloved namesake, my father, my dearest friend, Gregory C. Ellison Sr. was with us one moment and gone the next. Emotions of disbelief soiled the antiseptic-white room. The flatlining buzz could not outpitch my mother's wailing tears. Yet in the frenzy of the ER for a moment's time the world around me slowed. Though devastated, flattened, and overwhelmed, I beckoned the call of what I perceived to be my pastoral duty to care for the throngs who would gather to mourn the loss of our patriarch.

From the gallows of the hospital, I set my internal clock and began preparation to offer my father's eulogy in seven days' time. As expected, within hours of

---

[3] HT, "What Do I Want, Really?" in *The Living Wisdom of Howard Thurman: A Visionary for Our Time*, Sounds True Audio Learning Course (Boulder, CO: Sounds True, 2010).

Dad's passing, cars lined the driveway at our family home. By midweek, dozens upon dozens of loved ones trafficked in and out of the house. In search of space to breathe, mourn, and write the eulogy, I placed a call to Luther and Helen Smith. Without hesitation, the Smiths prepared their guest bedroom and cleared a table for me in the basement where Luther keeps his home office.

Surrounded by Luther's collection of ceramic turtles, a makeshift altar, family photos, and books from Howard Thurman's own library, I found the stillness palpable in the Smiths' subterranean sanctuary. Numbed by grief, I closed my eyes and let out a deep sigh of the sorrow that had settled in the pit of my being. When I inhaled I felt my chest rise and my internal reservoir expand. This rhythmic cadence of release and replenishment continued for minutes on end. Upon opening my eyes, an all-familiar passage in Thurman's *For the Inward Journey* came to view: "A Good Death." Here, Thurman likens life and death to identical twins. He further suggests that these seeming polarities may be felt as "a single respiration—the ebb and flow of a single tide." While the body may fail, a good death comprises the same elements of a good life—a deep acceptance of one's purpose and a yielding to the will of God.[4]

In the refuge of the Smiths' subterranean sanctuary a creative tension surfaced. The weight of my namesake's departure unearthed complex emotions around my own mortality. Drafting my father's eulogy not only prompted reflection on the qualities of his good death, but it also initiated self-scrutiny on the conditions for me to live a good life.

Months after the eulogy I still puzzled, *What must I do to die a good death?* A corner piece of this existential quandary was placed before me in what I perceived to be a most unlikely locale—an academic conference. At a sparsely attended Thursday morning panel, a Buddhist monk offered a lesson on humility that taught me how the cultivation of God-given gifts is central to living a good life and ultimately dying a good death. The monk explained, "Humility is not the act of dimming one's light through deflection or self-deprecation. Humility is an accurate assessment of one's gifts." There is no need to boast or belittle, but one must own the gifts uniquely bestowed by God. Such accurate assessment and unapologetic acceptance of gifts squarely position one to live a life devoted to growth, learning, and a humble pursuit of God's will.

For me to die a good death, I must live into my gifts as an artist without shame or reservation. I must walk humbly with God. To this, I commit. *My friends, what must you do to die a good death?*

---

[4] HT, *For the Inward Journey: The Writings of Howard Thurman* (Richmond, IN: Friends United Press, 1984), 71.

Not for Rent

Fifteen months had passed since Dad joined his walk with the ancestors, yet grief lingered and I found myself hanging on by a thread. After decades of striving for excellence, I found my body broken, my spirit saturated, my mind *macerated*.[5] Even more devastating, I stood directionless. Unlike many of my faculty peers, in high school I never envisioned myself a professor. Yet positive momentum drove me forward from a top-tier university to grad school, doctoral study, and a renowned teaching post. However, after tenure I had no goals for which to quest. I published without perishing, so I continued to feverishly write. I taught with abandon and earned a third faculty teaching award. I offered service to the university and the profession. But to what end? My body broke. My spirit anguished. My mind *fractalized*. Somehow, in my striving I had lost my way.

In search of a compass, a colleague made mention of a scantly referenced theme in the voluminous library of Howard Thurman, "the working paper." As the phrase seemed rife with meaning, I grew unsatisfied with the small handful of paragraphs on the topic in Thurman's texts *Disciplines of the Spirit, Deep Is the Hunger,* and *Jesus in the Disinherited.* In pursuit of a more robust understanding of the working paper, I consulted my mentor-teacher, and editor of the Howard Thurman Papers Project, Walter Earl Fluker. Within moments, he emailed three of Thurman's unpublished sermons. Each bore in its title, "Your Working Paper." Little would I have known that those handful of published paragraphs and three uncirculated sermons would launch me on a mission to find my true north.

According to Thurman, "The working paper is a creative synthesis of what you are in all your parts, [it patterns] how you react to the living process ... and [it provides] the framework [by] which [you] live [your] days moment by moment."[6] The working paper is far more than a goal or an end located far off in the future. To the contrary, it is a living, breathing document that expands and constricts; it grounds purpose and clarifies vision. For Thurman, such grounding and clarity are the direct result of sustained introspection on hard questions, such as the following:

1. What are the lines along which you are living your life?
2. What are you trying to do?

---

[5] For more on the perils of maceration, see Bonnie J. Miller McLemore, "Contemplation in the Midst of Chaos: Contesting the Maceration of the Theological Teacher," in *The Scope of Our Art: The Vocation of the Theological Teacher*, ed. Gregory L. Jones and Stephanie Paulsell (Grand Rapids: Eerdmans, 2001), 53.

[6] HT, "Your Life's Working Paper—Introduction," unpublished sermon, Marsh Chapel, September 26, 1954, 1, HTC, Box 11, Folder 101:99.

3. Are there any guiding principles that you preach about or that you talk about?
4. What does it mean to commit your life?
5. At what point and with reference to what do I compromise?
6. What does life mean to you?
7. Do you have your own working paper or are you using one that you just borrowed from somebody?[7]
8. What part must others play in my working paper?[8]

For Thurman, every person—regardless of rank, title, or status—is born with a unique idiom and must face a similar bevy of questions to live out his or her working paper. Further, Thurman states, "If you do not make formal decisions about the lines along which you will live your life, then all sorts of things and people are constantly inciting, without your leave, notions and schemes and plans on the basis of which you live."[9] That summer, it struck me that since earning tenure I had made no formal decisions about the lines along which to live my life, and the constant inciting of others led me down a path not of my own choosing. More devastatingly, I stood at a crossroad when I recognized that my trained mind was for rent.

In an unpublished 1954 Boston University Marsh Chapel sermon titled "Your Life's Working Paper—Commitment," Thurman articulates that tragic consequence of a mind uncommitted to a strong pure purpose.

> There is nothing more tragic in human life than to see the trained mind, the mind that has mastered the discipline or the particular area of human knowledge, and at the center of that trained mind there is no fundamental commitment; no hard core of metaphysical purpose. The result is the trained mind is for rent. Anyone who is able to pay enough money can rent the trained mind and use the fruits of the creative process of mind for ends with which the mind itself has nothing in common.[10]

At the high cost of pleasing others, I had allowed my body to be mortgaged, my spirit to be compromised, and the creative processes of my mind to be let to the highest bidder.

---

[7] Ibid., 2–5.

[8] HT, "Your Life's Working Paper—Human Relations," unpublished sermon, Marsh Chapel, May 8, 1948, 1, HTC, Box 11, Folder 12:12.

[9] HT, "Your Life's Working Paper—Introduction," 2.

[10] HT, "Your Life's Working Paper—Commitment," unpublished sermon, Marsh Chapel, October 10, 1954, 5, HTC, Box 14, Folder 5:81.

Standing at the tensive crossroad of a rented mind with no discernible commitments to my own future, I entered into a series of soul-plumbing conversations with my spiritual guide, Elesa Commerse. In her customary monkish chant, Ms. Elesa intoned, "If people can take your time, they can deplete your energy. When your energy is diminished, you have no life. To guard your time is to guard your life." She then posed a question that I could not answer: "Greg, do you value yourself?" I stopped. An uneasy quiet hung in the air. I closed my eyes and felt the darkness envelop me. Time passed as I reckoned with this question that was not academic, but existential. Minutes later I responded, "I do not." As a result, the working paper was borne in an effort to guard my time, dedicate my energies to a God-inspired audacious goal, and fully value the life I have been gifted.

My Working Version of My Working Paper

The working version of my working paper appears below. I classify this iteration as a working version because the working paper is a living document that is subject to revision and refinement as dictated by the Spirit of God and the daily lessons of life. Of equal note, to my knowledge, Thurman does not provide a template to organize one's working paper.

For clarity of frame, I structure this working version of my working paper around the classic organizational tenets of mission, vision, objectives, and values. This framework is dually helpful. On one hand, this classic structure helps serves as an umbrella to centrally organize and guide my multifaceted roles as educator, minister, activist, author, and artist. On the other hand, the structure provides a comparative model for me to discern if I align with the organizational tenets of the institutions or individuals with which I affiliate. Should I discern that the tenets of the institution or individual are at cross purposes with the tenets of my working paper? I must find ways to remove myself from such commitments or work tirelessly to restate its terms, for to stay in step with an institution or individual that contradicts my own working paper is to devalue my time, my energy, my life. In this regard, the working paper serves as a tool of discernment that offers clarity and liberation. Here is the working version:

Vision	To catalyze change for the generational good, three feet at a time.
Mission/Call	Bring people together, by modeling togetherness. (Togetherness is much more than gathering persons in a physical space. Togetherness connotes living an undivided life.)

Objective	Create spiritually charged interactive learning environments that stimulate wonder and spark conversation for local and global leaders.
Values	To achieve this vision, mission, and objectives in my working paper I have outlined six values that situate me to be a living V.E.S.S.E.L. for God's work.

Value	Live humbly by accurately assessing my gifts, ensuring that others do the same, and supporting leaders to see the intrinsic worth in those around them.
Excellence	Fill each moment with dignity and every encounter with grace, so that the highest quality is evident and God is glorified. Excellence in this regard is not to be confused with the strictures of perfection.
Storytelling	Employ the power of story in mixed media (e.g., oral, written, artistic, technological) to teach empathy, embolden care, and vitalize hope.
Synthesis	Make it plain so that the unfamiliar becomes familiar and invite awe so that the familiar becomes unfamiliar.
Ecosystem	Cultivate the relationship between my center and the center of all things living, ancestral, and Eternal.
Legacy	Move with intention and discipline such that with God's grace, I can live a good long life, die a good worthy death, and leave a better world for my great-great grandchildren.

The final element of my working paper is a mantra. In a recent session with Ms. Elesa, she explained that in Sanskrit the word *mantra* can be translated as "mind protection." One might imagine that enacting the tenets of a working paper could put one at odds with neighbors, loved ones, and colleagues, who have their own desires, ambitions, and wants for your life. The mind committed to the working paper must be protected. To my delight an eight-sentence mantra came from afar and landed in my spirit after a particularly vexing therapy session on June 4, 2019. Feel these words:

> *Know this.*
> *I am with you.*
> *God is with you.*
> *I am with me.*
> *God is with me.*
> *God is in us.*
> *God is near.*
> *Know this.*[11]

Again, Thurman posits, "If you do not make formal decisions about the lines along which you will live your life," you risk renting your mind and remaining susceptible to imposing others' working papers on you. Therefore, I commit to a lifelong revision of my working paper and a daily walk with its complementary mantra. To this, I commit. *Now to you, beloved, I ask: What working paper guides your life?*

Beloved, as you find yourself at the crossroads of life, stand at the intersection and discern the creative tension. Listen deeply, for the journey from head to heart is paved with question marks. When Thurman appears, declare your commitment and walk humbly with God. May you find peace on your journey.... This is the unfinished search.

---

[11] Gregory C. Ellison II, "My Working Paper: Beyond the Mule's Path," *Pastoral Psychology* 69 (2020): 354–59.

4

From Prodigals to Good Samaritans

*One Path to Common Ground in
Howard Thurman's Life and Thought*

David B. Gowler

Every [person] is potentially every other [person's] neighbor.[1]

Jesus of Nazareth was a first-century apocalyptic prophet of Jewish restoration theology who, like many other Jewish prophets before him, proclaimed a message of social and economic justice for his oppressed people. Jesus's teachings are also Torah-centered and incorporate aspects of Jewish Wisdom traditions, the ethical import of which represents a "voice from below," a humane, commonsense approach of a first-century Jewish non-elite person.[2]

What does this understanding of Jesus of Nazareth have to do with Howard Thurman's unfinished search for common ground? Thurman's *Jesus and the Disinherited* depicts Jesus's first-century context in ways that many New Testament scholars still do not (cannot?) understand about how Jesus's religion and ethical vision are embedded in his first-century context: he was a Jew living in poverty, a member of a minority group with their "backs against the wall," suffering oppression from a dominant, controlling group, the Romans.[3]

---

[1] HT, *Jesus and the Disinherited* (Boston: Beacon Press, 1976), 79.

[2] For an introduction to the ethics of Jesus, see Gerd Theissen and Annette Merz, *The Historical Jesus: A Comprehensive Guide* (Minneapolis: Fortress Press, 1998), 347–403.

[3] This inability or unwillingness to understand Jesus's status, perspectives, and teachings is even more pronounced among white Christians in the United States, especially white evangelicals. See, for example, Anthea Butler, *White Evangelical Racism: The Politics of Morality in America* (Chapel Hill: Ferris and Ferris Books / University of North Carolina Press, 2021); Robert P. Jones, *White Too Long: The Legacy of White Supremacy in American Christianity* (New York: Simon & Schuster, 2020); Katherine Stewart, *The Power Worshippers: Inside*

In addition, in my experience, *Jesus and the Disinherited*, a book published in 1949, remains the best explanatory bridge for making the ethics of a first-century Jewish prophet understandable and relevant for twenty-first-century readers. Students in my Ethics of Jesus course at Oxford College of Emory University, for example, are often stunned by how many of Jesus's teachings are not relevant to life in the United States today. Jesus of Nazareth was immersed in the legal debates of his fellow first-century Jews by his concern with Mosaic Law and Torah observance—questions of practice arising from it (e.g., Sabbath observance and purity rules), topics that are of little interest or relevance to the vast majority of my students.

As *Jesus and the Disinherited* clearly demonstrates, though, Thurman realized that Jesus, a poor first-century Jew, spoke to an overwhelming number of first-century Jews who, like him, were poor, oppressed, disinherited, and dispossessed—those with their "backs constantly against the wall." Then Thurman asks the crucial question: "what does our religion say to them?" In contrast to much of what passes for Christianity today—which, as Thurman also correctly notes, all too often has betrayed the religion of Jesus by becoming the established religion of nations whose use of power and violence violated the essence of his message—Thurman argues that we have to return to the teachings and religion of the historical Jesus: "It is necessary to examine the religion of Jesus against the background of his own age and people, and to inquire into the content of his teaching with reference to the disinherited and the underprivileged."[4]

By highlighting Jesus's message to the oppressed, Thurman made the teachings of Jesus again relevant for the struggle for civil and human rights and revealed a path for seeking common ground. The fact that Jesus spoke as a member of an oppressed group with their backs against the wall provides a bridge to subsequent centuries, because, as Thurman observes, "This is the position of the disinherited in every age."[5] In my course, we spend a week mid-semester reading and discussing *Jesus and the Disinherited*, and it has been the most effective way for my students to begin to understand the implications and contemporary relevance of Jesus's teachings, both for the "disinherited" and the "inherited."

Key to Thurman's understanding of parables, the religion of Jesus, and religious experience itself is his insistence that personal transformation—the coming to oneself and therefore coming to God—is the foundational first step that leads to all other transformations of self and society. One's personal, inner transformation

---

the Dangerous Rise of Religious Nationalism (New York: Bloomsbury, 2019). The search for common ground remains an urgent and difficult task.

[4] HT, *Jesus and the Disinherited*, 5.
[5] Ibid., 12.

should lead to social action, and social transformation is possible because of our own inner transformation and the guiding hand of God. We also see more clearly how the parables of the Prodigal Son and Good Samaritan are foundational to Thurman's life and thought, and in our continuing search for common ground, these two parables exemplify a path that Thurman also recommends: *reconciliation, restoration, and community* with God and our fellow human beings.

Two Foundational Parables

Thurman's sermons on the parables include reflections on their *meanings*, but his interpretations primarily focus on how parables should be applied in one's life—what they *want* from us.[6] In addition, his sermons also include insightful observations about how parables *work*—how they are effective rhetorically by their use of particular words, images, or other aspects of their composition, including their dialogical nature and ambiguity that stimulate our imaginations and, hopefully, our actions. Thurman admires, for example, the genius in Jesus's stories, the turn of phrase—such as the priest in the parable of the Good Samaritan "walking by the other side"—or the mysterious and curious absences—where is the mother, for example, in the parable of the Prodigal Son? Such details, Thurman argues, give ample evidence of Jesus the storyteller's "consummate touch of genius."[7]

These sermons, especially the meditations and prayers that preface them, reflect Thurman's belief that a fundamental aspect of "the religion of Jesus" is to meditate in the quietness so that one can experience the spirit of God. For Thurman, that time of quietness, that time of listening to the spirit of the living God, necessarily leads to a deeper awareness of who we are as human beings and our interconnectedness with God. Those foundational experiences of "coming to ourselves and therefore coming to the father" (see the Prodigal Son discussion below) lead to a profound understanding of our interrelatedness to other human beings, to all other children of God. We are all interconnected and therefore have responsibilities to one another:

---

[6] Beginning with this section, the rest of this chapter is a significant revision of David B. Gowler, "Sit and Listen; Go and Do: The Parables of the Good Samaritan and Prodigal Son in Howard Thurman's Life and Thought," in *Anatomies of the Gospels and Beyond the Gospels: Essays in Honor of R. Alan Culpepper*, E. J. Brill Biblical Interpretation Series 164, ed. Elizabeth Struthers Malbon, Mikeal C. Parsons, and Paul N. Anderson (Leiden: E. J. Brill, 2018), 434–51. Used with permission. The insights in this chapter also form a major part of the foundation for my book tentatively titled *What Do Parables Want?: Howard Thurman's Search for Common Ground*, under contract with Paulist Press.

[7] HT, *Sermons on the Parables*, ed. and intro. David B. Gowler and Kipton E. Jensen (Maryknoll, NY: Orbis Books, 2018), chapter 3, "The Prodigal Son" (preached on September 23, 1951); and chapter 5, "The Good Samaritan" (preached on October 7, 1951).

No one of us can live unto himself no matter how hard he tries. We are so deeply involved in each other and in others that often it is difficult to determine where we begin and the other leaves off. And perhaps in the quietness we may sense the mystery and the wonder and the magic of our relatedness, and in that relatedness become aware each after the pattern of his own sensitiveness of the emergence in our midst of the living spirit of the living God in whom we live and move and have our being. What we discover here in the quietness may inform all of the boundless, limitless spread of mankind everywhere to the end that what we do we know must be done with an eye singled to its bearing upon the least and the greatest, the wisest and the most foolish, the meanest and the righteous of all the children of men.[8]

Coming to oneself and coming to God, then, have significant implications. The awareness of our interconnectedness with God necessarily leads to an awareness of our interrelatedness as human beings with other human beings in what Thurman calls our "central cores" as children of God and, therefore, that understanding of interconnectedness should lead to ethical actions:

Do not shrink, then, from that which turns up in your road, suddenly making of you an ultimate demand. Know that if you respond with all that you have, your little life takes on a meaning in the light of which even death itself is a little thing. To miss it because of fear, timidity, pride, arrogance, self-righteousness, deceit, to miss it is to wander down your road in darkness, and what a darkness, what a darkness it is for you.

Go thy way, all things say. Thou hast thy way to go. Thou hast thy time to live. Do thy thing. Know thou this that there is no other who can do for thee that which is appointed thee of God. So go thy way and do thy thing.[9]

The profundity of Thurman's insights into the parables—what he often calls "simple stories"—deserves further exploration. The best starting point for these explorations is a more detailed look at Thurman's understanding of the Prodigal Son and Good Samaritan parables, how they are fundamental to his life and

---

[8] HT, *Sermons on the Parables*, chapter 7, "The Rich Fool," 68–69. Although HT's life and work bear witness to his belief in gender equality, his use of masculine nouns and pronouns is disconcerting if not offensive to modern readers. After much reflection, however, I transcribed HT's sermons as he delivered them in the 1950s and ask readers to remember that the most recent sermon HT preached cited in this chapter was over sixty years ago.

[9] HT, *Sermons on the Parables*, 115; Richard Watson Dixon, "Love's Consolation," in *Christ's Company: And Other Poems* (London: Smith, Elder, 1861), 97.

thought, and how the process of moving from the prodigal to the good Samaritan reveals aspects of Thurman's thoughts on how to search for and work toward common ground.

The Prodigal Son (Luke 15:11–32)

In the context of Luke's Gospel, the younger son represents such people as the tax collectors and sinners who are coming to Jesus and "acknowledged the justice of God," and the elder son illustrates some characters in Luke's narrative who oppose Jesus and therefore "rejected God's purpose for themselves."[10] Jesus tells the three "lost" parables of Luke 15 (lost sheep, lost coin, and lost sons), in fact, to those opponents in Luke who grumble about Jesus welcoming and eating with sinners (15:1–2), analogous to how the older son gets angry and refuses to join the celebration over his sinful brother's return.

The parable, as it is found in Luke, portrays God as a father welcoming back the prodigal with joyous, compassionate, and loving arms *and* as a father who shows love and forgiveness to his elder son by seeking him out, assuring him ("all that is mine is yours"; 15:31), and urging him to celebrate his brother's return. He reminds his elder son, who had refused to acknowledge the prodigal as his brother ("this son of yours"; 15:30), that the two sons are indeed brothers ("your brother"; 15:32), thus gently reinforcing family ties, underlining the necessity of reconciliation, and attempting to reestablish community—a fact that is extremely important to Thurman.

This open-ended parable—we are not told whether the older son joins the celebration after his father's pleas to do so—reflects the still unanswered question in Luke of whether Jesus's opponents will respond positively to Jesus's invitation. The lack of resolution also functions as a powerful way to ask readers of Luke the same question: will they join God their father and celebrate the return of "prodigal" sinners?

---

[10] Luke labels these opponents "Pharisees and scribes," but because of centuries of anti-Judaism and the historical inaccuracies involved in their subsequent negative portrayals, I instead designate them as "many of Jesus's opponents in Luke." HT also recognizes this bias, noting, for example, that the "judgmental attitude" toward Pharisees is a "kind of prejudice" and does not accurately reflect "the genius of the Pharisaical movement in Israel": HT, *Sermon on the Parables*, 40. For a discussion and refutation of the common, inaccurate negative stereotypes of the Pharisees, see Joseph Sievers and Amy-Jill Levine, eds., *The Pharisees* (Grand Rapids: Eerdmans, 2021). An analysis of the function of Pharisees *as characters in Luke's narrative* is found in David B. Gowler, *Host, Guest, Enemy, and Friend: Portraits of the Pharisees in Luke and Acts* (1991; repr., Eugene, OR: Wipf and Stock, 2008).

Thurman's Interpretations—A Redemptive Experience

While a graduate student at Rochester Theological Seminary, Thurman spent his summers as an assistant pastor at a church in Roanoke, Virginia, where his duties included leading vacation Bible school for the youth in the church. One summer, Thurman several times had to exclude one particularly difficult boy from class because he was creating an intolerable situation for the other youth. As a result of being dismissed on previous occasions, on the last day of the program, the boy refused to attend the final party no matter how much Thurman urged him to participate. As Elizabeth Yates describes it, Thurman felt as if he had failed the boy:

> What was involved, Howard asked himself, in the loss of an opportunity to relate meaningfully to another human being? Even if the boy might sometime feel sorry, that would not redeem the time that had been lost now. When the prodigal son returned to his father—and Jesus had ended his story at the point where his hearers could pick it up—did he wrestle till he died with the problem of how he could ever redeem the time interval during which his relationship with his father had been ruptured? The wheel of time could not be made to turn back, *but any experience could be made redemptive* [emphasis added].[11]

This illustrates how the parable of the Prodigal Son is a recurring emphasis in Thurman's thought, one that continually compelled him to explore how to create redemptive experiences in order to build community. His reflections on community that are inspired by the parable of the Prodigal Son unsurprisingly revolve around the family relationships of the three main characters in the story. In this light, the poem "The Prodigal Son" by a friend of Thurman's, James Weldon Johnson, provides an apt introduction to the ways in which Thurman interprets this parable:

> *But Jesus spake in a parable, and he said:*
> *A certain man had two sons.*
> *Jesus didn't give this man a name,*
> *But his name is God Almighty.*
> *And Jesus didn't call these sons by name,*
> *But ev'ry young man,*
> *Ev'rywhere,*
> *Is one of these two sons.*[12]

---

[11] Elizabeth Yates, *Howard Thurman: Portrait of a Practical Dreamer* (New York: John Day, 1964), 73–74.

[12] James Weldon Johnson, "The Prodigal Son," in *God's Trombones* (New York: Penguin, 1990), 21.

As Johnson suggests, an examination of the three main characters of the parable of the Prodigal Son is key to understanding the parable, and it is a path that Thurman follows, albeit with some distinctive contributions.

God the Loving Father

In his interpretations of the parable, Thurman stresses that the father illustrates the love, compassion, and forgiveness of God, as well as God's desire to restore community with and among human beings. The stress on community in Thurman's sermons on the three lost parables is palpable. In the sermon on the Lost Sheep and Lost Coin preached on September 16, 1951, the Sunday before the Prodigal Son sermon in the seven-sermon series on the parables,[13] Thurman argues that the sheep became lost because it became "out of touch with the group that sustained him, the group that fed him, that gave him a sense that he counted." Even the coin, which, as Thurman notes, couldn't think, feel, or wander away on its own, was, like many human beings a victim of circumstances over which it had no control. He uses these two parables to explore how best to answer the question "What is God like?" He concludes that the parables demonstrate that God is like both the shepherd and the woman because God does not passively wait for the lost to return—and the coin itself could not! God takes the initiative and actively searches for all who are lost. God wants to do what the shepherd does for the sheep—find and restore it to community—and what the woman does with the coin—restore it to its place of "usefulness." That is what God is like, and as Thurman explores the implications of Jesus's understanding of God's nature and resulting activity, he concludes:

> Now, Jesus says that God is like the shepherd, seeking always to find those who are out of community with their fellows, and when they have found it, when they have found their community with their fellows, then all the world seems to fit back into place, and life takes on new meaning.[14]

All three lost parables in Luke 15, then, tell us what God is like: God is like a shepherd who loves, actively searches for, and rejoices when he finds a lost sheep; God is like a woman who searches for and rejoices when she finds her lost coin; God is like a loving father who runs out to greet his returning prodigal son, forgives him, and restores him to his proper place in the family. God is like a loving father who goes out to entreat his elder son to join in the familial celebration of restored fellowship. God, whether we are like the prodigal or like

---

[13] HT, *Sermons on the Parables*, 17–36.
[14] Ibid., 24.

the older brother—and we can be both at different stages in our lives—always makes the first move, Thurman argues: seeking, searching, finding, welcoming, and urging us to rejoin that family relationship with God and our fellow human beings. God is like the father who is so anxious to welcome the prodigal home that when the prodigal returns, the father does not even give him time to finish his prepared speech, but instead, Thurman observes,

> His father fell on his neck and kissed him. He was so glad to see him that in that swirling moment of heightened ecstasy, he said to his servants, "get the special garment. Kill the fatted calf, wash [my beloved prodigal], and bring him in here so that he can know that he is at the center of my heart where he's been all the time."[15]

Restoration of the Younger Son

Many if not most interpreters understand the "came to his senses" in Luke 15:17 as indicating that the younger son repented. Thurman recognizes, however, that the parable itself is ambiguous about whether the younger son actually repents; although the Lukan context certainly implies it, the parable leaves open the possibility that the younger son may again be manipulating his father. When the younger son asked for his inheritance prematurely, for example, he plays his father for a fool. Likewise, the wording in the parable makes it unclear whether his realization (when he "came to himself") constitutes repentance or is merely a plan of action to make sure he does not starve; readers of the parable can raise significant questions about his motives and sincerity.[16] Thurman, however, does not explicitly question the prodigal's sincerity; for him, the main problem, the most important thing, is that the son had forgotten that he was his father's son. He had lost his family and his community, but now he was home where he belonged.

Thurman continually stresses that the younger son was restored to community. A distinctive element in his interpretation of the younger son, however, stems from his mysticism-guided vision: that human beings discover God within themselves.[17] Thurman relates this insight in a conversation he had with a Buddhist man in Colombo, Sri Lanka, in 1924–25. The man commented that

---

[15] Ibid., 31.

[16] HT, for example, ambiguously paraphrases "came to himself" as "it occurred to him": HT, *Sermons on the Parables*, chapter 3, "The Prodigal Son," 30. For an argument that "biblically literate" readers would suspect that the prodigal is still insincere and connivingly returns home so that he will not be hungry anymore, see Amy-Jill Levine, *Short Stories by Jesus* (New York: HarperOne, 2014), 53–54.

[17] See HT's appropriately titled *The Inward Journey* (New York: Harper & Row, 1961).

the Buddhist students he knew who attended Christian schools in Sri Lanka became "spiritual drifters," people who not only abandoned their own faith but also did not become Christians. Thurman's response is fundamental to understanding his Christian mysticism and the impact it had upon his interpretation of the Bible:

> It seems to me that Christian education has succeeded if it makes a man an authentic Christian, or it may make him a better and more completely devout Buddhist. For I believe that Jesus reveals to a man the meaning of what he is in root and essence already. When the prodigal son came to himself, he came to his father.[18]

He also uses those exact words in his 1951 sermon "The Prodigal Son," where he is even more explicit about its implications. After noting that the famine in the far country that produced physical hunger in the prodigal reflected the famine inside the prodigal, the spiritual hunger he was experiencing in his own heart, Thurman says, "When [the prodigal] came to himself," he came to his father. "That when I ... come to the very center, the very core of myself, then I come face to face with God. That God is, God is within me. That he is the very point of my being and existence ... That there is that of man which is God. Not a reflection of God. Not some staggering accent of God, but that which is God."[19] For Thurman, then, it is in the quietness that we can "center down in the stillness," as he says in the meditation and prayer before the sermon, to listen and perhaps to hear a deeper note than we have ever heard before, when we are "quiet enough to hear the whisper in our heart," when God can be revealed within us and to us.

Call to the Older Son to Celebrate the Restoration of Community

Like most interpreters, Thurman spends a great deal of time reflecting on the younger son but very little time discussing the older son. Both sons, the parable makes clear, became at different times estranged from their father—out of a true family relationship and fellowship with God their Father—and both need to be

---

[18] HT, WHAH, 114–15.

[19] HT, *Sermons on the Parables*, chapter 3, "The Prodigal Son," 34. The effect of reading those words in print can be substantial, but when I read them again, I always hear HT's voice echoing in my ears from the recording of the sermon that I transcribed for our book. Such is the power of Thurman's spoken word. As HT noted, reading his written sermons does not offer the "benefit of the magic of the spoken word, the creative pause, and the lifted countenance." HT, *The Growing Edge*, x. Fortunately, the recorded and written sermons are now publicly available online in PITTS (the quote above starts just after 28:30 in the recording): https://thurman.pitts.emory.edu/items/show/912.

restored into God's family, into fellowship with their father and into fellowship with each other. Thurman, as always, emphasizes the restoration and preservation of *community*. He also stresses that this lack of fellowship with God impacts our relationships with other human beings—a loss of the community that sustains us.[20] The younger brother is restored; whether the older brother is truly restored remains to be seen, although God the father searches for his son, assures him of his love, and entreats him to rejoin the family.

Thus, along the lines of Johnson's poem, Thurman indicates that anyone can be a prodigal returning—or needing to return—home to the father, and anyone can be the elder brother being asked to join the celebration. If we are similar to or identify with the younger brother, what does the parable *want* from us? Thurman asks. It wants us to "come to ourselves," to return to fellowship with God. If, however, we are like the elder brother, the parable wants us to join in and celebrate the restoration of community, a move that also involves ending our estrangement from God.

In the many times Thurman refers to the parable of the Prodigal Son, the focus is always on God's love and the implications of that love for human existence. His sermon "The Love of God" is an example of how his concern about *the experience of love* greatly outweighs any concern about the nuances of the Scripture text itself:

> Jesus, as he began to think aloud of how the love of God operates, told the story about the prodigal son.... [T]he creative attitude of his father's love held firm the context, the climate, the atmosphere, in which the boy could work out his salvation.
>
> It seems to me that this points up an important thing about the love of God. In the religious experience, the individual finds fulfilled what he has glimpsed in his other experiences of love: namely, that in the presence of his God he becomes aware of being dealt with totally. Whether he is a good person or a bad person, he is being dealt with at a point beyond all that is limiting, and all that is creative, in him. He is dealt with at the core of his being, and at that core he is touched and released. With insight, with wisdom, with patience, with courage, with devotion, with commitment, he can now deal with the facts of his own life; and he will seek to introduce all these qualities into his relationships with his fellows.[21]

---

[20] In a 1957 sermon on the Lost Coin and the Lost Sheep, Thurman argues that fundamental to the religious experience and insight of Jesus is that the loss of community can be a "deadly thing": HT, *Sermons on the Parables*, chapter 8, "The Lost."

[21] HT, *The Growing Edge*, 67–68.

Thurman's final sentence is a clear call to action, and this application leads to another dialogic aspect in his approach to the Bible in general and to the parables in particular. On the one hand, his sermons engage with fundamental, universal realities of human and religious experience, yet on the other hand, they translate those ultimate realities into concrete, practical messages for his congregation to apply in their daily lives. Thurman's sermons are never merely instructional: they also involve guidance, inspiration, conviction, and dedication in the communal experience of God's all-embracing presence in the worship service. In addition, his sermons, as do the parables of Jesus, challenge his listeners, as he notes about his ministry in the Church for the Fellowship of All Peoples:

> The core of my preaching has always concerned itself with the development of inner resources needed for the creation of a friendly world of friendly men.... It was my conviction and determination that the church would be a resource for activists—a mission fundamentally perceived. To me it was important that individuals who were in the thick of the struggle for social change would be able to find renewal and fresh courage in the spiritual resources of the church. There must be provided a place, a moment, when a person could declare, "I choose!"[22]

Those words illustrate how Thurman envisions the transition from sitting and reflecting in the quietness to concrete actions in the world, the processes of social action involved with *reconciliation, restoration, and community* that become even clearer in his interpretations of the Good Samaritan parable.

The Good Samaritan (Luke 10:25–37)

The second parable foundational to Thurman's life and thought is the Good Samaritan. His interpretations of this parable illustrate how he envisions moving from the spiritual aspects of religious experience to the practical needs in the lives of his congregation and then to the needs of the local and larger community. The motivation for such actions comes from within, from the recognition, as proclaimed by Jesus of Nazareth, that one's religion should be "God-centered," that we should expect "God to invade the normal processes of life," and that "we are called upon to work with [God]" to further God's kingdom, a kingdom that is present among us, within us, and in our "community relatedness."[23] The best lens through which to interpret Thurman's understanding of the importance of this parable is the perspectives of its various characters and how people should or should not identify with them.

---

[22] HT, WHAH, 160.
[23] See HT, *Sermons on the Parables*, chapter 13, "Who Is My Neighbor?"

The Perspective of the Wounded Man

Thurman does not often dwell on the parable from the point of view of the wounded man by the side of the road, but this perspective is at the heart of his own life and religious experience. The most apparent evidence for this can be found in a seminal event in his early youth that Thurman relates numerous times throughout his career. He even dedicates his autobiography to this mysterious person: "To the stranger in the railroad station in Daytona Beach who restored my broken dream sixty-five years ago." This stranger—whom he had never seen before and to his knowledge would never see again—functions as a paradigmatic good Samaritan whose benevolent actions, Thurman believes, totally changed his life.

One of the times Thurman relates this story is in a 1953 broadcast of *Face to Face* on NBC, a version that is more expansive than most of his retellings of the encounter. He begins and ends by acknowledging how all of us are indebted to "a host of others" before relating how this unknown stranger came to his rescue:

> I remember many, many years ago, when I was just beginning to enter high school, and I was going from the little town in which I lived to a larger city where I would have the opportunity for attending a high school, because, at this period in my state, which is the state of Florida, there were only two public schools in the entire state that were open to me.... When I went to check my trunk, I was told by ... a rather unsympathetic ticket agent, "You will have to send this to Jacksonville by railway express." I only had enough money to buy a ticket and, perhaps, a dollar and fifteen or twenty cents left over, and when he said this, I found that the cost of expressing the trunk was about a dollar and seventy-five cents. So my dreams were gone, and I sat on the steps of the railway station, weeping, as we say, crying my eyes out.
>
> And then, when I opened my eyes so that I could see just a little, I saw two rather large feet just in front of mine. And then my eyes crawled all the way up the full height of this man whom I had never seen before. He was in the act of taking a bag of Bull Durham smoking tobacco out of the jacket that he was wearing, and he opened this bag of tobacco, and then he reached in another pocket and took out a cigarette paper, and all with one hand, the left hand, he emptied some tobacco in the paper, rolled it rather deftly, sealed it with saliva, put the cigarette in his mouth, took his teeth and pulled the cord of the sack of tobacco until it was tight, put the tobacco in his pocket, took a match out of another pocket, struck the match on his thumbnail, lighted the cigarette, took a deep draw, and then he said to me, "Boy, what are you crying about?" And then I told him. And he said, "How much does it cost?" I said,

"Oh, about a dollar seventy-five cents." And then he said, "Come with me. If you're trying to get out of this town, to get an education for yourself, the least I can do is to help you." So he paid for the express charges on the trunk. When the receipt was given to him, he handed it to me, and then he wished me well, turned, disappeared out of the door, walking down the railway track.

I had never seen him before, nor have I seen him since, but because of what he did that particular morning, it was possible for me to begin the long pilgrimage which has led to all of the variety of experiences of my life....

This idea that our lives are lived open to the world without this feeling, without this experience, life would not be possible at all. I am not myself alone, but I am a part of all the life that breathes through me and through which I breathe. We are all of us indebted to a vast host by which we are surrounded.[24]

Thurman observes that our knowledge of being indebted to God and being indebted to other human beings should fill us with a sense of gratitude for these blessings and, as a result, a spirit and a desire to help others just as we have been helped: "Anything less than this is unworthy of our creation as children of God."[25]

The Good Samaritan Perspective

An interpretation of the parable that focuses primarily on the wounded man seeks to answer the lawyer's question in Luke 10:29: "And who is my neighbor?" The answer, of course, is that our "neighbor" in this instance is the wounded man by the side of the road. Jesus, however, asks a different question in Luke 10:36, one that is the flip side of the same coin: "Which of these three, do you think, [proved to be] a neighbor to the man who fell into the hands of the robbers?" That question focuses on the role and responsibility of the Samaritan, as the lawyer reluctantly admits (i.e., he cannot even bring himself to say the word "Samaritan"; instead, he says, "The one who showed him mercy"). In response, Jesus tells the lawyer that he has the same role and responsibility to all human beings: "Go and do likewise" (Luke 10:37).

The majority of Thurman's interpretations focus on this aspect of the parable: our responsibilities to and for other human beings. This approach is based on his belief that the transformation of society ultimately depends upon the transformation of individual human beings, and that personal transformation—the

---

[24] Transcribed from the audio of this broadcast housed in PITTS.
[25] HT, *Sermons on the Parables*, 131.

actualization of the presence of God in one's life—includes the building of human relations and true community, and further, it could be achieved through the life, message, and personal example of Jesus of Nazareth.

An essential element of this creation of community is Thurman's insistence that we should act as "Good Samaritans" because we are truly "related" to each other as children of God in a sacred community of humanity. We are not related by race, creed, or nationality, and we should not act simply because there is need, no matter how great. We act because we become involved in an encounter from the core of ourselves to the core of other human beings, an inward community that then manifests itself as an outward community. He thus uses the parable to challenge our assumptions about our relatedness, our community, our family. Jesus had insisted that "true family," for example, was determined by working relationships (e.g., Mark 3:35: "Whoever does the will of God is my brother and sister and mother").[26]

Compare Thurman's recollection from his summer work in a church in Roanoke in 1924, of how a Muslim from Africa reacted when he found out that there was a Baptist church for whites only and a Baptist church for Blacks only: "In the Moslem religion there would be no such distinction made.... Allah laughs aloud in his Mohammadean heaven when he sees the Christian spectacle: the First Baptist Church White, and the First Baptist Church Colored."[27] As Thurman's ministry at the groundbreaking of the Church for the Fellowship of All Peoples demonstrates, he strove to obliterate such human-erected boundaries between people and the construction of in-groups and out-groups, but he started first and foremost with the transformation of individual human beings and the community that arose from that transformation.

The Priest and Levite Perspective

Thurman also does not often dwell on the perspective of the priest and Levite in his interpretations of the parable of the Good Samaritan; he tends to focus on the positive aspects of community. But in his autobiography, he wryly relates how one of his students reminded him of the possibility that any person, including respected religious figures, could act as the priest and Levite did in the parable. When Thurman became dean of Marsh Chapel at Boston University and professor in the School of Theology, he was asked to teach a homiletics class, and in the second half of the semester he required his students to give extemporaneous short sermons. He relates what one student said in his sermon on the parable of the Good Samaritan:

---

[26] HT, WHAH, 194.
[27] Ibid., 195.

I will give you a modern version of that story. Two days ago, just as it was getting dark, a man was walking by the School of Theology, when another man jumped from behind the hedges and attacked him. He was assaulted and robbed, then pulled off the sidewalk. In a few minutes, the dean of the School of Theology came out of the building and passed where the man lay. He was on his way to a meeting of the Ecumenical council downtown and his mind was full of agenda items. He did not see the man at all; he did not even hear his groans. The next person to come by was the dean of the chapel [i.e., Thurman]. He had just finished a discussion on Meister Eckhart. His mind was trying to work out the difference between God and the Godhead in Eckhart's interpretation. He did not see the man at all; he did not even hear his groans. The next man to come along was Bob Ward, the custodian at the chapel. Bob saw this man and said, "My God! What the hell happened to you?" He called to a security guard and said, "Call the hospital and get an ambulance over here right away. I'll try to make him comfortable until the ambulance comes." When it came, Bob said, "Take care of this man. I am due at the hospital for my own treatment tomorrow and I'll drop in the emergency room and take care of the bill."[28]

He relates the story partly because he found it humorous, but what is also interesting—besides the way in which the young man both implicated Thurman as being the Levite in the parable and relieved Thurman of some of the negative implications in the parable (e.g., in the parable, both the priest and Levite see the wounded man and move to the other side as they pass by him)—is that his retelling of the parable incorporates a significant switch in the character with which people, especially Christians, tend to identify. Instead of being identified with the wounded man who is saved (often interpreted allegorically as Christians being "saved" by Jesus) or with the good Samaritan (by showing mercy to others in God's name), Thurman is identified instead with the Levite, and his error (or sin) is simply being too preoccupied with aspects of his daily life even to take notice of someone in need. Although the parable is still domesticated of most of the radical message inherent in it (the context of hatred between Jews and Samaritans made the "good" Samaritan a character whose inclusion and actions in the story would be shocking to most if not all of Jesus's listeners), it still retains the important warning that all human beings should "Go and do likewise" by showing such mercy to all human beings whenever possible.

---

[28] Ibid., 176–77.

Reconciliation, Restoration, and Community

One of my father's favorite sayings was, "If all else fails, read the instructions." That humorous advice is both insightful in its analysis of human behavior in general and applicable in many areas of human endeavor. One must know what to do before one can go and do it effectively.

In a similar way, Thurman argues that the proper response to the teachings of Jesus is, first, to sit in the quietness, to listen, reflect, experience, and understand. Yet, as Thurman also contends, an encounter with the teachings of Jesus—truly understanding his message—involves more than intellectual assent; it means "to go and do likewise." Jesus's teachings, including these two central parables of the Prodigal Son and Good Samaritan, not only *challenge* us to act; they *demand* that we act. Understanding must lead to concrete action in the world, because truly understanding Jesus's radical message creates in us a profound moral obligation to reflect, decide, and act accordingly, whether by working for civil and human rights, promoting justice in the midst of oppression, seeking peace among those who advocate for war or in other words, proclaiming good news to the poor, release to the captives, and liberation of the oppressed (Luke 4:18).

As Thurman says about love being an "encounter that leads from the core of me to the core of you":

> What about it? Now, I don't know whether it makes sense to you or not, but that isn't important either. Are you willing to try that? Are you willing to try it, really? To work at it? And if you work at it—*really* work at it, despite all the things that we know about the psychology of relations and all the learned things—if you really work at it, you can depend upon this: That there will open up to you, more and more, the strength to keep on working at it. Not to achieve it—that is beside the point—but that is the *assignment of man*, and the degree to which he stays in school and works at it, to that degree is it a reasonable thing to dream about a time when this world will be a decent place for friendly men underneath a friendly sky. Let's try it and see.[29]

---

[29] HT, *Sermons on the Parables*, chapter 5, "The Good Samaritan," 56.

Part Two

Apostles of Sensitivity

Ecclesial and Nonecclesial Communities and Interfaith Practices

5

Eccentric Apostles

Leading from the Growing Edge

Barbara Brown Taylor

"Look well to the growing edge," Howard Thurman said to the congregation of Fellowship Church in February 1949:

> All around us worlds are dying and new worlds are being born; all around us life is dying and life is being born. The fruit ripens on the tree, the roots are silently at work in the darkness of the earth against a time when there shall be new leaves, fresh blossoms, green fruit. Such is the growing edge! It is the extra breath from the exhausted lung, the one more thing to try when all else has failed, the upward reach of life when weariness closes in upon all endeavor.... Look well to the growing edge![1]

Almost seventy-five years later, at the conference "The Unfinished Search for Common Ground" at Emory, the freshest flow of that edge, brought together premier scholars of Thurman's work with people who might have just discovered him. Whatever their connection, chances are that they too were drawn to him for reasons that feel deeply personal and globally urgent all at the same time. This essay focuses on one of Thurman's more peculiar phrases—"apostles of sensitiveness"—by which he meant people alive at their nerve ends, alive in their connective tissues, alive in their ability to feel what others were feeling and to discern the deep contradictions in an established order that was unjust in its reward system. They would be the dramatizers of the growing edge, Thurman said, "the sensitive nerve ends for the body politic"[2] making a track to the edge that others might follow.

---

[1] HT, "The Growing Edge," in PHWT 3:303.
[2] HT, "Cultural and Spiritual Prospect for a Nation Emerging from Total War" (1945), in PHWT 3:108.

For this reason, he recognized that racial minorities—those most exposed to the daily realities of injustice—were uniquely equipped to become apostles of sensitiveness. But "uniquely equipped" did not mean "singularly responsible for." In Thurman's vision, the vitality of the growing edge depended on people from all walks of life, from every class and culture—you, in other words—bringing their conscience of heart and mind into the public sphere wherever they were best able to bend the arc toward more justice, more love.

In the following, I have tweaked his phrase, substituting "eccentric" for "sensitive"—because "sensitive" can mean "delicate" in our time, and apostles are not that. At the same time, their keen receptivity can make them seem more than a little eccentric: nearer the edge than the center, even when they are at the center of something—disrupting business as usual at the center or leaving their desks at the center to set up a card table nearer the growing edge, where they mess with people's sense of where the center really is. I examine this notion of "eccentric apostles" in three acts. In act 1, I look at Thurman's life—his vocational choices in particular—to see what can be learned about an eccentric apostle from the source. In act 2, we hear from him directly about what sets such apostles apart. In act 3, I point to some places where I see apostles at work today, in ecclesial, nonecclesial, and interfaith settings. To do this in such a short time means dipping one cup out of the Thurman freshwater ocean, so that the reader is still thirsty at the end.

Act 1:
What Made Thurman an Eccentric Apostle?

Thurman distinguished himself in so many ways that calling him "eccentric" sounds more than a little off-center itself. He was the valedictorian at both his college and seminary graduations. He was the first dean of Rankin Chapel at Howard University in his early thirties, cofounder of one of the nation's first interracial churches in his forties, and the first Black dean of a chapel at a majority-white university in his fifties, when he arrived at Boston University in 1953. That same year—eleven years before the passage of the Civil Rights Act—*LIFE* magazine named him one of twelve great preachers who were bringing Americans back to church. Thurman was the only Black man on the list, sharing honors with Norman Vincent Peale, Fulton Sheen, and Billy Graham, among others.[3]

Yet this is the same person who, when he was seven years old, said, "One thing is for sure. When I grow up and become a man, I will never have anything

---

[3] "Great Preachers," *LIFE*, April 6, 1953, https://oldlifemagazine.com/april-06-1953-life-magazine.html.

to do with the church."⁴ He was sitting in a buggy with his mother and grandmother at the time, headed home from the cemetery where they had just buried his father, a laborer on the Florida East Coast Railway. Young Thurman's head was still ringing with what he had heard the preacher say about his father, who was not a churchgoer—that he died "out of Christ" and was going straight to hell. Five years later Thurman decided to give the church another try. He went before the deacons and asked to join, but they found fault with his reasons and turned him down. When he went home and told his grandmother, she had the deacons straightened out before the afternoon was over. Still, when he was baptized in the Halifax River on Sunday, he knew it was not by the grace of God embodied in the church but in his formidable grandmother.⁵

His hometown was no kinder to him than his home church. Though Daytona had a sizeable Black population living in three different neighborhoods, the boundaries between Black and white Daytona were so clear that they might as well have been painted on the ground. Thurman could work in Daytona Beach, but he could not spend the night there. It was a "sundown town" where he would be threatened if he stayed after dark. Once, when he was raking leaves for a white family in town, a girl came up and stuck him with a straight pin. When he yelled, she was surprised, saying she thought Black people could not feel pain.⁶ Stories like these make plain that eccentric apostles do not always choose the edge; plenty are driven there. When you are excluded from the center by those who preside there, with power to say who may enter and who may not, you learn your way around the edges by default. Small wonder, then, that between the religious chauvinism of his church and the racial chauvinism of his town, Thurman "found more companionship in nature than [he] did among people."⁷

His friendship with an oak tree in his backyard is legendary by now. When storms blew through, the heavy lower branches of the oak would snap and fall, while the upper ones swayed enough to keep themselves from breaking. "I needed the strength of that tree," Thurman wrote later, "and, like it, I wanted to hold my ground."⁸ Leaning against its trunk, he felt at peace. Talking aloud to it, he felt understood. This sense of connection would stay with him for the rest of his life, expanding his sense of common ground to include all forms of life. So would his sense of being called to the edge.

---

⁴ HT, WHAH, 6.
⁵ Ibid., 18.
⁶ Peter Eisenstadt, *Against the Hounds of Hell: A Life of Howard Thurman* (Charlottesville: University of Virginia Press, 2021), 26–27.
⁷ HT, WHAH, 7.
⁸ Ibid.

Trace his career and you see the pattern emerge. In 1944 he left a tenured position at Howard University to work for half pay as cofounder of an interracial church start-up in San Francisco. Before he had been there a year, he led the congregation in cutting loose from the Presbyterian-funded vision of who they were—a move that cost them both their annual budget and Thurman's Presbyterian co-pastor Alfred Fisk. Though Fellowship Church stayed smallish as a result, never becoming a lightning rod for the political concerns of the Black community, Thurman's commitment stayed firm for another eight years. When he left in 1953 to go back east, it was because he believed Boston University was offering him a chance to do what he was doing in San Francisco at a major university, where there was "the maximum possibility of contagion."[9]

As it turned out, what looked like a move from the edge to the center put him back on the edge again—in an institution he did not head, with an understanding of Christian worship he did not share, and a system of governance that required him to ask permission to go where the Spirit led. Since all his colleagues and higher-ups were white, it was hard for Thurman to parse how much of their resistance to his proposals was based on his race, his theology, his impatience with institutional life, or his spiritual fluidity.[10]

In his annual report of 1961, Thurman reported that the trustees had rejected his proposal for a chapel fellowship modeled on Fellowship Church. In response, he resigned as dean of Marsh Chapel and became university minister-at-large, beginning a four-year period of withdrawal from campus to what he called his "Wider Ministry."[11] This was his last move from the center to the edge, at least at the institutional level. After his formal retirement in 1965, he became CEO of his own foundation—the Howard Thurman Educational Trust—a job he kept until his death in 1981.

Click on any of these vocational stops and you find more eccentricity in Thurman's leadership style, especially in worship. Would he invite a rabbi to give the Sunday sermon? Would he ask a dancer to embody the four universal moods of the human spirit—or show a movie, or stage a play? Those may not sound like edgy options now, but they were in the mid-twentieth century, especially since Thurman was such a compelling speaker that most people would have been happy just to hear him preach. One of his former students at Howard University, James Farmer, wrote that when Thurman preached, Rankin Chapel was packed.

> Though few but theologians and philosophers comprehended what he was saying, everyone else thought that if only they had understood it

---

[9] Eisenstadt, *Against the Hounds of Hell*, 275.
[10] Ibid., 305–7.
[11] Ibid., 306.

would have been wonderful, so mesmerizing was his resonant voice and so captivating was the artistry of his delivery. Those who did grasp the meaning of his sermons were even more ecstatic.[12]

At Fellowship Church, one of the edges Thurman explored took him away from the sound of his own voice. In 1948 he introduced a half-hour period of meditation before the regular service began. He said this quiet time "communicated in vital currents the smell of life in the aura of the worshippers. I would sniff this, somehow, and react to it."

> Sometimes the whole experience would be a prayer. At other times I would move from the depths of my reflection, and the next thing I knew I would hear myself talking [out loud] to God. They were not two separate experiences; there was no boundary. It was one accent, one synthesis. I felt the hearts and minds of the worshippers were receptive to whatever insight my mind and my heart could share with them. This form obtained in the worship Sunday after Sunday.[13]

The language in this passage sounds like someone in a rare state of divine union with God and his congregation, in which all the usual binaries blurred. Yet the fact that this melding happened Sunday after Sunday distinguishes it from most mystical experience. This was more than a rare gift of the Spirit; it was the reliable fruit of a pastor's lifetime practice of availability to the Spirit in whatever form it came.

He was a gardener who patted his roses when they were not doing well, going out to them at night to express his concern for their well-being. He was an animal lover who befriended snarly dogs by telling them more than they wanted to know about the Dalmatian that had bitten him when he was a boy, how he had overcome his fear well enough to have two dogs of his own named Barriemore and Kropotkin, and how he was sure the unfriendly dog would like him once they got to know each other better.[14] Which the dog did, of course, whether it understood one word Thurman was saying or was as taken by his resonant voice as anyone listening to it on a Sunday morning.

Stories like these are so charming that it is easy to miss what Thurman made of them. Here is how he put it in *The Search for Common Ground*: "If one form of life can transcend or get beyond the wall, barrier, or context that separates it from another form of life, then essential unity of life is confirmed to that extent."[15] An ailing rose, a snarly dog, an old oak tree, a pillaged creation, a society sick with

---

[12] Ibid., 148.
[13] Ibid., 172 (brackets added).
[14] HT, SCG, 60.
[15] Ibid., 67.

racism, along with churches mirroring that—these forms of life are not the same, but the life in them is the same—or at least that was the conviction that funded Thurman's reverence for all living things. His decision to focus his energy on the suffering of *human* living things was a matter of urgency, not hierarchy, because an apostle of sensitiveness must make choices. "There can never be a substitute for taking personal responsibility for social change," Thurman wrote.[16] His way of inviting people to do that was so powerfully indirect, so focused on the development of thick relationships across cultural boundaries, and so firm about the need for a strong inner life that it is not a natural match for many of the social movements of our day—but that makes it more important, not less, for us to notice.

Act 2:
What Did Thurman Say about Apostles of Sensitiveness?

He started talking about "apostles of sensitiveness" near the end of World War II, when he believed there was a huge opening for the future to unfold in a new way. All the human energy and imagination that had been consumed by war would soon be freed up again. There was a chance for the nation to be born again. *New leaves. Fresh blossoms. Green fruit.* Looking around for who could help that happen, Thurman came up with the phrase "apostles of sensitiveness," by which he meant people who *were* awake and whose senses were finely tuned. They did not have to know each other. They did not have to quit their jobs or start wearing special clothes. They just had to stay alert to the ideals of democracy that were being threatened right in front of them, doing whatever they could to protect those values at the points where they had power or could exert influence.[17] They were especially needed near the end of the war, Thurman believed, because when people walked out of the rubble and the radiation, the future was going to be there, standing wide open. It was the perfect time for apostles of sensitiveness to get to work, recapturing human energy and imagination for something more than a scramble back to business as usual.

A pandemic is not a world war, but there is a lot in Thurman's description that sounds familiar. Surviving COVID took all the energy and imagination most of us had over the past two years. While our divisions grew deeper, our resources for dealing with them became shallower, with so many demands on them. Now that we are beginning to stick our heads out again, we have a chance to do things differently, if we choose.

---

[16] HT, WHAH, 161. See also HT, "The Light That Is Darkness," June 1940, in PHWT 2:256; and HT, "Mysticism and Social Change," February 13–16, 1939, in PHWT 2:218.

[17] HT, SCG, 67.

Thurman's clearest exposition of what he meant by "apostles of sensitiveness" came in a sermon by that title that he preached in 1946 at the Cathedral of Saint John the Divine. First, he said, "The apostle of sensitiveness must have a highly developed sense of fact with reference to other people."[18] Most of us are specialists in the facts of our lives. We know something about who raised us and what they did for a living. We know which boxes to check on forms that ask about our race or origins. We know why we lean left or right. Those of us who identify with a religion know the basic teachings of it and when the holidays are. We know our zip code and have a general idea what houses in our neighborhood are worth.

At the same time, most of us do not know those facts about other people. We are specialists in our lives, not theirs. Some of theirs are so different from ours that we grab a few impressions and come up with labels that put them at a distance: foreigners, rednecks, snowflakes, liberals, conservatives, elites. Thurman lived with labels much stronger than those, and he knew they came from people who were short on facts about anyone but themselves. Apostles of sensitiveness are not only curious about the facts of other people's lives; they are also alive enough in their imaginations to practice a kind of self-projection by which they enter other people's experience. Thurman called it "a sense of fancy." Without trying to colonize other people's experience, apostles can sense other people's hopes and fears. They can tell what makes others "go," what is vital to them—and within them—that makes them who they are. Having a highly developed sense of fact regarding other people, Thurman said, means meeting them where they are and treating them as if that is where they ought to be. "By so doing," he wrote, "one places a crown over their heads that for the rest of their lives they are trying to grow tall enough to wear."[19]

The second thing Thurman said about apostles of sensitiveness is that they must have a keen sense of alternatives, because where there is no sense of alternatives, there can be no freedom. To say, "There is nothing that can be done about this" or "It's too late to change," is to admit no alternative. *Alternatively*, to say, "What if we sold the building?" or "Why don't we host a radical puppet show in the park instead of planning another march?"[20]—those are things an apostle of sensitiveness might say, alert to seeing a way where there is no way, and to making use of the energy that a creative alternative opens up.

---

[18] HT, "The Apostles of Sensitiveness," in PHWT 3:171.
[19] Ibid., 172.
[20] The Bread and Puppet Theatre was founded in 1963 by Peter Schumann on New York City's Lower East Side as a way of dramatizing "rents, rats, police, and other problems of the neighborhood." See https://breadandpuppet.org.

This requires a sense of the future, Thurman said, which is the third quality he named for apostles of sensitiveness. While the guardians of the status quo work hard to secure the truth they have received from their predecessors against winds of change in the present—with established orders of service, mimeographed organizational charts, and carefully worded creeds of all kinds—apostles of sensitiveness are happy to nod their heads and keep walking. This is not because they disrespect the old truths but because they are sure there is more truth to be found up ahead, in what happens next at God's creative, growing edge.[21]

Act 3:
Where Are Such Apostles at Work Today?

That is a question for everyone who asks it to answer, since the possibilities are vast and as likely to be local as they are to be widely known. They will also reflect different areas of concern (which raises the question of how far from Thurman's concerns we may go without losing him as mentor). William Barber will top one list of super-apostles, while Richard Rohr tops another. Greta Thunberg and Eboo Patel will show up on some lists, Laverne Cox and Tarana Burke on others. Eccentric apostles are all over the place, and they do not always stay put.

Since my focus is on ecclesial, nonecclesial, and interfaith settings—another ocean from which to dip one cup—I do that by tagging a few initiatives that have caught my attention, and invite you, the reader, to do the same so that you can note how they are different from yours. In cases where I only mention one person's name, it is because that person is part of a movement.

In an ecclesial setting, I recognize an apostle in Adam Bucko, cofounder and director of the Center for Spiritual Imagination. Bucko emigrated to the United States from Poland when he was seventeen—old enough to know what it was like to live under a totalitarian regime and to recognize the anarchist youth movement there as a force for social change. After a period of homeless wandering on several continents, he began working with homeless youth in New York City, establishing an ecumenical fellowship for those drawn to what he called "radical spirituality and sacred activism."[22] Now he directs the Center for Spiritual Imagination, hosted at the edge of the Episcopal Cathedral of the Incarnation in Garden City, New York. According to its website, "Our practice exists at the margins of the church (or at its heart) where communion with God and each other eclipses religious affiliations—where the spiritual needs of

---

[21] HT, "Apostles of Sensitiveness," 173.
[22] "Adam Bucko," HuffPost, https://www.huffpost.com/author/adam-bucko, accessed March 14, 2022.

seekers, doubters and religious practitioners converge."[23] It is easy to imagine Thurman nodding at that.

I am also aware of a new initiative by Resist Harm and other progressive caucuses in the United Methodist Church, to create space for those both here and abroad who have no Christian community, or who may not have one soon as the denomination splinters. It will be a virtual space at first, with a vision of the future that includes home churches, affinity groups, and intentional communities. According to Pat Luna, one of the leaders of the movement, it is not about bolstering the institution but about leading from the edge, in a Wesleyan-based community that celebrates the belovedness of every person without exception.

In nonecclesial settings, Volodymyr Zelenskyy has leaped onto the world stage as an eccentric apostle of sensitiveness—the first Jewish president of his country under attack, taking on giants in the tradition of his ancestor David. Between his surprise appearance at the 2022 Grammys and his fiery speech before the UN Security Council during the same week, he excused no one from the call to *do something* to end the war between Russia and Ukraine. Thurman also believed that there can never be a substitute for taking personal responsibility for social change.

Closer to home, I recognize an apostle in Greg Ellison, creator of Fearless Dialogues, who has led scores of organization- and life-changing dialogues with his team of animators since 2013. At the moment I cannot think of another seminary professor who has been invited to work with the Houston Rockets, Chicago Bulls, and Miami Heat as well as Delta, Shell Oil, the American Conference of Cantors, and the Young People's Chorus of New York City. Since Thurman was a believer in the arts, I wish he could see the posters created for these events, each worthy of a framed spot on the wall.

The largest group of apostles I have encountered are younger people who identify as postevangelical.[24] Put off by the politics, racism, and heterosexism of the churches they grew up in, they have decamped—but they have taken their love of Jesus, their commitment to social change, and their desire for soulful community with them. I met a lot of them at the 2019 Wild Goose Festival in Hot Springs, North Carolina, where more than four thousand people converged on a campground by the French Broad River for four days of music, art, worship,

---

[23] The Center for Spiritual Imagination, "Our Community," https://www.spiritualimagination.org/our-community, accessed March 13, 2022.

[24] Bradley Onishi, "The Rise of #Exvangelical," *Religion and Politics,* April 9, 2019, religionandpolitics.org; Kenneth E. Frantz and Samuel L. Perry, "The Unignorable Plight of the Exvangelicals," Real Clear Religion, August 28, 2019, realclearreligion.org; Scout Brobst, "'Evangelicals' Are Living a Uniquely American Crisis," Vice, March 16, 2021, https://www.vice.com/en/article/akdbee/what-its-like-to-leave-the-evangelical-community-exvangelicals.

main stage talks, tent-sized workshops, and small-group meetings designed for spiritual orphans. At Wild Goose, it is not unusual to see a Black Buddhist monk in orange robes walking with a couple of face-painted twenty-somethings in rompers, while an older couple with hiking poles get as close as they can from behind to eavesdrop on what is being said.

Later that same year, I went to the Evolving Faith conference in Denver, where Rachel Held Evans's fast friends Sarah Bessey and Jeff Chu carried on after Rachel's unexpected death in May 2019. "Welcome home," the online invitation read, "Question-asker, status-quo upender, church kid, bible nerd, rebel, yes, you. You wonderer, spiritual refugee, weary one, idealistic cynic and disappointed disciple. *Hello, we see you.*"[25] So many people signed up for that pre-COVID conference that we met in a hockey arena, where twenty-five hundred exvangelicals sang old gospel hymns with new words and soaked boxes of Kleenex with their tears.

The high energy and commitment to change at annual gatherings like these—including the Proctor Institute for Child Advocacy at Haley Farm and Richard Rohr's CONSPIRE conferences in Albuquerque—remind me of a medieval pilgrimage route, traveled by budding apostles who cannot get enough spiritual decentering or strange company where they live. So they leave home instead, seeking those sacred disrupters at marked stops on the pilgrim's way.

Speaking of stops, I have one more to make before I am through. What are apostles of sensitiveness up to in interfaith settings? *So many things* that there is no more room in my cup for even a few of them—so the only stop I will make is the college classroom where I taught world religions for close to twenty years.

Since I went straight from parish ministry to that classroom, the first thing I noticed was that students could have conversations about faith in the secondary, nonecclesial space of a classroom that they were not having in the primary, ecclesial spaces of their home congregations. I do not know how things were going for them in their history, psychology, or statistics classes, but in their religion class they were a little twitchy asking questions they had been taught not to ask and being curious about things they had been told to avoid.

When I first read about Thurman's interfaith programs at Fellowship Church, it was thrilling to see international dinners, painting exhibits, drama, dance, and music programs on the calendar. In his effort to establish common ground, he gave priority to bodily experience when he could have circulated handouts instead; he trusted the arts to take people places their reason might not go. A classroom is not a church, but the first time I invited students to design mandalas, translate sacred songs, or draw floor plans for an interfaith chapel instead of producing five-page papers for a grade, it felt like letting them down.

---

[25] Evolving Faith, https://evolvingfaith.com, accessed March 14, 2022.

Shouldn't they be working on their MLA citation skills instead? But when I saw what they created and heard them talk about the lasting impact of it later, the sun came out. I could not grade their hearts like I could grade their heads, but both belonged in class.

Still, we learned more by leaving the classroom than we ever did by staying put. Site visits to Atlanta-area masjids, synagogues, temples, and gurdwaras became the most popular part of the course by far (and not only because I bought dinner afterward). The first time we traveled to Drepung Loseling Monastery in Atlanta, Geshe Lobsang Tenzin Negi[26] was the Tuesday night teacher, offering us a taste of Tibetan Buddhism we could never have gotten from a book. Though the students could hardly take their eyes off him, everything in that strange-to-them dharma hall blew their minds: the *thangkas* on the walls, the golden figures on the altar, the other students sitting around them on zafus, stiller and more focused than any human beings they had ever seen. One student who was particularly anxious about going on the trip wrote this in the afterword: "There may have been some rituals and ceremonies that I was not sure I wanted to take part in ... but when we arrived it was different." To his surprise, he was able to clear his mind during the meditation periods, reaching a place of calm that was new for him. "The whole experience made me think about changing my perspective on what is going on in my life," he wrote. "Not about changing my religion, but the way that I look at things. This may be what we have been learning in class about different worldviews, but I did not understand the concept until I saw it firsthand at the monastery."[27]

That is one of those papers a teacher keeps for twenty years. It persuades me that the main thing I was up to in that course was wooing more apostles of sensitiveness, if they were open to being wooed—to prick their consciousness, excite their fancy, increase their sense of alternatives, support their eccentricity, deepen their sense of kinship with perfect strangers, and shoo them out the door to create the future in all their different ways.

Epilogue: Apostles Are Never Finished

When I first accepted this assignment, I worried about the word "Unfinished" in the title of the conference. Was the search for common ground supposed to be finished? Were we supposed to outline how that could be done? Nothing sounded more unlikely to me, or more outside my experience. Everything that

---

[26] See Lobsang Tenzin Negi's essay, "Apostles of Sensitiveness: The Buddha Crown and Howard Thurman's Growing Edge," in the present volume.

[27] Quoted in Barbara Brown Taylor, *Holy Envy* (New York: HarperOne, 2019), 58.

has ever mattered to me is still fluorescently *unfinished*. Every time I think I am getting anywhere close to a conclusion, the Spirit moves, and it is back to the drawing board again. Whether the bottom just dropped, or the ceiling just rose, the measurements on the old draft are no longer accurate. It is time to begin again.

How wonderful, then, to discover this passage in Thurman's sermon on "The Growing Edge":

> So the paradox is that the growing edge is always working to be finished, to stop being a growing edge, to settle down and be; and yet the very nature of the growing edge makes that state forever impossible.... Nature is always finally against that which has arrived, that which is ripe, that which has completed itself.... If I want to live, life seems to suggest, I must always be working toward completing something that I never complete, for if I complete it, life is through with me. So when I round out this little dream that I have brooded over with all the creative processes of my mind until at last it begins to realize itself, in its full orbed stature then I know that I had better begin looking beyond.[28]

Whew. That sounds more like it. What a pleasure, then, to be at the end of this unfinished paper, as part of this unfinished conference, on the unfinished search for common ground. I take that as proof that life is not finished with us and that there is still time for us to keep looking beyond—together.

---

[28] HT, "The Growing Edge," 304.

6

Creating Little Islands of Goodwill and Fellowship in a Sea of Hatred

Amanda K. Brown

In 1947, in response to the United States' emergence as a global democratic leader after the Second World War, the Fellowship Church issued a pamphlet that stated, "The United States cannot take to the peoples of the world what we do not practice at home. Democracy and brotherhood may be inherently excellent, and we may extol them to the skies but if we do not live by them, we cannot teach other peoples to do so. World community begins at home."[1] The comment was both a dig at the nation's comprehensive failure to uphold its own founding principles—the law of the day supported numerous institutions and discriminatory practices that negated many people's basic rights—as well as a call to private citizens to take seriously their own power and role within a functioning democratic society.

As a student of American social movements, I am interested in understanding how and why certain expressions of democratic activism emerged and, from a pragmatic standpoint, curious about how some of the ideas and tactics employed within them are potentially useful for us today. This is one of the reasons I was initially drawn to Howard Thurman. When I first encountered his work, his philosophy that large-scale social change could not only start on the local level but that recognizing and building community was an inherently spiritual matter stood out to me as provocative—yet accessible—and altogether appropriate for our own moment.

I should make the point that I come to Thurman from a completely secular background. I was not raised in any type of formal religion, and by the time I was in college and graduate school I was particularly suspicious of religion, especially coming of age in a post-9/11 culture where the most glaring expression of American Christianity—at least through my own perspective and experiences—was

---

[1] HT and Alfred Fisk, "The Church for the Fellowship of All Peoples," in PHWT 3:212–21.

the maturing Religious Right that appeared to be anything *but* inclusive. Yet there I was, and here I am, a nonreligious white millennial intrigued by and invested in this mid-twentieth-century African American Christian theologian. Thurman helped lower my blinders and consider how elements of religion, particularly the cultivation of the inner life, could be functional or useful in dealing with the contemporary affronts to democracy like racism, bigotry, violence, and dogmatism with which I initially thought religion to be wholly complicit.

Thurman saw oppressive belief systems and institutions as spiritual crises disrupting the fundamental wholeness of the human experience, and he thought a hopeful desire to achieve social harmony was a natural impulse. Highly critical of organized religion's divisive tendencies, he cultivated and wielded a spiritual program that was philosophically accessible to individuals from diverse backgrounds, geared to transcend barriers that prevent authentic community. His work fits within the tradition of modern liberal theology—a reformist culture within American Protestantism that balances Christian orthodoxy with rationalism, knowledge, and ethics. It emerged as a compromise between turn-of-the-twentieth-century secularism and long-standing American religious tradition, and its practitioners—focused on empiricism and personal experience—judged ancient biblical texts by standards of modern intellectual inquiry and sought out the usefulness of religious ethics to contemporary life. The intellectual tradition was compatible and often interchangeable with the culture of twentieth-century spiritual "seeking" that provoked a peaked interest in mysticism, Eastern religious practices like yoga and meditation, and a widespread embrace of the idea that the spiritual quest is a universal impulse. The idea that historical scrutiny of Scripture and personal religious experience could serve the goals of social progressivism motivated intellectuals, like Thurman, to theorize about the relationship between religious experience and social change.[2]

William James's *The Varieties of the Religious Experience* (1902) established religion and religious experience within the scholarly community as both relevant and useful aspects of human life, and cleared a path for serious contemplation of the personal and social benefits of spiritual insight.[3] The tradition of mysti-

---

[2] See Amanda Brown, *The Fellowship Church: Howard Thurman and the Twentieth-Century Religious Left* (New York: Oxford University Press, 2021); Gary J. Dorrien, *The Making of American Liberal Theology: Idealism, Realism, and Modernity, 1900–1950* (Louisville, KY: Westminster John Knox Press, 2003); Matthew Hedstrom, *The Rise of Liberal Religion: Book Culture and American Spirituality in the Twentieth Century* (New York: Oxford University Press, 2013); Leigh Eric Schmidt, *Restless Souls: The Making of American Spirituality* (San Francisco: HarperSanFrancisco, 2005).

[3] William James, *The Varieties of Religious Experience* (New York: Longmans, Green and Co., 1902).

cism, what historian Gary Dorrien called "the realization that all life is one," fit firmly within modern American thought. American mystics like Thurman were, as historian Hal Bridges noted, "intensely interested—as mystics the world over have always been interested—in timeless questions of good and evil, of the nature of God or ultimately reality, and of the 'imprisoned splendor' within man and how it may be found."[4]

Thurman subscribed to affirmation mysticism—the idea that once a person experienced wholeness with the rest of the universe, that they would be motivated and even responsible for attempting to create the same synchronicity within society. He defined religious experience as the "conscious and direct exposure of the individual to God."[5] This definition could be problematic to the secularist, but Thurman's conception of God was universal and inclusive. His God was an abstract yet powerfully binding force of love that connected all living things—a force that reveals "that there is at the heart of life a Heart."[6] Thurman surmised that, amid the grasp of heightened spiritual consciousness,

> the individual is seen as being exposed to direct knowledge of ultimate meaning, *ne plus ultra* being, in which all that the individual is, becomes clear as immediate and often distinct revelation. He is face to face with something which is so much more, and so much more inclusive, than all of his awareness of himself that for him, in that *moment*, there are no questions. Without asking, somehow he knows.[7]

Thurman's notion that mystical experience exposes the inherent truth that all life is interconnected and interdependent was something he suspected humans inherently know but are often disconnected from, largely because of how disconnected modern life is from the natural world.[8] He said that "despite the fact that man is a part of nature he sees himself always as in one sense standing over against the world of nature," and theorized that civilization's thrust into industrial life created a kind of internal discord as the constraints of modern society affirmed separateness instead of connection. Given that he interpreted the natural world as harmonious, he understood human beings to have an inherent longing to sustain peaceful community. In *The Search for Common Ground*, he wrote, "In human

---

[4] Dorrien, *The Making of American Liberal Theology*, 564; Hal Bridges, *American Mysticism: From William James to Zen* (New York: Harper & Row, 1970), 9.
[5] HT, *The Creative Encounter: An Interpretation of Religion and the Social Witness* (New York: Harper & Row, 1954; Richmond, IN: Friends United Press, 1978), 20–21.
[6] HT, *Deep River: Reflections on the Religious Insight of Certain of the Negro Spirituals* (New York: Harper, 1955), 95.
[7] HT, *The Creative Encounter*, 20.
[8] HT, "The Inner Life and World Mindedness," in PHWT 3:108–13.

society, the experience of community, or realized potential, is rooted in life itself because the intuitive human urge for community reflects a characteristic of all life." He noted, "In the total panorama of the external world of nature, there seems to be a pattern of structural dependency and continuity, or what may be called an inner logic, that manifests itself in forms, organizational schemes, and in a wide variety of time-space arrangements."[9] Thurman thought that his contemporaries' oversight of this sense of knowing was an essentially spiritual problem, and firmly believed that spiritual *work* was required to rescue it.

He thought that different factors could contribute to one's ability to attain mystical insight. First, he saw certain personalities to be more likely to enter the proper headspace. He thought those who deeply contemplated the state of the world and had a desire to improve problematic conditions were most prepared, and observed that the individual enters religious experience "with the smell of life heavy upon him."[10] The world-weary seeker is therefore primed to reevaluate himself and his issues and is open to a new perspective that will allow him to better cope with his environment. Furthermore, Thurman believed certain endeavors like meditation, prayer, communal worship, and artistic expression serve in the readying process for religious experience. Along those lines, he even thought it was possible to engineer spaces or environments to help dislodge people from their preconceived notions in order to better grasp the connection of all life. Catching this glimpse of mystical insight was imperative to social change because it could compel people to then recognize social inequalities and ultimately confront systems, behaviors, and beliefs that disrupted the natural order. He argued that the mystic "is forced to deal with social relations because, in his efforts to achieve good, he finds that he must be responsive to human need by which he is surrounded, particularly the kind of human need in which sufferers are victims of circumstances over which, as individuals, they have no control."[11]

Thurman's faith in the transformative power of heightened spiritual consciousness—that vertical exposure to a divine truth could spur feelings of horizontal connection with other beings—was, given the circumstances of the early and mid-century, a viable and accessible option for spurring social change. Because oppressive systems like racism were so damaging to the psychological and emotional well-being of those who lived under them, he saw it to be imperative to focus efforts on the inner life. He reflected,

---

[9] HT, SCG, 5.

[10] HT, *The Creative Encounter*, 40.

[11] HT, *Deep Is the Hunger: Meditations for Apostles of Sensitiveness* (New York: Harper & Brothers, 1951), 44–45.

> The cruel vicissitudes of the social situation in which I have been forced to live in American society have made it vital for me to seek resources, or a resource to which I could have access as I sought means for sustaining the personal enterprise of my life beyond all the ravages inflicted upon it by the brutalities of the social order.[12]

Although he was acutely aware of tight grip racism had on American life and that common beliefs and practices, not to mention laws, collectively reinforced social division, he was hopeful. Despite the bleak social state, he resolved,

> Nevertheless, a strange necessity has been laid upon me to devote my life to the central concern that transcends the walls that divide and would achieve in literal fact what is experienced as literal truth: human life is one and all men are members of one another. And this insight is spiritual and it is the hard core of religious experience.[13]

As I state in *The Fellowship Church*,

> To Thurman, the impetus for change would come from something far more powerful and personal than human-made laws or policies. Those things were, of course, necessary but he thought the unseen realities of life were not only *real* but were far more potent than outward constructions. Thurman thought that broad social transformation would spring from the inner life and that democracy would be driven by human consciousness. Feelings, emotions, and beliefs were the true battlegrounds, and if the mind could elevate above superficial barriers, the rest would follow.[14]

One thing I particularly enjoy about studying Thurman, and what has made it challenging from a historian's perspective, is that he lived, worked, and thought on the fringes. He was forward-thinking and experimental, constantly pushing boundaries and evolving the realms he operated within to be more open and inclusive. He was, as Barbara Brown Taylor aptly proposes, an eccentric. And that eccentricity made some of those around him and many who have looked back on him somewhat—confused.

Much of the confusion surrounding Thurman's life and legacy is, in part, due to his place within mid-century African American intellectual culture and

---

[12] HT, *Mysticism and the Experience of Love* (Wallingford, PA: Pendle Hill Pamphlet 115, 1961), 4–5.

[13] HT, *The Luminous Darkness: A Personal Interpretation of the Anatomy of Segregation and the Ground of Hope* (New York: Harper & Row, 1965), 30.

[14] Brown, *The Fellowship Church*, 57.

within the long civil rights movement. Although he fits snugly within the tradition of modern liberal theology, his ideas took some time to fully blend with modern Black activism. He spent his early academic career pushing back against naysayers of religion as a legitimate resource for social change; his peers within the talented tenth preferred to work in more "serious" fields like economics, sociology, and history. Even after he was instrumental in advancing the spiritually based philosophy of Gandhian nonviolence—a tradition that aims to alter society through consciousness transformation—some within the early civil rights struggle were disappointed that he never sought to take the reins of a protest movement. One young activist remarked, "We thought we had found our Moses in Thurman, but he turned out to be not Moses, but a mystic!"[15] Some who have studied and historicized Thurman have even gone as far as to call him "ahead of his time."[16]

But I offer that it's the outsiders and outliers—the confusing or eccentric characters of our history—that we need to pay closest attention to. Thurman was, by no means, ahead of his time—he was right on time—a distinctly American thinker who was shaped by and a shaper of a nexus of ideas that grew up in the early twentieth century. The fringes that he occupied were also the vanguards of leading modern intellectual movements. He straddled the growing edges of modern Black activism, Christian liberalism, pacifism, cosmopolitanism, and nonviolence, and embraced the modern experimental spirit of pragmatism. Viewing him through a singular lens will always make him seem a little bit out of place. For someone like Thurman, we are better off looking through a prism, seeing his light as a broad range of intersecting colors.

I emphasize the timeliness of Thurman's thought because the fact that he was so representative of his own moment is important to our quest in figuring out if and how we should or can apply his ideas today. The staged demonstrations of the civil rights movement stand out as the primary examples of modern nonviolent activism within our historical memory, but Thurman offers us another side of nonviolence. He was primarily interested in experimenting with human potential and the long-term work of *building* something. While the strategies and tactics of Martin Luther King Jr. and the likes were *reactive* to various oppressive systems, Thurman was invested in proactively creating communities that could provide examples of how individuals and groups can embody authentic democratic life. Perhaps the best example of this, and the example we may really be able to draw

---

[15] PBS, "The Legacy of Howard Thurman: Mystic and Theologian," January 18, 2002, http://www.pbs.org/wnet/religionandethics/2002/01/18/january-18-2002-the-legacy-of-howard-thurman-mystic-and-theologian/7895/.

[16] Scott Olster, "Bringing Folks Together on Sunday," *SF Gate*, November 13, 2000.

from right now, is the Fellowship Church—the eccentric, often misunderstood, physical embodiment of Thurman's thought.

Thurman cofounded the Church for the Fellowship of All Peoples—the United States' first interracial, intercultural, and interfaith church—in San Francisco in 1944. The institution emerged at a paradoxical historical moment: the United States was waging war on behalf of democratic values while it maintained the practice of Jim Crow segregation and controversially relocated around 120,000 Japanese Americans from the Pacific Coast to government-mandated internment camps.[17] Racial tensions ran high, especially in wartime industrial cities like San Francisco, but at the same time many liberal leaders were increasing their focus on civil rights and interracial cooperation. Amid the growing nationalism of the World War II era and the heightened suspicion of racial and cultural others, the Fellowship Church successfully established a pluralistic community based on the idea "that if people can come together in worship, over time would emerge a unity that would be stronger than socially imposed barriers."[18] Rooted in the belief that social change was inextricably connected to internal, psychological transformation and the personal realization of the human community, it was an early expression of Christian nonviolent activism within the long civil rights movement. The Fellowship Church attracted influential local, national, and international social leaders from the time of its inception, and the ideas behind it were so potent and relevant that it still operates at 2041 Larkin Street in San Francisco's Russian Hill neighborhood.[19]

Thurman's vision for it was born from his desire to "test whether a religious fellowship could be developed in America that was capable of cutting across all racial barriers, with a carry over into the common life, a fellowship that would alter the behavior pattern of those involved."[20] It was something of a laboratory—a space for Thurman to experiment with his theory that creative, interfaith practice, interdisciplinary intellectual inquiry, and strategically engineered pluralistic spaces could initiate both vertical and horizontal mystical experiences. "The God of the Fellowship Church," as Thurman often stated, "was neither male nor female, black nor white, Protestant nor Catholic nor Buddhist nor Hindu." The church employed its spiritual cosmopolitanism in worship and in study. Thurman borrowed techniques and spiritual practices from different faiths and set up a meditation room equipped with materials from varying traditions for members

---

[17] National Archives and Records Administration, "Japanese Relocation during World War II," https://www.archives.gov/education/lessons/japanese-relocation.
[18] Ostler, "Bringing Folks Together on Sunday."
[19] Brown, *The Fellowship Church*.
[20] HT, *Footprints of a Dream*, 24.

to examine. The congregation engaged in a multitude of ancient texts that highlighted the social concern and activist nature of historical religious practitioners and considered how various spiritual insights could have contemporary relevance. In addition to worship and formal study groups, members of the church transcended racial, cultural, and religious lines by attending interracial and intercultural dinners, workshops, artistic performances, and lectures—all aimed at emphasizing diversity and tolerance.

Membership in the Fellowship Church was open "to any person who is willing to accept its commitment, to participate in its program and to share in its responsibilities," and the option of a "dual membership" allowed people to participate both in the unique spiritual experiment while maintaining status within their original denomination.[21] It also allowed for members at large who lived in different parts of the world, and the congregation eventually grew to include people from India, Japan, South Africa, Iran, Formosa, and the British Isles.[22] The Fellowship Church's network included laypeople as well as influential public figures. First Lady Eleanor Roosevelt, educator and humanitarian Mary Beth McLeod Bethune, African American intellectuals Benjamin Mays and Mordecai Johnson, South African author Alan Paton, jazz artist Josephine Baker, and civil rights attorney Pauli Murry, among other leading figures, all threw their weight behind the fledgling institution. Members set an example of radical love and inclusivity in the face of widespread oppression and inequality.

To Thurman and others who supported it, the Fellowship Church represented "an authentic growing edge for far-reaching social change in making possible communities of friendly men in a world grown gray with suffering and hate."[23] Its activist impetus was rooted in the idea that the love encountered through moments of heightened spiritual consciousness would reproduce itself, transforming individuals until the social whole changes for the better. Sociologist Alton Pollard called this process "social regeneration." On the regenerating nature of such mystical insight, a pamphlet published by the church stated,

> We can create little islands of goodwill and fellowship in the seeming sea of hatred. The islands will grow and become linked together until a veritable continent is born. The tiniest island is important. It may be but a couple of neighborhood children taken to the Zoo together. But

---

[21] Unknown, the Church for the Fellowship of All Peoples, pamphlet, HTC, Box 187.

[22] Editors of *Christian Century*, "Trumpet Ready in the West," *Christian Century*, September 12, 1951, 1040–45; in PHWT 3:32.

[23] "The Fellowship Church of All Peoples," Spring 1945, in PHWT 3:127. Originally published in *Common Ground* 5 (Spring 1945): 29–31.

if a sense of oneness grows up between those two, it is an achievement on a small scale of the very thing we long for, in bringing this nation together.[24]

While its model for social change is less familiar to us, the Fellowship Church's history illuminates the ways in which people have imagined initiating social activism from a grassroots level during times when government has failed to protect its citizens' civil liberties, safety, and overall well-being through judicial safeguards. Thurman's efforts to affect individual consciousness in the midst of the broad and complicated systemic failures and contradictions of his own historical moment are particularly important, at least in my mind, in the conflicted social climate of the twenty-first century. His belief that "a major revolution in the human spirit" could begin at the local level was indicative of the time in which he lived and worked and is still pertinent and applicable today.[25]

Now, while "little islands of goodwill" can really be developed anywhere on any scale, I wonder what formally establishing a larger intentional community similar to the Fellowship Church would look like today. The theme of this book initially compelled me to think about *how* we could implement a new and contemporary "island of goodwill" to aid in the unfinished search. What kind of space would it occupy? Who would be involved? What kind of spiritual language would be used? How could it be pitched in a way that appealed to a modern demographic? How could a spiritually conscious community appeal to a religious "none" like myself? I quickly became overwhelmed with just the how.

I actually think the how is up for discussion—and that's really the question that I want to pose here. I want to know, from a practical standpoint, how new, alternative expressions of Thurman's search for common ground—similar to that of the Fellowship Church—can be employed today. What, exactly—and I'm sure there are several answers—would this look like? Before we can really get into the how though, I will offer a little insight into the why—*why* contemporary expressions of such communities might not only be necessary but especially possible right now. To unpack this, we need to delve into a few similar hospitable conditions that our culture shares with that of 1940s America.

First, there is the matter of relevant ideas. The ideas Thurman worked with and applied at the Fellowship Church were already in the air and compatible with the evolving culture of twentieth-century spiritual seeking. From the notion that historical examples within ancient religious texts can be applied to address pressing contemporary social issues, to the experimental, pluralistic embrace

---

[24] HT and Fisk, "The Church for the Fellowship of All Peoples."
[25] Brown, *The Fellowship Church*, 8.

of a multitude of religious perspectives, to the idea that mystical experience or heightened consciousness can benefit not only the individual but the democratic whole—all concepts were well established within the mid-century American intellectual tradition. Thurman did not pull anything he implemented at the Fellowship Church out of thin air. It was all in the Zeitgeist, and still is.

The tradition of religious liberalism that spanned the twentieth century is still very much with us, perhaps in an even stronger state than when the Fellowship Church was founded. Currently, 29 percent of American adults identify as religiously unaffiliated, and that number is growing. That doesn't mean that the United States is headed in the direction of total secularism, however—only about 4 percent of Americans identify as atheist, and that appears to be unwavering. In contrast, the country is becoming increasingly theologically cosmopolitan, as 27 percent of adults identify as "spiritual" instead of religious and feel more comfortable borrowing aspects of a number of belief systems.[26] Many modern Americans have turned away from formal religion for political and ethical reasons, especially those within Christianity, as the organized church has in recent history touted conservative and exclusivist values. The majority of my millennial cohort, although "turning away from religion faster than any other age group" (likely never to return), apparently still believes in some kind of universal spirit and is "hungry for meaningful connection," and many within Gen Z are following suit.[27]

It should also be mentioned that there has been a markedly noticeable interest in the exploration of inner life within contemporary secular culture. The wellness industry, medical and scientific communities, and academic circles like our own are all considering the benefits of consciousness transformation in various ways. The liberal religious project of the long twentieth century—the task of cutting away the fat of organized faith in order to locate the core of religious experience and universal truths shared by the human family—is ongoing. Given this reality, Thurman's spiritual program is not without a potential audience.

---

[26] "About Three-in-Ten U.S. Adults Are Now Religiously Unaffiliated," Pew Research Center, December 14, 2021, https://www.pewforum.org/2021/12/14/about-three-in-ten-u-s-adults-are-now-religiously-unaffiliated/; "When Americans Say They Believe in God, What Do They Mean?," Pew Research Center, April 25, 2018, https://www.pewforum.org/2018/04/25/when-americans-say-they-believe-in-god-what-do-they-mean/.

[27] "Millennials Haven't Forgotten Spirituality, They're Just Looking for New Venues," PBS News Hour, March 3, 2017, https://www.pbs.org/newshour/show/millennials-havent-forgotten-spirituality-theyre-just-looking-new-venues; "Generation Z and the Future of Faith in America," Survey Center on American Life, March 24, 2022, https://www.americansurveycenter.org/research/generation-z-future-of-faith/.

The Fellowship Church had the opportunity to emerge because of the disruptive moment created by World War II, and it is important that we consider how a society thrown off-kilter can be ripe for experimentation. The war's transformative effect on American demography and social politics gave Thurman's ideas teeth. While he was hesitant about the implications of war, he recognized opportunity within the cataclysm. He understood that the moment, with its contradictions and existential angst, was ripe for experimentation as it created a sense of urgency and motivation—a refreshed belief in human agency. He said, "When the war comes, something is at last at stake in the day's living.... The ordinary individual now counts in a strange new way.... No one is exempt. Everybody and everything counts.... A new kind of civic character appears sired by new and awful responsibilities. My country needs me—I fly to the rescue."[28] While Thurman emphasized that what the individual does matters every day, he was keen to pick up on the realization that, faced with nihilist destruction, people felt the meaning of their lives and their impact on the world more acutely.

Although the war exposed the worst of humanity, Thurman, ever astute at observing his environment, noticed that something was in the air. The experience of total war dislodged people from their routines. The details of their lives "shifted, thrown out of normal balance, readjusted," and shocked them into the realization that they had power and influence over their environment.[29] To Thurman, this recognition of personal agency, combined with the glaring fact that the United States still had some work to do on its great experiment in democracy, created an opportune moment. He remarked, "We are all of us in quest of a way of life that is worth living. We want to feel that we are engaged in a total enterprise that is meaningful" and hoped others would recognize each and every person's shared interest. He said, "For better or worse we are tied together in the world. I can never be what I ought to be until you are what you ought to be. The present global war is a tragic illustration of the modern version of this truth."[30]

As the war evoked individuals' most basic survival instincts, he was hopeful his fellow citizens would transfer some of their self-preservation energies to preserve the nation's democratic life force: "Survival for us to-day," he insisted, "means more than biology. It means the survival of certain ideas, ideals, ways of thinking, value qualities—vast overtones making up the American way of life."[31] To lead the way, he called upon "apostles of sensitiveness":

---

[28] HT, "Religion in a Time of Crisis," in PHWT 2:344–49.
[29] Ibid.
[30] Ibid.
[31] HT, "The Cultural and Spiritual Prospect for a Nation Emerging from Total War," in PHWT 3:105–8.

those individuals who by their ability and skills will be at work in various areas of the national life, doing their jobs but who at the same time are ever on the alert to preserve those ideals and ideas of democracy which are being directly threatened at the points where they themselves have power or can exert influence."[32]

While these individuals, "the sensitive nerve ends for the body politic," could be discouraged or feel as though they are "wasting their time and energies as they look out upon the destruction of much for what they stand," he made it clear that "whatever the world of the future will be like depends in no small part upon the spear head that will be provided by those who have worked out in a thousand social laboratories techniques and methods for implementing those ideals which are so seriously threatened at home and abroad."[33] Although they may be mislabeled or personally attacked for challenging the status quo, Thurman insisted it was their job to remain steadfast in order "to keep alive the growing edge of democratic life by insisting on the realization of national ideals of tolerance, courtesy, the three freedoms etc. at the points of greatest testing."[34]

As Barbara Brown Taylor mentioned, a global pandemic is not a world war, but it is certainly disruptive, and I agree with her points that it has put American values and democracy up on trial, just as the war did in Thurman's time. Because disruptive moments do that. As historians we look for them, not only because they help us locate where some major social and cultural shifts began, but because they help us see what was really going on at a particular time. Calamitous events pull at the threads of society, straining the fabric until the seams burst open, allowing us to see what's really underneath the surface—and sometimes it's a bit of a mess.

When the pandemic first started, I told my students to pay attention: that these are the times when our underlying issues present themselves in such a way that we have no choice but to look right at them and grapple with them. And I think it is safe to say that the past few years have pulled on the threads of our society quite hard—our guts are all over the floor—we can see and directly feel what our issues are as we teeter and try to move through this moment. Racism, bigotry, class inequality, violence, hatred rooted in misunderstanding—things that have been there all along—are on full display and it all feels heavy and in need of immediate attention. I write this as the flaws in our democratic life continue to be exposed, and I feel the "smell of life heavy upon" *me*. Yet another mass shooting this week and our lawmakers stand idly by. The Supreme Court has overturned

---

[32] Ibid.
[33] Ibid.
[34] Ibid.

Roe v. Wade. I wonder if we, like the founding members of the Fellowship Church, are also living in a time when government has failed to protect its citizens' civil liberties, safety, and overall well-being through judicial safeguards. I wonder how we will confront our underlying issues as the seams continue to burst.

The thing about a tear in the fabric of society, though, is that it can never be put together just as it was before. We cannot just stuff everything back in and perfectly mend it. It can never be exactly the same. With a bit of imagination and a creative touch, though, torn and frayed materials can be repurposed into something new—maybe even something better. So, what do we do with this current opportunity—with this culture on wobbly footing, bursting with all of our contradictions? What can we, as individuals, *do* to spur the creation of world community? Can we harness this energy, utilize the ideas that are already in the air, and seize the moment to experiment as Thurman did? Can we build our own islands of goodwill and fellowship? It seems possible. *How* do we do it? Well, I don't exactly know. I do think, though, that as we continue to contemplate Thurman with an eye on our own time and ask ourselves where his ideas might apply in our own small communities, we may just come up with a few suggestions.

7

Reimagining Howard Thurman's Use of Negro Spirituals and Hymnody

W. James Abbington Jr.

The collective wisdom of scholars in this volume on reimagining Howard Thurman's creative vision of common ground speaks in powerful ways to critical issues at stake in the contemporary context of churches, nonecclesial communities, and the state of democratic societies in the United States and around the globe. The quest for spiritual wholeness and social transformation will continue to be an important dimension of the struggles of disenfranchised and oppressed peoples everywhere. As the authors in this volume attest, this is indeed an "unfinished search for common ground," and most significantly, the quest for human and nonhuman flourishing. With the ongoing threats to human existence on this planet, we are all called to reimagine and reinterpret the role of traditions, institutions, and social practices that are vibrant and relevant. Churches are not exempt from the challenges that call for reimagining and dreaming of what Thurman called "a friendly world under friendly skies."

A critical and often neglected aspect of discussions such as these about Thurman's role as a liturgist, worship leader, and pastor is the aesthetic dimensions of his spirituality as a resource for continuing the search for common ground. In the following, I propose that a careful investigation of Thurman's experimentation with liturgy, music, and dance performances provides an important interpretative key to this continuing quest. We proceed by responding to several questions that Thurman raised regarding his liturgical vision.

In this chapter, I discuss ways in which Howard Thurman imaged and used Negro spirituals and hymnody in worship. He constructed services that are faithful to Scripture, historically conscious, theologically relevant, and that promoted the inclusiveness of all people. In doing so, he provided ecclesial and nonecclesial spaces that invited full, active participation for the worshiper.

First, I examine his own reimagining of the ministry of the church and creative considerations in worship through his pastoral experiences at the Church for the Fellowship of All People in San Francisco and Marsh Chapel at Boston University. Second, I explore two examples of his use of the Negro spiritual, "Deep River" and "Balm in Gilead," to reimagine worship from his *Deep River and The Negro Spiritual Speaks of Life and Death*,[1] which is a compilation of reflections on selected spirituals. Third, I illustrate his use of hymnody and the centering Negro spiritual "Were You There?" in his April 20, 1962 Good Friday service at Marsh Chapel at Boston University.[2] This annual service was often referred to as the "Good Friday Experiment" that attracted audiences from all over the city and the world. At the conclusion of the service, Thurman exhorted the congregants to leave the sanctuary and tell everyone that they encountered that "There's a man on the cross!" Finally, I offer ways that Thurman's reimagining of these musical elements can serve as instructional and inspirational guidelines for creative ways of reinterpreting and constructing worship by using Negro spirituals and hymnody.

Reimagining the Ministry of the Church

Walter Earl Fluker reminds us that for Thurman, the ministry of the church is twofold. It should provide for an environment of worship in which experiences of spiritual unity are achieved and serve as a pedagogical function by teaching and interpreting the religious and moral implications of political, economic, and social arrangements in which the church finds itself. A basic theme of Thurman's ecclesiology is that experiences of unity and fellowship are more compelling than the fears, dogmas, and prejudices that separate people. If spiritual experiences of unity could be multiplied over a time interval of sufficient duration, they should be able to undermine any barrier that separates one person from another.[3] The collective worship of God is the locus where experiences of inner unity are achieved. The primary questions that informed Thurman's liturgical vision were: "Is the worship of God the central and most significant act of the human spirit?" "Is it really true that in the presence of God there is neither male nor female, child

---

[1] HT, *Deep River and The Negro Spiritual Speaks of Life and Death* (Richmond, IN: Friends United Press, 1975).

[2] PHWT 4:xxx–xxxiv. See also "Text of Telegram to Shirley Katzander on the Good Friday Experiment," PHWT 4:335–36.

[3] Walter E. Fluker, *They Looked for a City: A Comparative Analysis of the Ideal of Community in the Thought of Howard Thurman and Martin Luther King Jr.* (Lanham, MD: University Press of America, 1989), 72–75.

nor adult, rich nor poor, nor any classifications by which humankind defines itself in categories, however meaningful?" "Is it only in the religious experience that the individual discovers what, ultimately, she, he, they amount to?"[4]

The Fellowship Church for All Peoples

While Thurman began his liturgical experimentations as early as his pastorate at Mount Zion Baptist Church in Oberlin, Ohio, and later as dean of Howard University's Rankin Chapel, his most daring adventure was the cofounding of the Fellowship Church for All Peoples with Alfred Fiske, a white Presbyterian minister and professor of philosophy at San Francisco State University. This period of his ministry as liturgist was a site of some of his most creative and imaginative experiments in the search for common ground. The formal statement of the Fellowship Church for All Peoples, titled "The Commitment," provides the rationale and purpose of the collective worship of a diverse assembly of congregants. It was created by the original members of the church and serves as the declaration that unites the present community of worshippers in San Francisco.[5] Thurman affirmed that

---

[4] HT, *Footprints,* 21, 69–70; HT, *Disciplines,* 120; HT, *The Creative Encounter,* 137.

[5] See "The Declaration," Fellowship Church, https://www.fellowshipsf.org/services. "The Commitment" reads, "The Church for the Fellowship of All Peoples is a creative venture in interracial, Intercultural, and interdenominational communion. In faith and genius, it is Christian. While it derives its inspiration primarily from the source of Hebrew-Christian thought and life, it affirms the validity of spiritual insight wherever found and seeks to recognize, understand, and appreciate every aspect of truth whatever the channel through which it comes. It believes that human dignity is inherent in man as a creature of God, and it interprets the meaning of human life as essentially spiritual. It recognizes and affirms that the God of Life and the God of Religion are one and the same, and that the normal relationship of people as children of one God and Father, is one of understanding, confidence, and fellowship." "The Commitment," as it was initially called, began as early as 1944, shortly after Thurman arrived at the Fellowship Church. During August 1944, he "preached a series of sermons on different aspects of the Commitment. At the end of that period, an invitation was extended for members of the congregation to sign the Commitment and formally affiliate with the Fellowship Church." PHWT, 3:xxxiv; HT, *Footprints of a Dream,* 51–52. The editors of PHWT indicate that "The Fellowship Church went through at least three versions of their Commitment between 1944 and 1949. Each draft reflected a different phase in the history of the church and had different emphases. Although the interracial nature of the church was mentioned in each of the drafts, the main purpose of the Commitment was to vouchsafe the religious mission of the church. With each restatement, the Fellowship Church moved further from explicit ties and links to traditional Christianity and toward a freer spirituality—Christian in its origins but not its destination." See "The Commitment 1944," in PHWT 3:25–26.

The basic conception was that the highest act of celebration of the human spirit is the worship of God. In the act of worship, the worshiper sees himself as being in the presence of God. In His presence the worshiper is neither male nor female, black nor white, Protestant nor Catholic nor Buddhist nor Hindu, but a human spirit laid bare, stripped to whatever there is that is literal and irreducible. This kind of worship inspires a quality of life that makes barriers of separateness among men increasingly and finally untenable. Worship therefore is central in the church.[6]

He often commented that in his judgment, the most significant result of the Fellowship Church was not participation by a cross section of people, but rather the quality of the individual's religious experience achieved through worship and the effect of that experience on daily behavior. "Worship is at once the source and dynamics both of religious inspiration and judgment."[7]

At the Fellowship Church, Thurman designed worship to be inclusive of hymns, silence, music, a period of prayer and meditation, the reading of Scripture, and the speaking of the Word. The order of service was carefully devised and is largely nonritualistic even today.[8] The part of the service that he felt the most important is the period of meditation preceding the sermon, called "The Centering Moment."[9] Thurman believed that "Here the congregation and the minister become still in the presence of God. This is the time when the innermost secrets of life are laid bare without pretense, when each one of us feels that he is in the presence of One who understands thoroughly and completely and, in whose presence, it is unnecessary to pretend anything."[10]

Boston University

Thurman became dean of Marsh Chapel at Boston University in 1952, and the following statement appeared in the Sunday morning bulletin on the first Sunday and throughout his ministry there:

The Sunday morning worship is so designed as to address itself to the deepest needs and aspiration of the human spirit. In so doing, it does

---

[6] HT, *Footprints of a Dream*, 69–70.

[7] Ibid.

[8] https://www.fellowshipsf.org/services.

[9] HT, "Some Centering Moment," in *The Centering Moment* (Richmond, IN: Friends United Press, 2000), 85.

[10] HT, *Footprints of a Dream*, 70.

not seek to undermine whatever may be the religious context which gives meaning and richness to your particular life, but rather to deepen the authentic lines along which your quest for spiritual reality has led you. It is our hope that you will come to regard the Chapel not only as a place of stimulation, challenge, and dedication, but also as a symbol of the intent of the university to recognize religion as fundamental to the human enterprise.[11]

This formal statement of the purpose of the chapel service hardly captures the deep, throbbing dynamic of Thurman's emphasis on the experiential and aesthetic dimensions of worship. "To experience one's self is to enter into a solitary world that is one's unique possession and that can never be completely and utterly shared," Thurman writes.[12] Yet the human spirit, he taught, cannot abide the enforced loneliness of isolation, "for mutual interdependence is characteristic of all of life."[13] In this sense, the search for the ground addresses both the independence of the self and the interdependence of all of life as a quest best undertaken through the agency of worship. In fact, Thurman's view of worship is qualified by his vision of the sacred—that is, the sacred as the unity that undergirds the diversity in human beginning, structures, dreams, forms of consciousness, and instances of identity. Accordingly, the search for the common and the unifying goal are profoundly sacramental and constitute both the parameters and essence of worship. It is along these lines that we best see the dynamic and interrelated elements at work in his construction of worship and liturgy as "sacred vision."

Thurman's Vision of the Sacred in Worship

In his article "Worship and Anti-Structure in Thurman's Vision of the Sacred," Robert C. Williams asserts that Thurman "was interested in that which takes human persons beyond cognition and beyond the ordinary categories of thought. Thus, his suggestion was that one be self-conscious about experience and reflect upon what one experiences—that one be willing to ponder all dimensions of experience, especially the spiritual aspect of experience as it is captured in worship."[14] According to Williams, Thurman's vision of the sacred is manifested in the gathering for worship as the dialectical interplay of "structure and anti-

---

[11] HT, WHAH, 171–72.
[12] HT, SCG, 2.
[13] HT, SCG, 3.
[14] Robert C. Williams, "Worship and Anti-Structure in Thurman's Vision of the Sacred," *Journal of the Interdenominational Center* 14, no. 1–2 (Fall 1986–Spring 1987).

structure"[15] that creates a liminal space, an opening, a gateway into the spiritual world. Similarly, Mozella Mitchell's depiction of Thurman as "a sophisticated modern-day shaman" and "a technician of the sacred" is helpful as we move into his understanding of the role of the Negro spiritual and worship in ecclesial and nonecclesial spaces where religious experience has practical and ethical implications for social justice.[16] Along with Mircea Eliade and Stephen Larsen, Mitchell makes a distinction between the role of the "priest" and "shaman," in that the former is concerned primarily with "traditional mythological forms" through which members of the community are periodically reawakened to the awareness of the sacred. The shaman, however, "is not satisfied celebrating encounter with the sacred that happened in the long ago but rather develops an affinity for renewing regularly the contact in his own person."[17] For Mitchell, Thurman stands somewhere between the priest and the shaman while maintaining a distinctive posture as a social prophet. Unlike the prophet who speaks to the community, "Thus says the Lord," the shaman leads the community to God by "giving others access to the spiritual world and effects a care for their ailing condition." According to Mitchell, "Thurman, in his shamanistic function, does not simply bring the message of truth from God to the religious community, but he leads individuals and the community to have an experience with the divine from which they may gain a sense of wholeness themselves."[18] Fluker writes, "Mitchell's description of Thurman places him alongside a company of African American healers and teachers whose roots reach beyond the American clime and find affinity with a long and neglected tradition."[19]

---

15 Victor W. Turner, *The Ritual Process Structure and Anti-Structure* (New York: Routledge, 2017).

[16] Mozella G. Mitchell, "Techniques of Myth and Ritual in Thurman," in *Debate and Understanding: Simmering on the Calm Presence and Profound Wisdom of Howard Thurman*, ed. Ricardo A. Millett and Conley H. Hughes (Spring 1982 special edition), 28, claims that "most of Thurman's power stems from his mythical-ritual technique combined with the use of powerful intellect in phenomenological explorations and religious and cultural studies. In his functions as a religious authority and in his mythic-ritual technique, Thurman shares much in common with the shaman of archaic societies. I maintain that his appropriation and use of such techniques is conscious and deliberate, a natural outgrowth of his style of practical mysticism. He becomes in large measure a sophisticated modern-day shaman, and he does so in order to penetrate behind the wall of Christian orthodoxy and to get at and utilize genuine religious experience as a cure for many of the ills of our day. He becomes, then, a self-styled sophisticated shaman." See Mozella G. Mitchell, *Spiritual Dynamics of Howard Thurman's Theology* (Bristol, IN: Wyndham Hall Press, 1985), 88; and Stephen Larsen, *The Shaman's Doorway: Opening the Mythic Imagination to Contemporary Consciousness* (New York: Harper and Row, 1976), 9–10.

[17] Mitchell, "Techniques," 29.

[18] Mitchell, *Spiritual Dynamics in Howard Thurman's Theology*, 88.

[19] Walter Earl Fluker, "Howard Thurman as Opener of the Way," in *Ethical Leadership:*

Deep River and
The Negro Spiritual Speaks of Life and Death

Thurman used the content of Negro spirituals to create sacred space, many of which are included in his awe-inspiring book *Deep River and The Negro Spiritual Speaks of Life and Death*. In the fall of 1928, shortly after his return to Atlanta after spending a semester studying under Rufus Jones at Haverford College, Thurman gave his most extended lecture series, a five-part exposition titled "The Message of the Spirituals," delivered at Spelman College's Sisters Chapel.[20] This became a theme to which Thurman returned time and again, culminating in the 1947 Ingersoll Lectures at Harvard Divinity School titled "Immortality of Man," later published in *Deep River* in 1955.[21]

Throughout *Deep River and The Negro Spiritual Speaks of Life and Death*, Thurman uses literary arts to help illustrate the religious lessons in the Negro spirituals. In the spiritual "Deep River," he opens the reflection with Langston Hughes's 1920 poem "The Negro Speaks of Rivers," which serves as the epigraph to this essay.[22]

> *I've known rivers ancient as the world and*
> *older than the flow of human blood in human veins.*
> *My soul has grown deep like the rivers.*
> *I bathed in the Euphrates when dawns were young,*
> *I built my hut near the Congo, and it lulled me to sleep,*
> *I looked upon the Nile and raise the Pyramids above it.*
> *I heard the singing of the Mississippi*
> *when Abe Lincoln went down to New Orleans,*
> *And I've seen it muddy bosom turn all golden in the sunset.*
> *I've known rivers; ancient, dusky rivers.*
> *My soul has grown deep like the rivers.*

The poet was a close friend of Thurman, whose poetry he admired greatly. One of the key poems of the artistic and literary movement known

---

The Quest for Character, Civility and Community (Minneapolis: Fortress Press, 2009), 19; Joyce Elaine Noll, *Company of Prophets: African American Psychics, Healers, and Visionaries* (St. Paul, MN: Llewellyn Publications, 1991); Malidoma Patrice Some, *Of Water and the Spirit: Ritual, Magic, and Initiation in the Life of an African Shaman* (New York: G. P. Putnam's Sons, 1994).

[20] HT, "The Message of the Spirituals," *Spelman Messenger* 45 (October 1928): 4–12.

[21] See headnote "From George Thomas, 18 April 1947, Cambridge, Mass.," PHWT 3:222–23 for overview of "The Ingersoll Lectures."

[22] Langston Hughes, "The Negro Speaks of Rivers," in *The Dream Keeper and Other Poems* (New York: Knopf, 1932).

as the Harlem Renaissance, "The Negro Speaks of Rivers" traces Black history from the beginning of human civilization to the present, encompassing both triumphs like the construction of the Egyptian pyramids and the horrors of American slavery. The poem argues that the Black "soul" has incorporated all this historical experience, and in the process has become "deep like the rivers." The poem thus suggests that Black cultural identity is continuous, that it stretches across the violence and displacement of slavery to connect with the past—and that Black people have made vital, yet often neglected, contributions to human civilization.

In this collection, he includes prophetic insight and profound reflections for select Negro spirituals, including "The Blind Man," "Heaven! Heaven!" "A Balm in Gilead," "Deep River," "Jacob's Ladder," and "Wade in the Water, Children." He believed that "the genius of the slave songs is their unyielding affirmation of life defying the judgment of the denigrating environment which spawned them. The indigenous insights inherent in the Negro spirituals bear significantly on the timeless search for the meaning of life and death in human experience."[23] In *Footprints of a Dream: The Story of the Church for the Fellowship of All People*, Thurman describes how he used the Negro spirituals in public presentations and in worship. He says, "Several times during the years I preached a series of sermons on the religious insight of certain Negro spirituals. Each Sunday during this series, the choir would sing the spiritual as an anthem. This series was brought to a full-orbed climax in a public lecture on the theme, given at one of the large Jewish synagogues in the city."[24]

Reflecting on the Negro spiritual "Deep River," Thurman says, "This is perhaps the most universal in insight, and certainly the most intellectual of all the spirituals. In a bold stroke it thinks of life in terms of a river."[25] I read here his use and understanding of the spiritual as a sort of functional music, as music that is communicative, and in fact, music that is reflective of the system that produced them. When enslaved Africans sang spirituals, they were singing them from an inner feeling, no doubt a kind of outward manifestation of an inner-living essence, feeling something very deeply, real, and authentic *searching for common ground*, a place to stand amid the unrelenting tragic exigencies of their existence as chattel and disposable property.

---

[23] HT, WHAH, 216–17. See also PHWT 1:126–38; HT, "Religious Ideas in Negro Spirituals," *Christendom* 4 (Autumn 1939): 515–28. The remainder of the volume contains, in separate chapters, elaborations of his 1928 treatments of "Jacob's Ladder," "De Blind Man," "Heab'n, Heab'n," and "Deep River" and discussions of "A Balm in Gilead" and "Wade in the Water, Children."

[24] HT, *Footprints of a Dream*, 74.

[25] HT, *Deep River*, 66.

In "Deep River," his reflection is in close conversation with Langston Hughes's poem. The same speech also includes a quotation from the Greek philosopher Heraclitus, an excerpt from the poem "Ulysses" by Alfred Lord Tennyson, and the words of Jesus. Thurman even uses his own poetry to add yet another layer of insight and expression to his exposition of Negro spirituals:

> The fascination of the flowing stream is a constant source of wonder and beauty to the sensitive mind. It was ever thus. The restless movement, the hurrying, ever-changing stream has been the bearer of the longings and yearnings of mankind for land beyond the horizon where dreams are fulfilled, and deepest desires satisfied. It is not to be wondered at all that in this spiritual there is a happy blending of majestic rhythm and poignant yearning:
>
> *Deep River, my home is over Jordan.*
> *O, don't you want to go to that Gospel feast,*
> *That Promise Land where all is peace?*
> *Deep River, I want to cross over into campground.*[26]

The analogy is fruitful with great meaning: life, in all its tragic and fierce movements, itself is a deep river. I am interested here in how potential time as in-between-time allows for the reconstruction or revisability of language as sound, using jazz as a metaphor. We, through our agency, must "make the path" that leads to the river—"the river is timeless"—before and after time, and we are constantly in the stream of the river that flows inwardly and outwardly, forever ingressing and egressing, depicting two modes of reality, the inner and outer, which are inseparable but experienced as modes of consciousness. In engaging Thurman, then, one is driven to contemplate the relationship between time and infinity, and to register them as analogous to the flow of the river that empties itself into the sea. The analogy yields key insights from enslaved Africans and from their cosmological and theological perspectives; the river leads to a deeper appreciation of the African American past, which Thurman calls "flood time" in his reflection on death and freedom in the Negro spirituals.[27]

---

[26] Ibid.

[27] "Howard Thurman, Deep River," Louisville Chapel, Louisville Presbyterian Seminary, November 11, 1967, HTC, 74:28. I am indebted here to Fluker's discussion of Thurman's interpretation of the river as a metaphor for "re-membering our stories" as part of the critical task of Black churches for reviving prophetic discourse and practices. Walter Earl Fluker, *The Ground Has Shifted: The Future of the Black Church in Post-Racial America* (New York: New York University Press, 2016), 31–34, 41.

Thurman challenges the reader to reflect on a deeper meaning and says that to think of life as being like a river is a full and creative analogy. He continues with the first analogy:

> To think of life as being a river is an apt and almost universal analogy. The analogy is complete in the first place because the river has a very simple beginning, and it gathers in depth and breadth and turbulence, as it moves across the broad expanse of the continent till it gives itself up to the sea whose far-off call all waters hear. It is the nature of the river to flow. It is always moving, always in flux. It is small wonder that Heraclitus reminds us that no man bathes twice in the same stream.[28]

The analogy is complete in the second place because the river has flood times. There are times when the river ceases to be tranquil and easygoing and beneficent, spreading peace and helpfulness throughout the land that it touches, and becomes a monster, reckless and evil, spreading pestilence and destruction along its reckless way. It is the flood time of the river.

He presents the final analogy:

> The analogy is complete in the next place because the river has a goal. The goal of the river is the sea—that out of which the river comes and that to which the river goes is the sea. All the waters of all the lands comes from the sea, and all the waters of all the lands go to the sea. The source and goal of the river are the same.[29]

He concludes, "*Life* is like that. The goal of life is God. That out of which life comes and that into which life goes is God. We do not wonder, then, that Augustine says, "Thou has made us for Thyself, and our souls are restless till they find their rest in Thee."[30]

The analogy is complete in the last analysis because the river has a goal; the goal of the river is the sea. Thurman suggests, "All the waters of all the earth come from the sea. Paradox of paradoxes: that out of which the river comes is that into which the river goes. The goal and the source of the river are the same! From gurgling spring to giant waterfall: from morning dew to torrential down-pour;

---

[28] Heraclitus, from Plato, *Cratylus* 402A: "Heraclitus says somewhere that all things are in process, and nothing stays still, and likening existing things to the stream of the river he says that you would not step twice into the same river" (PHWT 1:138n14); see also HT, "Religious Ideas in Negro Spirituals," *Howard University School of Divinity Faculty Publications* (1939), paper 7, 524.

[29] Ibid.

[30] Ibid.

from simple creeks to mighty rivers—the source and the goal are the same: the sea."[31] This powerful statement reinforces and affirms Thurman's argument that the source and goal of life is *God*. He posits that all of humanity is created by God and in God's image (*imago Deo*), strengthened, fortified, and enabled by God throughout our lives—and that ultimately we return to God. Even for those who do not believe or acknowledge God as creator, Thurman invites an imaginative reading of a lineage and a kinship that goes beyond that of biological parentage. The source of life is God, and through death one returns to God to experience eternal life. This analogy, likening life to the flow of the river, is greater than race, ethnicity, gender, sexual orientation, age, class, or social status. One might think of water for bathing, cleansing, the elixir of life, as well as an element of good or bad realities. And all of these examples illustrate Thurman's understanding of humanity's own interconnectedness and relationality, akin to the flow of all of earth's waters through their various channels and canals.

On many occasions in worship, public performances, and in a recording of these spirituals, he interspersed the singing of the spiritual with a congregational hymn, a choral arrangement, or a vocal solo. The most popular and beloved of all of the arrangements was the setting by Harry T. Burleigh (1866–1949), the pioneer of the arranged-concert spiritual.[32] This engagement of hearing the music and spoken word paired together provided his audiences and congregations with an experiential, reflective, and insightful experience. As he reimagined the spiritual as worship, he knew that this method of engagement with music, alongside his own art throughout the collection, rendered his reflections more meaningful, vivid, applicable, relevant, and contemplative. In singing the spiritual, a person fosters a deeper understanding and interpretation of the texts toward more than a song of mere otherworldliness—rather as a communal experience of sacred space. Thurman's reflections expanded the mind and imagination in a way that simply performing the spiritual or simply hearing his words would never accomplish.

"A Balm in Gilead"

This would be the case for any of the other spirituals in the collection or spirituals that he chose to utilize as a resource for worship that invited the other to the timeless rhythm of the ebb and flow of life with all its vicissitudes and tragic character. Another example of this practice can be found in one of my favorite

---

[31] Ibid.
[32] Library of Congress, "H. T. Burleigh (1866–1949)," Biographies, https://www.loc.gov/item/ihas.200035730.

chapters in *Deep River and The Negro Spiritual Speaks of Life and Death*—his profound and prophetic reflection on "A Balm in Gilead." Thurman writes,

> The peculiar genius of the Negro slave is revealed here in much of its structural splendor. The setting is the Book of Jeremiah. The prophet has come to a "Dead Sea" place in his life. Not only is he discouraged over the eternal events in the life of Israel, but he is also spiritually depressed and tortured. As a wounded animal he cried out, "Is there no balm in Gilead? Is no physician there?" It is not a question of fact that he is raising—it is not a question directed to any particular person for an answer. It is not addressed either to God or to Israel, but rather it is a question raised by Jeremiah's entire life. He is searching his own soul. He is stripped to the literal substance of himself for an answer and is turned back on himself for an answer. Jeremiah is saying actually, "There must be a balm in Gilead; it cannot be that there is no balm in Gilead." The relentless winnowing of his own bitter experience has laid bare his soul to the end that he is brought face to face with the very ground and core of his own faith.
>
> The slave caught the mood of this spiritual dilemma, and with it did an amazing thing. He straightened the question mark in Jeremiah's sentence into an exclamation point: "There is a balm in Gilead!" Here is a note of creative triumph.[33]

Interspersed before or after this reading would be the singing of "Balm in Gilead" as a congregational hymn, a solo, or the rendering of a very popular and widely performed William L. Dawson (1899–1990) choral setting of the spiritual.[34]

"Were You There?" Good Friday Service

On April 20, 1962, Howard Thurman's Good Friday Service at the Marsh Chapel at Boston University was a masterful and thoughtful liturgy of hymns, silence, solos, readings, meditations, prayers, and several organ selections and improvisations. On his notes for the service, he carefully indicates what should be sung as a solo, what should be sung by the congregation, and what should be reflected upon in silence as the organist played the hymn. These hymns included

---

[33] HT, *Deep River*, 55–56.
[34] Vernon Huff, "William Levi Dawson (1899–1990): Reexamination of a Legacy," *Choral Journal* 59, no. 10 (May 2019): 20–33.

"My Times Are in Thy Hands," "Silent Night, Holy Night," "What Child Is This? (Greensleeves),"[35] "O Master, Let Me Walk with Thee," one of Thurman's favorites, "We May Not Climb the Heavenly Steeps," and the Negro spiritual "Were You There?" Three selections were rendered as solos: "What Child Is This?" "If with All Your Heart" from Felix Mendelssohn's *Elijah*, and "Were You There?"

The service was bookended with William Freeman Lloyd's hymn "My Times Are in Thy Hands," written in 1824 sung to the tune Ferguson.[36] It was sung by a soloist at the beginning and end of the service. Here are the texts to the less familiar hymn:

> *My times are in Your hand; my God, I wish them there!*
> *My life, my friends, my soul, I leave entirely to Your care.*
> *My times are in Your hand whatever they may be,*
> *pleasing or painful, dark, or bright, as You know best for me.*
> *My times are in Your hand; why should I doubt or fear?*
> *My Father's hand will never cause. His child a needless tear.*
> *My times are in Your hand; Jesus, the Crucified;*
> *those hands my cruel sins had pierced and now my guard and guide.*
> *My times are in Your hand; such faith You give to me*
> *that after death, at Your right hand I shall forever be.*

This text sets the mood and context for the service, and by using it to open and close the service, Thurman is musically capturing the theme of the day and allowing the congregant to reflect on his or her own life. Thurman was very sensitive to the fact that visitors and even regular congregants may not be as familiar with the hymns, therefore he used a soloist and directed the congregation to reflect on the text as they were being sung. This is an incredible insight for today as the hymnody of churches is more limited than ever.

Thurman's arrangement of these elements of song and word invites the listener to ponder not only the poignancy of personal and spiritual dimensions of worship, but they are also signals of commitment to social and political action.

---

[35] The hymn tune Greensleeves was the musical setting for the text "What Child Is This?" written by the nineteenth-century British hymn writer W. Chatterton Dix (1837–1898). There is a persistent belief that it was composed by Henry VIII in 1580 for his lover and future queen consort Anna Boleyn. While this probably isn't true, it is a traditional English folksong favorite with its roots in Tudor England, possessing elements of love and emotional declarations throughout. This very common pairing of W. C. Dix's text and the beloved English folksong melody Greensleeves was sung by a soloist in Thurman's Good Friday Service. For a detailed and scholarly examination of hymn tunes, see Paul Westermeyer, *Let the People Sing: Hymn Tunes in Perspectives* (Chicago: GIA Publications, 2005).

[36] The hymn tune Ferguson was the musical setting for the text "My Times Are in Thy Hand," written in 1824 by nineteenth-century British hymn writer William Freeman Lloyd.

Theological ethicist Cheryl J. Sanders asks, "Can a follower of Christ claim salvation through his crucifixion, but then consent to the suffering racial injustice imposed on others?" She continues: "The line of spiritual inquiry remains instructive for our time. If you were 'there,' did you identify with Jesus as the victim of state-sanctioned violence? Did you take note of His betrayal, arrest, trial, taunting, humiliation, torture, and execution by the ruling government at the bequest of the religious authorities? If you were 'there,' did you sympathize instead with those who crucified Him because you are convinced of the necessity to enforce the law and maintain order at any cost? If so, is your solidarity with Jesus and His cross or with those who put Him on the cross?"[37]

The message of "Were You There?" quickly expands beyond its initial historical context to include all who dare to commit to the spiritual and moral demands of its message. Thurman recalls being in a delegation that visited Mahatma Gandhi, and that this was a song that he requested them to sing for him. He said, "The insight here is profound and touching—at last there is worked out the kind of identification in suffering with Jesus which makes the cross universal in its deepest meaning. It cuts across difference of religion, race, class, and language and dares to affirm that the key to the mystery of the cross is found deep within the heart of the experience."[38]

> *Were you there when they crucified my Lord?*
> *Were you there when they crucified my Lord?*
> *Oh! Sometimes it causes me to tremble, tremble, tremble.*
> *Were you there when they crucified my Lord?*
> *Were you there when they nailed Him to the tree ... ?*
> *Were you there when they pierced Him in the side ... ?*
> *Were you there when the sun refused to shine ... ?*
> *Were you there when he hung his head and died ... ?*
> *Were you there when they laid Him in the tomb ... ?*

Thurman reflects, "The inference is that the singer was there: 'I know what he went through because I have met him on the high places of pain and I claim Him as my brother.' Here again the approach is not a conceptual one but rather an experimental grasping of the quality of Jesus's experience by virtue of the personal frustration of the singer."[39] At the conclusion of the almost three-hour Good Friday Service, he admonishes the congregation to "Run and tell everyone that they meet that there's a man on the cross."

---

[37] Cheryl J. Sanders, "Were You There?," *Christianity Today*, October 30, 2020.
[38] HT, "Religious Ideas in Negro Spirituals."
[39] Ibid.

An imaginative glimpse into Thurman's Good Friday Service suggests how George F. Handel's *Messiah* might have been a model for reimagining a Good Friday liturgy. After the spoken dialogue at the beginning of the service, Thurman begins with the carol "Silent Night, Holy Night." In his notes he writes, "The audience reads the Hymn while organist plays entire hymn." This is followed by the story of the birth of Jesus from Luke 2, Nativity selections, and a solo, "What Child Is This?": "Organ quietly—2 or 3 minutes of silence." Handel's *Messiah* draws from three parts of the Bible: Old Testament prophesies of the Messiah's birth; New Testament narratives of the birth of Christ, his life, death, and resurrection; verses relating ultimately to the Day of Judgment with final chorus texts drawn from the Book of Revelation. Because it is Good Friday, Thurman appropriately does not cover the resurrection of Christ but provides a full account of his life through his passion, crucifixion, and death. This is an extraordinary way of reimagining Holy Week and Good Friday specifically. His use of hymnody provides a wonderful blueprint for future services that could include Negro spirituals like "Calvary, Calvary," "Take My Mother Home," "He Never Said a Mumbling Word," and "Oh, That Bleeding Lamb" as solos, congregational hymns, or instrumental music with liturgical dance. There are endless contemporary hymns that could be used, such as "The Blood That Jesus Shed for Me," "Just for Me," "This Is Amazing Grace," "Christ Our Hope in Life and Death," "Stations of the Cross," "We Read the Cross So Many Ways," and many more.[40]

Conclusion

Thurman's work as a pastor, liturgist, and worship leader provides endless wisdom, models, inspiration, and possibilities for reimagining and creating new ways to tell and celebrate the "old story" for today's pastor, worship leaders, and liturgists. His liturgical experiments and practices in his positions as dean of Howard University's Rankin Chapel, pastor and cofounder of the Church for

---

[40] The contemporary hymns listed for reimagining a Good Friday Service are offered because of their lyrical content and all capture the passion, death, and suffering of Christ on Good Friday. Like the hymns in Thurman's service, they speak to congregations today by hymn writers who are committed to telling the story of Christ's crucifixion and death in contemporary language. These Good Friday hymns are filled with remembrance of how Jesus died on the cross for our sins, and with the sadness of Good Friday comes hope for Easter Sunday. For example, see an excerpt from Thomas Troeger's "We Read the Cross So Many Ways" written in 2015: "We read the cross so many ways: a sacrifice, a sign, A cause for grief, a cause for praise, a paradox to mine. A judgment on our lives of sin. A tool of death and pain, A junction where new lives begin, where grace and mercy reign."

the Fellowship of All People in San Francisco, and dean of Boston University's Marsh Chapel are full of guidelines, resources, and "tools" from his liturgical construction belt. *First*, he was willing to experiment with the liturgy and not be held hostage to the weekly rituals without reason, ceremonies without content, services without substance, and rubrics without relevance. Thurman, like Jaroslav Pelikan, clearly understood that "tradition is the living faith of the dead; traditionalism is the dead faith of the living; and unfortunately, it is traditionalism that has given tradition such a bad name."[41]

Second, his commitment to adequately planning worship is a critical lesson for worship leaders today. It is evident that he used a conversation model of planning worship with his team that included planning/possibilities, organizing/ordering, worshiping, and a most neglected element—reflecting on the liturgy.

Third, wherever liturgy happens, it should be understood as a means of creating a new kind of encounter with one's neighbor, knowing that through intentional encounter with one's neighbor—imagined and physical—the congregation comes into a new relationship with God. The use of hymnody and Negro spirituals—sacred folk songs produced by unknown, enslaved, oppressed, and marginalized Africans in America—the arts and literature gained power from the fact that Thurman understood which neighbors were not present in the room for whatever reason. Contemporary liturgists need to constantly assess which cultures, ethnicities, religions, and neighbors are unable to participate in the life of the liturgy because of prejudice, difference, and indifference. Once these communities are recognized, liturgists can use the space of their liturgy to bring other stories into the room. Thurman's use of the vesper and midweek services expose the congregation to so many aspects, avenues, and experiences that were a more informal style of liturgy, but liturgy all the same. These services can amplify the spiritual and intellectual formation of the congregants, understanding that liturgy is the "work of the people" which must be lived beyond the weekly one-to two-hour encounter at a designated time and place.

Thurman was thoughtful, pastoral, intentional, inclusive, and always seeking creative ways to make the encounter with God one that was a formative, transformative, cognitive, educational, and inspirational experience. Thurman's attempt was not to make worship fun, entertaining, or amusing. The temptation of many liturgists today is to entertain and amuse congregants. A. W. Tozer reminds us that "Congregations that have not been taught to worship, must be entertained. And those who lead the worship must provide that entertainment."[42]

---

[41] Jaroslav Pelikan, *The Vindication of Tradition: The 1983 Jefferson Lecture in the Humanities* (New Haven, CT: Yale University Press, 1986), 65.

[42] A. W. Tozer, *Tozer on Worship and Entertainment*, comp. James L. Snyder (Camp Hill,

Finally, Thurman's extensive use of silence is one that urgently needs to be reimagined and incorporated in our worship encounters. In a world full of noise, swift-moving soundbites, nonstop social media, sirens, and marketing, reimagining his use of silence would bring a much-needed sense of calm, awareness, creativity, concentration, and productivity in our public and private worship. Remembering Thurman, Reverend Dr. Dorsey Blake, the current pastor of the Church for the Fellowship of All People says,

> Thurman orchestrated worship as a complete, grand, profound meditation including meditation, music, readings, silences, and the spoken word from him. This included his nonverbal assistants—gestures, hands, pauses.... He was skilled at reading the congregation.... You felt that he was speaking directly to you. It was as if you had had a previous conversation [with him] and he knew where you were in your life and what you needed. You were affirmed and felt special in the worship experience and beyond.[43]

Thurman clearly understood that worshipful spirituality is far deeper and more complex than simply doing for the other. A worshipful spirituality might be described as "worship in action"—which means that our whole lives become an act of worship. Everything we do ultimately goes to God's honor and glory, whether we are consciously aware of it or not. "Worship spirituality suggests to us that Christian living is shaped primarily not by morality, fear of punishment, or specific religious practices, but by worship itself. Worship is the primary locus for discerning our stance before God and each other, and the two cannot be separated or be different from each other," says Joyce Zimmerman.[44] She continues, "Moral and virtuous living is the fruit of good worship; when separated from worship, morality by itself does not function very well to motivate us to wholeheartedly choose a gospel way of living. This is perhaps the most radical challenge

---

PA: Christian Publications, 1977), 102.

[43] James A. Abbington, telephone interview with Reverend Dr. Dorsey Blake, pastor of the Fellowship Church, September 2018 [brackets added]. At another place, Thurman writes, "As we worship God in silence, external layers of personality seem to fall away and the mechanics of the process become remote and irrelevant. As we move into the conscious awareness of the Irreducible Element of Self at our centers and identify with it, our consciousness expands until it becomes all-inclusive. Time stands still. The past and the future are wedded in the Now. There are no Christians, Jews, Buddhists, Moslems, or Hindus, as such, only children of God joined together in His Presence in a moment of high celebration. His all-pervading Spirit, moving at this level, transcends all mundane difference." HT, *Footprint*, 77–78.

[44] Joyce Zimmerman, *Worship with Gladness: Understanding Worship from the Heart*, Calvin Institute of Christian Worship Liturgical Studies (Grand Rapids: Eerdmans, 2014), 129.

of worship that transforms: an unprecedented deep entry unto the very heart of the Christian mystery, which is Jesus's very life and ministry as a pattern for our daily living. This vision of worship in action offers us insight into who we are, why we are, and how we ought to be."[45] It has been said that Thurman was a creative and a serious thinker. These attributes—creativity and serious thinking—have provided us with endless possibilities, perimeters, and liturgical treasures by which we can enliven and enhance worship through the use of the Negro spiritual and hymnody, which are both handmaidens of the spoken word.

---

[45] Ibid., 129–30.

8

APOSTLES OF SENSITIVENESS

The Buddha Crown and Howard Thurman's Growing Edge

Lobsang Tenzin Negi

"Apostles of sensitiveness" is a term Thurman used during World War II and the immediate postwar years to refer to small groups of individuals who felt the contradictions of society more acutely than others and who would take the lead in addressing society's ills. These small groups of individuals needed to work from the ground up to ensure that America lived up to its political and spiritual potential. Racial minorities, those most "exposed to the effects of the breakdown of the democratic ideals," Thurman believed, were in a "unique position" to become apostles of sensitiveness.[1] Apostles of sensitiveness—or as Barbara Brown Taylor calls them in her excellent essay in this volume, "eccentric apostles"—lead not from the center but from the always growing and unique edge of human experience. They are eccentric in the sense that their unconventional positioning disrupts how others perceive the location of society's center.

In the following discussion, I identify parallels between Thurman's creative conception of the apostles of sensitiveness and specific Buddhist teachings to illustrate ways in which ecclesial, onecclesial, and interfaith dialogue and practices might instruct diverse communities in the search for common ground. I briefly discuss several important intersections between Thurman's conceptualization and Buddhist practices. These include the symbolism of nature, especially trees, as a spiritual resource for refreshment and renewal; Buddhist-Christian relations and interfaith dialogue; a comparison of the Bodhisattva ideal to the apostle of sensitiveness; the importance of the education of the heart and mind; the complementary nature of compassion and wisdom; and the spiritual-emotional problem of self-absorption (excessive self-focus). My discussion is of the latter points to the relationship between compassionate motivation and

---

[1] HT, "The Cultural and Spiritual Prospect for a Nation Emerging from Total War" (1945), in PHWT 3:108.

discernment, and how it informs our behavior. Additionally, I draw attention to the Dalai Lama's vision for secular (universal) ethics and how it can empower apostles of sensitiveness in contemporary settings where they can address the concerns of both religious and nonreligious people—working toward what Thurman often called "a friendly world underneath friendly skies."[2]

Spiritual Trees of Refreshment and Renewal

With their presence and in their refreshing silence, trees nourish all life on earth. Without judgment or bias, they provide refuge for those seeking both physical shelter and spiritual inspiration. Reverend Thurman and the Buddha both experienced this special connection, a kind of mystical relationship supporting deep insight while providing solace. The Buddha, born as a prince under the trees in Lumbini Grove, awakened to the reality of suffering and the way to end suffering only after meditating for six years under a bodhi tree. For Reverend Thurman, the companionship of an oak tree taught him to contemplate both suffering and joy, described in his autobiography in this way:

> Eventually, I discovered that the oak tree and I had a unique relationship. I could sit, my back against its trunk, and feel the same peace that would come to me in my bed at night. I could reach down in the quiet places of my spirit, take out my bruises and my joys, unfold them, and talk about them. I could talk aloud to the oak tree and know that I was understood. It, too, was a part of my reality, like the woods, the night, and the pounding surf, my earliest companions, giving me space.[3]

This experience is reflected in Reverend Thurman's habit, later in life, of sitting in silence with his congregants for periods of contemplation and quiet reflection, so reminiscent of the Buddha and his sangha.[4] As with the Buddha's famous Flower Sermon, delivered in silence by holding up a flower, Reverend Thurman found nature to be a source of spiritual experience, a path to becoming an apostle of sensitiveness.

What insights can be gained here from the Buddhist tradition? What perspectives and practices can Buddhists recommend for those on such a path? How might they engage with *samsara*, that is, the conditioned world of suffering?

---

[2] HT, *The Greatest of These* (Oakland, CA: Eucalyptus Press, 1944), ix.
[3] HT, WHAH, 9.
[4] Buddhist monastic order, traditionally composed of four groups: monks, nuns, laymen, and laywomen. The sangha is a part—together with the Buddha and the dharma (teaching)—of the Three Refuges, a basic creed of Buddhism. *Encyclopedia Britannica*, "Sangha," March 6, 2020, https://www.britannica.com/topic/sangha.

Buddhist-Christian and Interfaith Dialogue

In his 1951 work *Deep Is the Hunger: Meditations for Apostles of Sensitiveness*, Reverend Thurman writes in the preface that he was "deeply of the mind that there is a need for materials of refreshment, challenge and renewal for those who are intent upon establishing islands of fellowship in a sea of racial, religious and national tensions."[5]

Buddhist-Christian dialogue is one such island of fellowship, and the promotion of interreligious dialogue is one of the three main commitments of His Holiness the Dalai Lama. His book *The Good Heart: A Buddhist Perspective on The Teachings of Jesus*[6] is an important offering to that conversation, which includes an array of other spiritual leaders and theologians, such as Thomas Merton, Jean-Yves Leloup, Brother David Steindl-Rast, and Thich Nhat Hanh. Despite what the media might have us believe, faith communities remain a force within human society, with 84 percent of the world's population identifying with some form of religion.[7] Working together, people of faith can transform society; if divided, they fuel suspicion and the conflicts that tear at the very fabric of humanity.

In his book *Toward a True Kinship of Faiths: How the World's Religions Can Come Together*,[8] His Holiness the Dalai Lama encourages religious leaders and practitioners around the world to have regular contact and conversations to learn about each other's beliefs and practices. He sees these gatherings as a way to promote understanding and respect for each other's traditions, which is the only way for different religions to coexist in harmony.

The Bodhisattva and the Apostle of Sensitiveness

Reverend Thurman defines the apostle of sensitiveness in the *Deep Is the Hunger* epigraph titled "Concerning Apostles of Sensitiveness." There, he paraphrases the Apostle Paul: "to have a sense of what is vital, a basic and underlying awareness

---

[5] HT, *Deep Is the Hunger* (New York: Harper & Brothers, 1951), ix.

[6] Dalai Lama, *The Good Heart: A Buddhist Perspective on The Teachings of Jesus* (Boston: Wisdom Publications, 1996).

[7] "Worldwide, more than eight-in-ten people identify with a religious group. A comprehensive demographic study of more than 230 countries and territories conducted by the Pew Research Center's Forum on Religion & Public Life estimates that there are 5.8 billion religiously affiliated adults and children around the globe, representing 84% of the 2010 world population of 6.9 billion." Pew Research Center, "The Global Religious Landscape," December 18, 2012, https://www.pewresearch.org/religion/2012/12/18/global-religious-landscape-exec/.

[8] Dalai Lama, *Toward a True Kinship of Faiths: How the World's Religions Can Come Together* (New York: Doubleday Religion, 2010).

of life and its potentialities at every level of experience, this is to be an Apostle of Sensitiveness."⁹

When I reflect upon this definition as well as Barbara Brown Taylor's notion of eccentric apostles, I am reminded of a fundamental premise of *Mahayana* Buddhism,[10] the Bodhisattva ideal.[11] The Sanskrit term *"Bodhisattva"* means a being who is seeking full awakening in order to liberate all sentient beings from their suffering. This extraordinary commitment is grounded in the Bodhisattva's unconditional love and compassion for other beings regardless of their particular character or circumstances. This profound wish to relieve other beings of their suffering compels a Bodhisattva to seek Buddhahood so that they have the ability to help all according to their diverse dispositions, interests, and needs.

Like Thurman's apostles of sensitiveness, a Bodhisattva meets people in need where they are and does not impose their own views and agenda. While attaining full enlightenment is their ultimate goal, the Bodhisattva's courageous heart moves them to take compassionate action against the injustices and suffering of the world at every stage of their journey. In Reverend Thurman's terms, Bodhisattvas "have come alive," or in the Buddhist framework, they are the ones who can "see things as they really are." Thurman's apostles of sensitiveness and the concept of a Bodhisattva seem to me to be congruent. Barbara Brown Taylor tells us in her essay that apostles of sensitiveness "practice a kind of self-projection by which they are able to enter other people's experience." They feel what others are feeling, what we call empathy, the foundation of compassion. Like a Bodhisattva, an apostle of sensitiveness is motivated to help through their experience of the suffering of others.

The Buddha Crown and Our Spiritual Aspirations

A quote from Thurman's "Apostles of Sensitiveness" sermon strikes me as particularly significant. He says such apostles have a "highly developed sense of fact with regard to other people." He explains that apostles of sensitiveness are "meeting people where they are and treating them ... as if they were where they ought to

---

⁹ HT, *Deep Is the Hunger*, xi.

[10] Mahayāna (Sanskrit: "greater vehicle") Buddhism refers to a branch of Buddhism whose adherents seek enlightenment for the benefit of all sentient beings. Central to the teachings is the idea of the Bodhisattva, that anyone can achieve full awakening. See https://www.britannica.com/topic/Mahayana.

[11] "Bodhisattva (Sanskrit), Pali bodhisatta ('one whose goal is awakening'), in Buddhism, one who seeks awakening (*bodhi*)—hence, an individual on the path to becoming a buddha." J. A. Silk, "Bodhisattva," *Encyclopedia Britannica*, updated September 26, 2022, https://www.britannica.com/topic/bodhisattva.

be. By so doing, one places a crown over their heads that for the rest of their lives they are trying to grow tall enough to wear."[12]

When considering this passage, the Buddhist concept of Buddha nature comes to mind. Buddhists believe all beings, not just humans, have Buddha nature, or the seed of enlightenment. The Buddha "crown" is already above our heads; it is up to us to grow into it, to actualize our full potential by uniting compassion and wisdom in our lives. This is something that must be cultivated and expanded; it is our growing edge. Our old habits of thought about who we are must be unlearned. It is a process of deconditioning to help us rediscover our true nature.

Coming Alive as a Bodhisattva and Apostle of Sensitiveness

How are apostles of sensitiveness able to realize their true potential and "come alive," as Reverend Thurman might say? Remember that Bodhisattvas are those sentient beings who deliberately engage with the suffering of the world in order to transform it, one sentient being at a time. In preparing for the "growing edge" of this work, one must extend one's love and compassion to all beings without bias or conditions.

Expanding Compassion and Thurman's Growing Edge

Great compassion is the seed of a Bodhisattva's aspiration to attain full enlightenment for the sake of all sentient beings, the moisture that nourishes and sustains the seedling of that altruistic resolve, and the proper ripening that supports the continual urge to help once enlightenment is achieved. As the sixth-century BCE philosopher Chandrakirti wrote,

> *As compassion alone is accepted to be*
> *The seed of the perfect harvest of buddhahood,*
> *The water that nourishes it, and the fruit that is long a source of enjoyment,*
> *I will praise compassion at the start of all.*[13]

To extend compassion to all sentient beings is much easier said than done. However, as His Holiness the Dalai Lama points out in his teachings, it can be achieved by relying on two pillars: (1) an awareness of our common humanity and (2) a realization of our interdependence.[14]

---

[12] HT, "Apostles of Sensitiveness," in PHWT 3:172.

[13] *Illuminating the Intent: An Exposition of Candrakirti's Entering the Middle Way*, Library of Tibetan Classics, trans. Thupten Jinpa (Somerville, MA: Wisdom Publications, 2021), 45.

[14] Dalai Lama, *Beyond Religion: Ethics for a Whole World* (Boston: Houghton Mifflin Harcourt, 2011), 19.

Finding Common Ground

Like Reverend Thurman, His Holiness appeals to our "common ground" and a sensitiveness to others. When we see others as "just like me," in that they want to be happy and to be free of suffering, they become part of our in-group. In other words, we relate to them as one of us. This sense of identification is what Dr. Frans de Waal, a renowned primatologist, calls "a key portal to empathy."[15] In the Buddhist tradition, one meditates on our shared human reality to continually expand this circle of concern. A verse by the first Panchen Lama from Tibet encapsulates this poignantly:

> *As for suffering, I do not wish even the slightest;*
> *As for happiness, I'm never satisfied,*
> *There is no difference between others and me.*
> *Bless me so that I may take joy in others' happiness.*[16]

Seeing Our Interdependence

The second pillar of compassion is a recognition of our interdependence, which helps us deepen our sense of connection to others. This takes our social reality into account; each one of us is dependent on countless beings for our survival. Making this reality visible leads to a sense of gratitude that deepens our warm-hearted feelings toward others and increases our sense of connection to them. As social beings, we need and seek connection, and this warm-hearted feeling is the catalyst for empathy—a sensitiveness to the needs of others. Reverend Dr. Martin Luther King Jr., who was mentored by Reverend Thurman, put it this way:

> And before you finish eating breakfast in the morning, you've depended on more than half the world. This is the way our universe is structured. It is its interrelated quality. We aren't going to have peace on earth until we recognize this basic fact of the interrelated structure of all reality.[17]

More than ever, an apostle of sensitiveness must internalize this insight and fully embody it in order to counter a growing sense of disconnection that is impacting our well-being as individuals, communities, and nations.

---

[15] Frans de Waal, *The Age of Empathy* (New York: Harmony Books, 2009), 213.

[16] As quoted in Dalai Lama and Desmond Tutu with Douglas Abrams, *The Book of Joy: Lasting Happiness in a Changing World* (New York: Avery, 2016), 218.

[17] From Martin Luther King Jr.'s "A Christmas Sermon on Peace" (1967), in Martin Luther King Jr. and James Melvin Washington, *A Testament of Hope: The Essential Writings of Martin Luther King Jr.* (San Francisco: HarperSanFrancisco, 1991), 253.

The Problem of Self-Absorption

Both Reverend Thurman and His Holiness the Dalai Lama anticipated what contemporary research is demonstrating: that excessive self-focus exacerbates many of our modern problems, including the alarming rates of loneliness, depression, burnout, and self-harm, as well as the prevalence on a global level of social conflict, injustice, and ecological destruction. Dr. Daniel Goleman, a psychologist and the author of *Emotional Intelligence* and other books examining how we can expand our circles of caring, puts it this way:

> Self-absorption in all its forms kills empathy, let alone compassion. When we focus on ourselves, our world contracts as our problems and preoccupations loom large. But when we focus on others, our world expands. Our own problems drift to the periphery of the mind and so seem smaller, and we increase our capacity for connection—our compassionate action.[18]

Our society today more than ever needs this altruistic outlook as envisioned by Reverend Thurman for his apostles of sensitiveness. For this reason, His Holiness the Dalai Lama has called for a "compassion revolution." His Holiness adds, "Compassion and love are not mere luxuries. As the source both of inner and external peace, they are fundamental to the continued survival of our species."[19]

Compassionate Motivation, Discernment, and Taking Action

It is important to remember that Bodhisattvas are those sentient beings who deliberately engage with the suffering of the world in order to transform it, one sentient being at a time. It starts with a motivation inspired by compassion and is complemented by the application of discernment (i.e., wisdom), resulting in constructive action. In order for a bird to navigate to its destination, it must rely on both wings equally. Similarly, a Boddhisattva relies on the integration of compassion and wisdom to attain their goal of full enlightenment and to benefit beings according to their needs and dispositions. His Holiness the Dalai Lama points out in his book *Beyond Religion* that compassionate motivation must be complemented by discernment:

> Until now I have emphasized the importance of compassion—a motivation of genuine concern for others' welfare—as the foundation of ethics

---

[18] Daniel Goleman, *Social Intelligence: The New Science of Human Relationships* (New York: Bantam Dell, 2006), 54.

[19] Dalai Lama, *Ethics for the New Millennium* (New York: Riverhead Books, 1999), 130.

and spiritual well-being and even the basis for understanding justice. Recognizing our shared humanity and our biological nature as beings whose happiness is dependent on others, we learn to open our hearts, and in so doing we gain a sense of purpose and that connection with those around us. Broad, unbiased compassion, I have also suggested, is the ground from which all positive inner values—patience, kindness, forgiveness, self-discipline, contentment, and so on—emerge.

However, while sound compassionate motivation is the foundation of ethics and spirituality, a further factor is crucial if we are to achieve a balanced and genuinely universal system of ethics. While intention is the first and most important factor in guaranteeing that our behavior is ethical, we also need *discernment* to ensure that the choices we make are realistic and that our good intentions do not go to waste.... What is required, therefore, in addition to good intention, is the use of our critical faculty, our discernment. The exercise of discernment, which enables us to relate to situations in a manner that is in tune with reality, enables us to translate our good intentions into good outcomes.[20]

Methods for Taking Action as a Bodhisattva or Apostle of Sensitiveness

Several techniques are available in Buddhism for uncovering and then cultivating our fundamental nature in order to become Bodhisattvas. Bodhisattvas are not finished "beings"; they are in a transformative state. In Buddhism, everything is dynamic, including what we call the person or self. Bodhisattvas are always on Reverend Thurman's growing edge. They are transformers of suffering, transmuting that distress and destructive emotions through the practice of compassion and wisdom.

Transforming Suffering: The Practice of Tong-Len

One of the core practices used to transmute suffering in the Tibetan Buddhist contemplative tradition is called *tong-len,* or "giving and taking." A spirit of *tong-len* involves a deeply felt sense of love and compassion. Love is a desire to see another flourish, while compassion is the desire to alleviate another's suffering. They are, in essence, two sides of the same coin. The experience of love, for example, allows a parent to happily sacrifice their own happiness for the sake of their child's happiness and well-being. Similarly, the experience of compassion

---

[20] Dalai Lama, *Beyond Religion*, 73–74.

allows a loving parent to willingly endure suffering if it will relieve the suffering of their child. This is the essence of *tong-len*.

By practicing *tong-len*, a Bodhisattva deepens one's spirit of love and compassion by attuning to the suffering of other beings to the point that Bodhisattvas are willing to take that suffering onto themselves. They visualize suffering being transformed into the source of happiness through the force of their deeply felt love and compassion. A Bodhisattva then visualizes sending those sources of happiness, along with their own virtues, to those lacking happiness and well-being. The First Panchen Lama encapsulates it this way:

> *Therefore, o venerable compassionate gurus,*
> *Bless me that all karmic obscurations and suffering*
> *Of mother migrators ripen upon me right now,*
> *And that I may give others my happiness and virtuous deeds*
> *In order that all sentient beings have happiness.*[21]

The practice of *tong-len* resonates with Reverend Thurman's idea of "meeting people where they are." He puts it this way:

> I see you where you are striving and struggling and in light of the highest possibility of your personality, I deal with you there. My religious faith is insistent that this can be done only out of a life of devotion. I must cultivate the inner spiritual resources of my life to such a point that I can bring you to my sanctuary before his presence, until, at last, I do not know you from myself.[22]

Starting from Where You Are

Bodhisattvas work to advance their spiritual capacity at the same time they are devoted to the welfare of others. It is a simultaneous process. As they engage in social justice, political, academic, or any other kind of work, they draw on their deep reservoir of love and compassion for all beings.

One does not have to become a Buddha before one can work to alleviate suffering in the world. We can start right now. The Bodhisattva, like the apostle of sensitiveness, starts from where they are, meets people where they are, and does so in a spirit of kindness and compassion for all sentient beings. Their altruistic

---

[21] Dalai Lama, *The Union of Bliss and Emptiness* (Ithaca, NY: Snow Lion Publications, 1988), 157.

[22] HT, *The Growing Edge* (New York: Harper and Row, 1956); paperback edition (Richmond, IN: Friends United Press, 1974), 27–28.

intentions are based on the recognition that all beings, like themselves, wish to be happy and free from suffering. Furthermore, that intention is grounded in their keen awareness of our interdependence. The illusion that any single person is a self-sufficient island must be abandoned. It is through this realization that one is able to make better choices; while no one can avoid all suffering in life, one can avoid the additional suffering brought about by destructive emotions such as greed, hatred, and jealousy.

Education of Heart and Mind

There are many parallels between Reverend Thurman's work and that of His Holiness the Dalai Lama. Like Reverend Thurman, His Holiness is very aware of the need to incorporate spirituality into societal institutions, including education. He attributes the many woes of our modern existence—such as the growing crises of mental health, political divisiveness, social injustice, and environmental degradation—to a loss of spirituality. He does not see spirituality as a strictly religious practice, but rather a practice of basic human values such as love, compassion, forgiveness, and tolerance that are shared by both the religious and nonreligious.

His Holiness has written extensively about the need to incorporate these values into education. In advocating for the inclusion of these universal values, what he calls "secular ethics," in education, he suggests that there is no need to rely on a particular religious framework. Rather, we should see these values in the context of common sense, common experience, and modern scientific evidence. For the Dalai Lama, universal values "are not mere luxuries, but necessities" for the continued survival of humanity. He suggests that what is needed is a "spiritual revolution," a revolution that is "beyond religion" in the sense that all people who value compassion can support such an approach, one that is not dependent upon any specific faith tradition. Secular ethics is complementary to all the major faith traditions in that it emphasizes concern for others' well-being.

This view aligns with the approach that Reverend Thurman ascribes to his apostles of sensitiveness or Reverend Taylor to her eccentric apostles; they are on the leading edge of the work necessary to solve today's human predicaments.

Finding Common Ground

As the Dalai Lama has engaged the teachings of Christ to find common ground between the traditions, so Reverend Thurman engaged the Buddha's teachings. In their editorial notes to the transcript of a sermon Reverend Thurman preached addressing the life of the Buddha, Peter Eisenstadt and Walter Earl Fluker discuss how Reverend Thurman sought to find the common ground between Buddha's message and the message of Jesus:

> At the same time, though [Thurman] worried about the implications of the Buddhist doctrine that "you cannot be free until you are free of the necessity even of being yourself," he saw affinities between his understanding of non-violence, as expounded in *Jesus and the Disinherited* and elsewhere. The de-emphasis on the self properly placed attention on the "event, the act and its results." It is not enough to oppose evil in one's heart; one must take action.[23]

In an excerpt from this same lecture, Reverend Thurman explained his reading of the Buddha's message in terms of morally and ethically purifying oneself as a crucial step before one can effectively engage in social transformation.

> "Therefore," [the Buddha] said, "the responsibility of the individual becomes a double responsibility. I will purify myself that I may get from under the necessities of existence. But in the purification of myself I recognize the responsibility to radiate a quality of living that will influence the minds, the thinking, and the processes of the people around me." And [the Buddha's] great contribution to ethics is at that point he defines direct action in terms that have to do with the inner purity of the life. And after all these centuries we still do not dare try the thing that he suggested: to make an attack on moral disorder in the world by the purification of one's own life on the theory and in the faith that something redemptive in character can be radiated from that.[24]

In conclusion, I believe Reverend Thurman's vision for the Apostles of Sensitiveness is beautifully reflected in these two prayers, one by a Christian, Saint Francis of Assisi, and the other by a Buddhist, Acharya Shantideva of Nalanda, an eighth-century CE Indian philosopher, Buddhist monk, poet, and scholar. Both prayers express a deep love and compassion for humanity, and the desire to alleviate whatever suffering they may encounter and to fulfill whatever needs there may be.

First, Saint Francis:

> *Lord, make me an instrument of your peace:*
> *where there is hatred, let me sow love;*
> *where there is injury, pardon;*

---

[23] HT, *Walking with God: The Way of the Mystics*, vol. 2, ed. Peter Eisenstadt and Walter E. Fluker (Maryknoll, NY: Orbis Books, 2021), 26.

[24] Ibid., 32–33.

> *where there is doubt, faith;*
> *where there is despair, hope;*
> *where there is darkness, light;*
> *where there is sadness, joy.*[25]

And Shantideva:

> *Just like the earth and space itself*
> *And all the other mighty elements,*
> *For boundless multitudes of beings*
> *May I always be the ground of life,*
> *The source of varied sustenance.*
> *Thus, for everything that lives,*
> *As far as are the limits of the sky,*
> *May I be constantly their source of livelihood*
> *Until they pass beyond all sorrow.*[26]

These prayers from two different faiths reveal a similar openness and responsiveness to the possibility and potential for transformative action. Such catalysts for change are required at the growing, leading edge. This location is where our apostles of sensitiveness and our Bodhisattvas will always find themselves working, with love, compassion, and wisdom. I can imagine Reverend Thurman nodding his head with us in agreement.

---

[25] Prayer of Saint Francis, https://en.wikipedia.org/wiki/Prayer_of_Saint_Francis.
[26] Shantideva, *Bodhicaryāvatāra* 3.21, as cited in Dalai Lama with Thubten Chodron, *Following in the Buddha's Footsteps* (Boston: Wisdom Publications, 2019), xvi.

9

INTERRELIGIOUS HOSPITALITY

Howard Thurman and Zalman Schachter-Shalomi

Or N. Rose

Rabbi Zalman Schachter-Shalomi (1924–2014), founder of the Jewish Renewal Movement, was a leading interreligious practitioner in post–World War II North American life.[1] By the time of his death at age eighty-nine, he was widely regarded as a leading interpreter of Judaism, particularly its mystical currents, and a wise religious bridge-builder. Rabbi Schachter-Shalomi participated in public and private gatherings with such renowned figures as His Holiness the 14th Dalai Lama,[2] Archbishop Desmond Tutu, and Father Thomas Keating.[3] From 1995 to 2002, he held the World Wisdom Chair at the Buddhist Naropa University in Boulder, Colorado. However, long before he grew into the role of international Jewish sage and spiritual elder, Schachter-Shalomi began an idiosyncratic journey that took him from the world of HaBaD-Lubavitch Hasidism into dialogue with an array of practitioners, practices, and texts from the world's religions.[4]

---

[1] Zalman Schachter added the name Shalomi ("of Peace") later in life. For an introduction to his life and work, including his interreligious expeditions, see *Rabbi Zalman Schachter-Shalomi: Essential Teachings*, ed. Or N. Rose and Netanel Miles-Yépez (Maryknoll, NY: Orbis Books, 2020). See, too, the extensive list of obituaries on the Yesod Foundation website, including pieces in the *New York Times*, the *Huffington Post*, and *Forward*. Also helpful are two pieces by Shaul Magid: "Jewish Renewal Movement," *Encyclopedia of Religion*, and "Jewish Renewal: Toward a New American Judaism," in *Tikkun* 21, no. 1 (January/February 2006): 57–60.

[2] On Schachter-Shalomi's most significant encounter with the Dalai Lama, see Rodger Kamenetz, *The Jew in the Lotus: A Poet's Rediscovery of Jewish Identity in Buddhist India* (San Francisco: HarperOne, 1994). See also Joy Levitt, "When Reb Zalman Met the Dalai Lama," *Forward*, July 4, 2014.

[3] For an intimate glimpse into the friendship between Keating and Schachter-Shalomi, see *The Kiss of God: A Dialogue on Science, Mysticism, and Spiritual Practice*, ed. Netanel Miles-Yépez (Boulder, CO: Albion-Andalus, 2020).

[4] HaBaD is an acronym for three Hebrew words: *Hokhmah* (wisdom), *Binah* (under-

In this brief essay, I examine Schachter-Shalomi's written reflections on his first encounters with the renowned African American spiritual polymath, the Reverend Howard Thurman, at Boston University (BU) in 1955.[5] At the time, Reverend Thurman served as dean of Marsh Chapel and professor of spiritual disciplines and resources at BU's School of Theology, and Schachter-Shalomi was a new student in the MA program in psychology and religion (with a focus on pastoral care), while also working as a pulpit rabbi in a small Orthodox congregation in New Bedford, Massachusetts. The rabbi repeatedly described this relationship as pivotal to his development as an (inter)religious leader and educator.[6]

As a scholar-practitioner in the burgeoning field of interreligious studies, I think it is crucial that we learn from the experiences of our forebears—theoreticians and practitioners alike—and those, like Thurman and Schachter-Shalomi, who moved between these distinct but related spheres of activity. Further, it is critical to examine not just the public but also (when evidence is available) the private efforts of such figures to better understand the efficacy of different forms of engagement and the connections among them. A robust and nuanced history of interreligious activity in North America (and elsewhere)—including successes, failures, and the many efforts in between—is a desideratum in the field.[7] I intend this essay as a historical case study: a close examination of an episode (in two parts) in interreligious leadership formation with the practice of hospitality emerging as its key feature.

---

standing), and *Da'at* (awareness). These reflect the intellectual-spiritual foundations of the group, based on earlier Jewish mystical teachings on the Godhead and the human soul. Lubavitch is the town in White Russia (the eastern part of present-day Belarus) where the now-dominant branch of the dynasty flourished from 1813 to 1915. The two names are often used together or interchangeably. See Naftali Lowenthal, "Lubavitch Hasidism," in *The YIVO Encyclopedia of Jews in Eastern Europe*, ed. Gershon David Hundert (New Haven, CT: Yale University Press, 2008). See also the entries on HaBaD (spelled Chabad) in *Hasidism: A New History*, ed. David Biale et al. (Princeton, NJ: Princeton University Press, 2018).

[5] This article is a revised and expanded version of my essay "Howard Thurman's Mentorship of Zalman Schachter-Shalomi," in *Interreligious Studies: Dispatches from an Emerging Field*, ed. Hans Gustafson (Waco, TX: Baylor University Press, 2020), 228–35. On Thurman's groundbreaking and challenging tenure at Boston University, see Peter Eisenstadt, *Against the Hounds of Hell: A Life of Howard Thurman* (Charlottesville: University of Virginia Press, 2021), 274–307.

[6] One simple demonstration of Schachter-Shalomi's abiding respect for and appreciation of Thurman is the fact that the rabbi dedicated his book *Davenning: A Guide to Meaningful Jewish Prayer*, with Joel Segel (Woodstock, VT: Jewish Lights, 2006), to his BU mentor and two of his spiritual guides from his days as a HaBaD yeshiva student.

[7] Two important examples of this type of research are Thomas Albert Howard, *The Faith of Others: A History of Interreligious Dialogue* (New Haven, CT: Yale University Press, 2021), and Kevin M. Schultz, *Tri-Faith America: How Catholics and Jews Held Postwar America to Its Protestant Promise* (New York: Oxford University Press, 2011).

A Chance Encounter?

As a commuter student, Schachter-Shalomi had to leave his home in New Bedford very early to avoid rush-hour traffic and arrive in time for morning classes. This meant that in the late fall and winter months he departed prior to sunrise and could not, therefore, recite the *Shaharit* (dawn, morning) service before heading off to Boston.[8] And so, after arriving at BU, he had to find an appropriate place to pray. According to the rabbi, the only building he could find that was open at that early hour was the university chapel. However, as Schachter-Shalomi writes, navigating this Christian holy space was challenging for him:

> In the main chapel upstairs were statues of Jesus and the Evangelists, and I didn't feel comfortable praying there. Downstairs was a smaller chapel for meditation, but I was inhibited by a big brass cross on the altar table. Finally, I chose a public room [the Daniel Marsh Memorabilia Room] … found myself a corner facing the east, toward Jerusalem, and used that as my morning prayer place.[9]

---

[8] There is extensive discussion among Jewish legal experts about when one may begin the morning service and which portions of it can be recited relative to the rising sun. See, for example, Isaac Klein, *A Guide to Jewish Practice* (New York: Jewish Theological Seminary of America, 1979), 13–14.

[9] Schachter-Shalomi told this story many times with minor variations. The following is a chronological listing of the written versions I have discovered in the course of my research: Zalman Schachter-Shalomi, "What I Found in the Chapel," *The First Step: A Guide for the New Jewish Spirit*, with Donald Gropman (Toronto: Bantam Books, 1983), 4. He republished the story in the same form and with the same title in an updated edition of the volume titled *First Steps to a New Jewish Spirit: Reb Zalman's Guide to Recapturing the Intimacy and Ecstasy in Your Relationship with God* (Woodstock, VT: Jewish Lights, 2003), xv–xviii (these are not the same as Schachter-Shalomi's 1958 meditation manual, *The First Step*). A slightly more detailed version of the story, with the same title, can be found in the anthology *My Neighbor's Faith: Stories of Interreligious Encounter, Growth, and Transformation*, ed. Jennifer Howe Peace, Or N. Rose, and Gregory Mobley (Maryknoll, NY: Orbis Books, 2012), 208–12. In his memoir, Schachter-Shalomi places the story within the broader narrative arc about his decision to attend the BU School of Theology and his desire to become a Jewish campus professional. He also adds a few details about his first meetings with Thurman not included in the versions listed above, as well as some illuminating comments about his experiences in Thurman's class and a later encounter (1963) between the two in Canada. See Zalman Schachter-Shalomi with Edward Hoffman, *My Life in Jewish Renewal: A Memoir* (Lanham, MD: Rowman and Littlefield, 2012), 87–92. Finally, Sara Davidson retells this story in *The December Project: An Extraordinary Rabbi and a Skeptic Confront Life's Greatest Mystery* (New York: HarperCollins, 2014), 75–77. The book is based on a series of dialogues between Davidson and Schachter-Shalomi, and her narration of the latter's first encounters with Thurman includes additional commentary from Schachter-Shalomi about this episode.

While the rabbi was apprehensive, a few previous constructive interfaith experiences helped him cross this threshold.[10] Still, he did not feel comfortable praying in the formal Christian worship spaces. Schachter-Shalomi continued to pray by himself in the Marsh Memorabilia Room for the next several days, before he attracted the attention of one of the chapel employees:

> One morning, when I'd just completed my prayers, a middle-aged black man came into the room and said in a casual way, "I've seen you here several times. Wouldn't you like to say your prayers in the small chapel?" I shrugged my shoulders, not knowing what to say. The man was so unpretentious that I thought he might have been the person who took care of the building. His offer was so forthcoming that I did not want to hurt his feelings—how could I explain that I couldn't pray in the chapel because of the cross on the altar? He looked at me and said: "Why don't you stop by the chapel tomorrow morning and see? Maybe you'd be comfortable saying your prayers there."[11]

Curious to see what his enigmatic host had in mind, the next morning Schachter-Shalomi went to look at the small chapel. To his surprise, it had been carefully reconfigured: "Two candles were burning in brass candleholders, and the big brass cross was gone. The ornate large Bible was open to the Book of Psalms. From then on, I understood that I was at liberty to move the cross and say my morning prayers in the chapel." In later written versions of the story, Schachter-Shalomi adds that the man did not simply open the Bible to the Book of Psalms—a biblical text that is foundational to Jewish and Christian worship—but

---

[10] Schachter-Shalomi with Hoffman, *My Life in Jewish Renewal*, chapters 10–14. Many Orthodox Jews will not enter a church because they view Christianity as an idolatrous religion (though usually distinguished from polytheistic traditions), based on Christian teachings on the triune nature of God and the divinity of Jesus of Nazareth. Christian houses of worship are, therefore, deemed loci of idolatrous ritual behavior. This is further compounded by the presence of the kind of iconography described above. See J. David Bleich, "Survey of Halakhic Periodical Literature: Entering a Non-Jewish House of Worship," *Tradition: A Journal of Orthodox Jewish Thought* 44, no. 2 (Summer 2011): 73–101. See also Alan Brill's broader treatment of Jewish understandings of Christianity in his monograph *Judaism and World Religions: Encountering Christianity, Islam, and Eastern Traditions* (New York: Palgrave Macmillan, 2012), 51–143. The fact that Schachter-Shalomi was even willing to enter Marsh Chapel is a sign of his emerging independence from the HaBaD and broader Orthodox community, which would unfold over the next decade. See my essay "Envisioning a *Jewish* Monastic Community: Zalman Schachter and the B'nai Or Fellowship," *Studies in Christian-Jewish Relations* (2022). See also Ariel Evan Mayse, "Renewal and Redemption: Spirituality, Law and Religious Praxis in the Writings of Rabbi Zalman Schachter-Shalomi," *Journal of Religion* 101, no. 4 (October 2021): 455–505.

[11] Schachter-Shalomi, *The First Step*, 4.

he specifically chose Psalm 139—"Wither shall I flee from Thy presence." As if with a wink, the "caretaker" sought to communicate to the rabbi that God—the Omnipresent One—was available to him even in this foreign house of worship. Further, to help ease the tension this Jewish devotee was experiencing, the man attempted to create a convivial worship space for him, including removing the "big brass cross" from the altar. Schachter-Shalomi also adds that when leaving the chapel each morning, he attempted to respond to these gestures of hospitality by returning the cross to its usual place and turning the Bible from Psalm 139 to Psalm 100—the "Thank you" psalm.[12] As he says to Sara Davidson in the *December Project*, he and his host were "sending messages to each other through the Bible," even though the rabbi still did not know the identity of this mysterious and considerate person.[13]

As Schachter-Shalomi would soon learn—much to his embarrassment—the man he originally mistook for the janitor was in fact the dean of Marsh Chapel: the Reverend Howard Thurman.[14] He discovered this sometime later when he met with the dean to discuss his course options for the coming semester.

> I read an announcement about a new course in spiritual disciplines and resources which would include labs for spiritual exercises, to be taught by

---

[12] Ibid. See also "What I Found in the Chapel," 209. Sara Davidson also includes this detail in her retelling of the story, *The December Project*, 76. Psalm 139 was one of Thurman's favorite texts as it speaks of the ubiquitous presence—including within the human being—of the Divine. See Walter Fluker's comments on Thurman's use of this psalm in the former's essay, "The Inward Sea: Mapping Interior Landmarks for Leaders," in *Anchored in the Current: Discovering Howard Thurman as Educator, Activist, Guide, and Prophet*, ed. Gregory C. Ellison II (Louisville, KY: Westminster John Knox Press, 2020), 59–60. Schachter-Shalomi found it a most fitting textual choice as a welcome psalm for an uneasy Orthodox rabbi entering an unfamiliar Christian prayer space. The following is a recording (and transcription) of Thurman briefly reflecting on this psalm: "Thou Has Searched Me," October 28, 1960, PITTS. See also examples of Thurman's poetic interpretations of Psalm 139 in the anthology *Howard Thurman: Essential Writings*, selected with and introduction by Luther E. Smith Jr. (Maryknoll, NY: Orbis Books, 2006), 41–42, 100–101, and 134–35.

[13] Davidson, *The December Project*, 75-77.

[14] Thurman was, in fact, the first African American clergyperson to serve as dean of a chapel at a major university in the United States, the first non-Methodist dean of Marsh Chapel, and the first African American to be a tenured professor and dean at BU. See Eisenstadt, *Against the Hounds of Hell*, 274–78. Given Schachter-Shalomi's love of and talent for storytelling and his decades-long commitment to fostering respectful and mutually enriching intergroup relations, I think he included this detail about his misguided racial assumption to gently prod his readers (primarily Jewish and white) to examine their own biases. I also think the story would have been stronger had Schachter-Shalomi shared more about this dimension of it, including his mindset at the time, his regret, and the impact of this experience on his work moving forward. I do not know if he and Thurman ever discussed the incident. Neither of them mentions doing so in their reports about their interactions. I have not found any comments by Thurman about this first meeting.

the Dean of the Chapel. The course intrigued me, but I was apprehensive about taking it. The Dean of the Chapel was also a minister and I worried that he might feel obliged to try and convert me. After some thought, I made an appointment to speak with him about my concerns.[15]

To Schachter-Shalomi's surprise, Thurman used a dramatic pedagogic tool to invite his apprehensive new student into the course:

> [Dean Thurman] put his coffee mug down on his desk and began to look at his hands. He turned them palms up, then palms down ... as if considering the light and dark sides of an argument.... This lasted for several minutes, but if felt like hours to me. He did what he was doing with such a calm certainty that he seemed to possess great power. Suddenly he spoke. "Don't you trust the *Ruach Hakodesh*?"[16]

And how did Schachter-Shalomi respond to this gesture? "I was stunned. He'd used the Hebrew for the Spirit of Holiness, something I had not expected from a gentile.[17] And in so doing, he brought that great question home to me in a particularly strong way."[18] It took Schachter-Shalomi some time to respond to Thurman's provocative question. In fact, the rabbi reports that he walked out of the office without answering and spent the next three weeks struggling with the question. But after careful consideration, the eventual answer was yes; he trusted that his relationship with God and commitment to Jewish life and practice—his "anchor chains"—were strong enough to take the risk of studying with this Christian teacher.[19] Clearly, he also trusted this kind, perceptive, and challenging man who had graciously welcomed him into the chapel, rearranging

---

[15] Schachter-Shalomi, *The First Step: A Guide for the New Jewish Spirit*, 5.

[16] Ibid.

[17] Ibid. See also "HT To Zalman M. Schachter, March 3, 1959, Boston, Mass.," in PHWT 4:xxix–xxx, 240–42. "Schachter-Shalomi wrote that he learned from Thurman that there were 'non-Jews who were wonderful, blessed souls' and that 'there are ways of loving and expressing God that are so simple.' Thurman, he concluded, 'wasn't interested in getting souls to Christ, but, like Jesus, he wanted to get souls to God'" (242n6). On the use of *Ruach Hakodesh*, a foundational theological term in Jewish and Christian contexts, see Alan Unterman, Howard Kreisel, and Rivka Horwitz, "Ru'ah Ha-Kodesh," in *Encyclopedia Judaica*, 2nd ed., ed. Michael Berenbaum and Fred Skolnik (Detroit: Macmillan Reference USA, 2007), 506–9, and Geoffrey Wainwright, "The Holy Spirit," in *The Cambridge Companion to Christian Doctrine*, ed. Colin E. Gunton (New York: Cambridge University Press, 1997), 280–85. I do not know if the two men discussed their understandings of this term, including similarities and differences (note, for example, that Schachter-Shalomi translates the term *Ruach Hakodesh* as "Spirit of Holiness" and not "*The* Holy Spirit").

[18] Schachter-Shalomi, *The First Step*, 5.

[19] Ibid.

the prayer space with great attention to religious and aesthetic detail.[20] Apparently, Thurman chose not to say anything about the chapel experience, letting his actions speak for themselves. Given Thurman's age and extensive experience in interracial and interreligious contexts, it seems more than likely that he was aware of Schachter-Shalomi's confusion and embarrassment about their first encounter in Marsh Chapel. In this delicate moment, the dean focused his pastoral energies on what he felt was an opportunity to help his new student deal with a faith challenge—as a Jew.[21] As Schachter-Shalomi later noted, Thurman "wasn't interested in getting souls to Christ; like Jesus, he was interested in getting souls to God."[22]

I wish to add that Thurman's gestures—both in the chapel and his office—could have easily fallen flat had his younger interlocutor not been receptive to his brand of hospitality. Other people may have not returned to the church building after their initial encounter—or, if they did return, might have felt that they still could not pray in the rearranged worship space. Further, Schachter-Shalomi seemed to delight in playing the nonverbal game of moving the cross and flipping from psalm to psalm.[23] Finally, other students may have found the dean's challenge about the *Ruach Hakodesh* too forceful, presumptuous, or even manipulative. But all these actions worked for this student at this life stage.

---

[20] Thurman had a passionate interest in religious aesthetics, including the use of the arts in worship services. See, for example, Amanda Brown, *The Fellowship Church: Howard Thurman and the Twentieth-Century Religious Left* (New York: Oxford University Press, 2021), 149–51. This was something he and Schachter-Shalomi shared in common. See my essay "A Mystical Reunion in Manitoba: Howard Thurman and Zalman Schachter (Shalomi)," in *Hiddushim: Celebrating Hebrew College's Centennial*, ed. Michael Fishbane, Arthur Green, and Jonathan Sarna (Boston: Academic Studies Press, 2022).

[21] I also think this was in keeping with one of Thurman's basic pedagogic commitments that a mentor must meet a student "where they are" and help the individual grow into their fuller or deeper selves. As he said many times, "A crown is placed over our heads that for the rest of our lives we are trying to grow tall enough to wear." As Thurman also notes, a mentor must carefully discern when and where to act with greater or lesser force in helping a student grow. See HT, *For the Inward Journey*, selected by Anne Spencer Thurman (Richmond, IN: Friends United Meeting, 1991), 247. See also Paul Harvey's comments on this maxim in *Howard Thurman and the Disinherited: A Religious Biography* (Grand Rapids: Eerdmans, 2020), 95–96.

[22] Unpublished interview with Zalman Schachter-Shalomi conducted by Peter R. Eisenstadt, June 28, 2012. My thanks to Dr. Eisenstadt for sharing his notes with me. For Thurman's own reflection on Jesus as a model of bringing others closer to God (and *not* as a part of the Godhead), see HT, *Footprints of a Dream: The Story of the Church for the Fellowship for All Peoples* (New York: Harper & Brothers, 1959), 129.

[23] In teaching this text, I regularly ask students to consider why Thurman did not introduce himself more fully to Schachter-Shalomi the first time they met. Was this deliberate? Why did the dean choose to say so little and express his intentions through his actions? Why not attempt to engage the rabbi in more conversation right away?

Since Thurman was an older, erudite, and charismatic religious leader, Schachter-Shalomi was perhaps more open to learning from him, given his rabbinical training and his relationships with his Hasidic teachers and mentors. Although he was expanding his religious horizons, the rabbi still greatly valued the guidance of a seasoned (male) teacher, even if that man was an African American progressive Baptist minister.[24] The private office meeting may have even felt familiar to Schachter-Shalomi from his experiences in *yehidut* (one-on-one counseling sessions) with his *rebbes* (Hasidic masters).[25] Thurman's understanding of and sensitivity to his new student's prayer needs and educational concerns were obviously very impressive to Schachter-Shalomi. While neither man says so in his writings, I wonder if the fact that both were from minority communities and had personally experienced the pain of marginalization and oppression also helped them forge a relationship.[26] It is worth noting that because of seeing the Ku Klux Klan burning crosses earlier in his life, Thurman carried with him great ambivalence about this ubiquitous Christian symbol. As he wrote a few years after this event, "Even to this day [1959], I find that whenever I see the cross my mind and my spirit must do a double take because the thing that flashes instinctively in my mind is that of the burning cross of the Klan."[27] This surely made it easier for him to move the large brass cross in the chapel, knowing that this weighty symbolic

---

[24] As Schachter-Shalomi would soon learn, Thurman was a highly unconventional Christian practitioner and leader, who drew creatively on a variety of spiritual traditions; he also strongly opposed Christian conversionary efforts aimed at Jews or other non-Christians. See, for example, HT, *The Creative Encounter* (New York: Harper & Row, 1954), 147–48. Dean Thurman was the rabbi's first significant heterodox religious mentor—Jewish or otherwise—following his ordination from HaBaD.

[25] Thanks to Netanel Miles-Yépez, a close student of Schachter-Shalomi, for our discussion of this matter. Schachter-Shalomi wrote his doctoral thesis about *yehidut* (Hebrew Union College–Institute of Jewish Religion, 1963–68). The project was informed both by his study and personal experiences as a Hasid and his growing interest and engagement in different forms of psychology (spurred by his studies at BU). He later published a version of the thesis as *Spiritual Intimacy: A Study in Hasidic Counseling* (Northvale, NJ: Jason Aronson, 1996).

[26] Thurman experienced the ills of racism from his earliest years in Daytona Beach, Florida (his grandmother, who played a key role in his upbringing, was a former slave). Schachter-Shalomi was a refugee from Nazi-occupied Europe, arriving in the United States in 1940 after a long and harrowing sojourn with his family through several countries. I do not know how much the two men discussed their biographies or if Thurman was aware of Schachter-Shalomi's experiences in Europe at the time of their first office meeting. HT did meet Schachter-Shalomi's parents and other family members a few years later in Winnipeg, Canada. See "A Mystical Reunion in Manitoba: Howard Thurman and Zalman Schachter (Shalomi)," in *Hiddushim*. See also, "II. A Conservative Rabbi and a Trappist Monastery in Winnipeg," in "Annual Report: The Wider Ministry, 1962–1963, September 1963, Boston, Mass.," in PHWT 5:23–25.

[27] See HT, *Footprints of a Dream*, 17.

object could alienate Schachter-Shalomi as a Jew whose people had lived in the shadow of the cross for centuries.[28] It is also the case that by this time in his career, Thurman was quite liberal and experimental in his liturgical leadership, seeking to create inclusive worship experiences for Christians and non-Christians alike at Marsh Chapel.[29]

Further, Thurman had an abiding interest in Jewish history and thought and forged meaningful relationships with several Jewish colleagues and students throughout his career.[30] To the best of my knowledge, however, Schachter-Shalomi was Thurman's only Hasidic student. Most of Thurman's Jewish colleagues and students were Reform Jews who did not have the same spiritual interests that he shared with Schachter-Shalomi; particularly, they lacked the minister's passionate interest in mystical texts and traditions and the use of such materials for personal and communal growth and transformation.[31] Further, both Jewish and non-Jewish seekers had far less access to Hasidic life and thought in the 1950s than they do today.[32] Thurman was clearly intrigued and impressed by

---

[28] See, among many works on the subject, James Carroll, *Constantine's Sword: The Church and the Jews: A History* (New York: Mariner Books, 2001). See also John Connelly, *From Enemy to Brother: The Revolution in Catholic Teaching on the Jews, 1933–1965* (Cambridge, MA: Harvard University Press, 2012).

[29] See, for example, Harvey, *Howard Thurman and the Disinherited*, 163–81, and Brown, *The Fellowship Church*, 199–208. Thurman's liturgical innovations flowed from his previous experience as pastor of the Fellowship Church for All People in San Francisco, where he carefully crafted worship services using a light Christian framework and including resources from other religious and secular traditions. His unconventional and eclectic prayer style was controversial at BU (even as church participation swelled during his tenure), as previous leaders of Marsh Chapel had all been Methodist and conducted services following denominational conventions. HT's successor restored the Methodist traditions of earlier eras. See Eisenstadt, *Against the Hounds of Hell*, 306.

[30] Eisenstadt, *Against the Hounds of Hell*, 475–76. See the tributes to HT by Rabbis Alvin Fine, Joseph Glaser, and Saul White in *Debate and Understanding: Simmering on the Calm Presence and Profound Wisdom of Howard Thurman*, ed. Ricardo A. Millett and Conley H. Hughes (Spring 1982 special edition): 76–78, 88.

[31] For Thurman's approach to the subject of mysticism (both personal and historical), see his collection of sermons in HT, *Walking with God: The Way of the Mystics*, vol. 2, ed. Peter Eisenstadt and Walter Fluker (Maryknoll, NY: Orbis Books, 2021). See also Anthony Sean Neal, *Howard Thurman's Philosophical Mysticism: Love against Fragmentation* (Lanham, MD: Lexington Books, 2019); and Kipton E. Jensen, "Reading Thurman as a Social Activist Mystic," in *Howard Thurman: Philosophy, Civil Rights, and the Search for Common Good* (Columbia: University of South Carolina Press, 2019), 89–104. For Schachter-Shalomi's views on the subject, see his *Credo of a Modern Kabbalist*, written with Rabbi Daniel Siegel (Victoria, BC: Trafford Press, 2005). See also chapters 2–5 and 8 in Shaul Magid, *American Post-Judaism: Identity and Renewal in a Postethnic Society* (Bloomington: Indiana University Press, 2013).

[32] Over the last several decades there has been a proliferation of multimedia materials

this unusual Hasid and burgeoning leader, who was both deeply steeped in his own religious tradition and increasingly open to learning from practitioners and teachers from other traditions.[33] Each man seemed attracted to the other based on a blend of mystery and familiarity. They were each lifelong seekers who had a penchant for the exotic and forging relationships with people—clergy, intellectuals, artists, and others—from different walks of life. As Peter Eisenstadt points out in his landmark biography of Thurman, through this unexpected turn of events, Schachter-Shalomi emerged as one of the dean's most enthusiastic and devoted students at Boston University; seeking to become, in Thurman's words, an "apostle of sensitiveness."[34] The rabbi made extensive use of his teacher's spiritual insights and pedagogical methods in his work as a Hillel professional and professor at the University of Manitoba (beginning in the fall of 1956), and in various other settings for decades to come.[35]

The Risks of Hospitality

One foundational teaching that emerges from this story is the power of *interreligious* hospitality. By this term, I mean a display of thoughtful welcome by a person from one religious tradition to someone from a different tradition, keeping in mind the specific religious needs of one's guest. As evidenced above, gestures of interreligious hospitality can be particularly important when forging

---

(popular and scholarly) on the origins and development of Hasidism and other forms of Jewish mysticism and piety. See, for example, *Hasidism: A New History*. Further, the HaBaD-Lubavitch dynasty has grown into a sophisticated international movement with deliberate and extensive interaction with non-Jewish entities throughout the world. Schachter-Shalomi was, in fact, among the first HaBaD emissaries sent forth by the sixth Lubavitcher Rebbe, Rabbi Yosef Yitzchak Scheersohn (d. 1950), in the mid-1940s. Schachter-Shalomi's eventual break with HaBaD in the mid-1960s involved his increasing experimentation with non-Jewish spiritual and North American (counter)cultural phenomena beyond the acceptable bounds of the HaBaD community and of Orthodox Judaism more broadly. See Or N. Rose and Netanel Miles-Yépez, "Rabbi Zalman Schachter-Shalomi: A Life of Renewal," in *Rabbi Zalman Schachter-Shalomi: Essential Teachings*, 4–19.

[33] One demonstration of the teacher's esteem for his student was HT's inclusion of Schachter-Shalomi's 1958 (self-published) manual on Jewish meditation, *The First Step: A Primer of a Jew's Spiritual Life*, in his Spiritual Disciplines and Resources course, which profoundly influenced Schachter-Shalomi. See Eisenstadt, *Against the Hounds of Hell*, 475–76. Schachter-Shalomi republished the manual several times in different forms. See Meshullam Zalman Schachter, *The First Step: A Primer of a Jew's Spiritual Life: 60th Anniversary Edition*, foreword by Netanel Miles-Yépez (Boulder, CO: Albion-Andalus, 2020).

[34] HT, *Deep Is the Hunger: Meditations for Apostles of Sensitiveness* (New York: Harper & Row, 1951); and Eisenstadt, *Against the Hounds of Hell*, 476.

[35] Schachter-Shalomi, *The First Step*, 6–7.

relationships across communities, whether individual or group, as they can help establish trust and respect. Of course, to serve as an effective host inter-religiously, one must be both knowledgeable enough about the needs of one's guest and willing to accommodate a person (or persons) whose beliefs and practices may differ from, even challenge, one's own. As the French monk Pierre-François de Béthune writes, "Offering such hospitality does involve a risk … [as evidenced by the fact that the words] 'hospitality' and 'hostility' share the same Indo-European root.… The guest, the stranger … always arouses a certain anxiety."[36] Further, the host also risks alienating the guest through their chosen gestures of hospitality, even when acting with the best of intentions. One must also carefully consider how much they can accommodate another without compromising their own integrity. In our case, Thurman's experience and commitment to Jewish-Christian relations, his ingenuity and generosity, and a developed sense of his own (quite permeable) religious boundaries all aided him in playing host to Schachter-Shalomi.

De Béthune also notes the importance of being able to *offer* and *receive* hospitality; learning to serve in both roles is crucial to this bridge-building work. As he writes, "The first side, the offering of hospitality, has been more often studied. But if this is the only kind of hospitality we are engaged in, we are running the risk of want of balance."[37] As noted above, I think Schachter-Shalomi's nonverbal responses to Thurman's rearrangement of the small chapel indicate that he was thinking carefully (and playfully) about how to serve as a respectful and attuned guest. Turning the Bible from Psalm 139—"Wither shall I flee from Thy presence"—to Psalm 100—the "Thank you psalm"—and returning the cross back to its usual place were deliberate expressions of his gratitude and of his understanding that he was a guest in a Christian worship space.

In exploring the dynamics of interreligious hospitality, it is also important to consider matters of power and privilege as they relate to religion, race, gender, and the like. Who can participate in such encounters? Who has the authority to lead or organize such meetings? Are these gatherings supported by communal authorities? The case of Thurman and Schachter-Shalomi is an interesting one given their respective identities, life stages, the roles each played in the context of their relationship at BU, and their positionality in the wider world.[38] Schachter-

---

[36] See Pierre-Francois de Béthune, "Monastic Inter-Religious Dialogue," in *The Wiley-Blackwell Companion to Inter-Religious Dialogue*, ed. Catherine Cornille (Chichester, UK: Blackwell, 2013), 45.

[37] Ibid., 48.

[38] In teaching about this relationship, I discuss with students the history and current uses of the term "intersectionality," inviting them to consider the different strands of their

Shalomi went on to study closely with Thurman while at BU and invited his teacher—whom he came to lovingly refer to as his "Black *Rebbe*" (spiritual master)—to lecture in Winnipeg in the spring of 1963. Both men wrote effusively about their reunion on the Canadian prairies.[39]

Conclusion

While Zalman Schachter-Shalomi and Howard Thurman are both well-known figures in their respective religious communities and increasingly so in related scholarly, spiritual, and activist circles, far fewer people are aware of their relationship. Thurman's thoughtful welcome of Schachter-Shalomi to BU and his subsequent mentorship of the emerging rabbi were decisive in the formation of this iconoclastic Jewish leader. While it is harder to evaluate the impact of this relationship on Thurman, as he was an older, well-established intellectual and leader when the two men met, he was intrigued by, took pride in, and felt a sense of spiritual kinship with Schachter-Shalomi. My hope is that by uncovering such stories of interreligious engagement, we can better understand the efforts of our forebears, including their struggles and successes. Otherwise, not only will we be doomed to repeat their mistakes, but also lose the opportunity to gain insight from their acts of courage and compassion.

---

identities, how they weave these together, and how others perceive and treat them in different contexts. See Kimberlé Crenshaw, *On Intersectionality: The Essential Writings of Kimberlé Crenshaw* (New York: New Press, 2017). See also Khyati Y. Joshi, *White Christian Privilege: The Illusion of Religious Equality in America* (New York: New York University Press, 2020).

[39] Schachter-Shalomi, *My Life in Jewish Renewal*, 91–92; HT, "The Wider Ministry and the Concept of Community," July 28, 1963 (unpublished sermon). My thanks to Dr. Eisenstadt for sharing this document with me, and for our ongoing discussions about HT and Schachter-Shalomi. A version of this fascinating text can be found in PHWT 5:14–18.

Part Three

America in Search of a Soul

Democratic Life and Practices

10

WE ARE NOT AFRAID

Howard Thurman and the Casting Out of Fear

Peter Eisenstadt

I am not a preacher, and this is not a sermon, but let me open as Thurman usually opened his sermons, with a reading:[1]

> I say to you Cast out fear. Speak no more vain things to me about the greatness of Rome. The greatness of Rome, as you call it, is nothing but fear: fear of the past and fear of the future, fear of the poor, fear of the rich, fear of the High Priests, fear of the Jews and Greeks who are learned, fear of the Gauls and Goths and Huns who are barbarians, fear of the Carthage you destroyed to save you from your fear of it and now fear worse than ever, fear of imperial Caesar, the idol you yourself have created, and fear of me, the penniless vagrant, buffeted and mocked, fear of everything except the rule of God: faith in nothing but blood and iron and gold. You, standing for Rome, are the universal coward: I, standing for the kingdom of God, have braved everything, lost everything, and won an eternal crown.

He did not write this, but it was a reading he often used. This is a dialogue between Jesus and Pilate taken from the preface from George Bernard Shaw's late and fairly obscure play, *On the Rocks*. I quote it because I think it expresses, perhaps in a more forceful and sweeping way than Thurman ever did himself, his own understanding of fear. Fear for Thurman was both a private emotion and

---

[1] George Bernard Shaw, *Too Good to Be True, Village Wooing, and On the Rocks: Three Plays* (New York: Dodd, Mead, 1934), 228. Thurman used this reading in "A Vision of God and Humanity," March 1939, in PHWT 2:231–32; in his 1978 lecture on Rufus Jones reprinted in HT, *Walking with God: The Way of the Mystics*, ed. Peter Eisenstadt and Walter E. Fluker (Maryknoll, NY: Orbis Books, 2021), 155; and doubtless on other occasions. The phrase "cast out fear" is a paraphrase of 1 John 4:18.

a shared and tangible social reality. He felt fear was the main building block of almost all of our social and political institutions, which he often saw as little more than molded fear, fear solidified and reified. If these structures are composed primarily by the fears of the dominant and powerful groups in society, they are often reinforced by the fears of the disinherited. I argue here that casting out fear is at the heart of Thurman's religious and social vision, and that for him, a society dominated by its fears can never be a true democracy, and a faith organized around fear can never be an authentic religion,

One opening qualification: Thurman detested fear, but he was not a campaigner against carefulness. He always recognized the importance of the proper recognition of potential dangers in one's physical or social environment.[2] But he was an enemy of the ways in which prudence and caution, all too easily, can curdle into timidity and cowardice, until one's life is trapped in its prohibitions and restrictions. It was precisely because the lives of the disinherited were suffused by legitimate fears that the need to fight fear was so imperative.

I am primarily concerned with Thurman's analysis of the fears of the disinherited, and the fears of Black Americans in particular, and their entanglement with the fears of white Americans. There is a burgeoning literature on the history of the emotions and of fear.[3] There is also a lively discussion about fear in contemporary political science and political philosophy.[4] For the most part, this literature has not focused on the question of a specifically African American analysis of fear and its broader influence on American social thought more generally. Howard Thurman needs to be seen as a central figure in this discourse.

His most extended treatment of fear is in his masterwork, *Jesus and the Disinherited* (1949), though he had been writing about fear since the 1920s.[5] At the core of the book are the three chapters on what Thurman calls the "three hounds of hell" that dog the steps of the disinherited: fear, deception, and hate. And of those three, fear is the first Thurman treats and is in many ways the first among equals. Deception, in his telling, as "the oldest of all techniques by which

---

[2] See, for instance, Thurman's discussion *The Temptations of Jesus* (September 1937) in PHWT 2:56–57.

[3] See Joanna Bourke, *Fear: A Cultural History* (Emeryville, CA: Shoemaker and Hoard, 2005); Peter N. Stearns, *American Fear: The Causes and Consequences of High Anxiety* (New York: Routledge, 2006). For an overview of the field, Rob Boddice, *The History of Emotions* (Manchester: Manchester University Press, 2018).

[4] See Judith Shklar's influential essay "The Liberalism of Fear," in Shklar, *Political Thought and Political Thinkers* (Chicago: University of Chicago Press, 1998), 3–20; Corey Robin, *Fear: The History of a Political Idea* (New York: Oxford University Press, 2004).

[5] HT, *Jesus and the Disinherited* (New York: Abingdon, 1949). For the evolution of Thurman's views on fear, see Peter Eisenstadt, *Against the Hounds of Hell: A Life of Howard Thurman* (Charlottesville: University of Virginia Press, 2021), 126–44, 217.

the weak have protected themselves against the strong," is pretty clearly a subcategory of fear.[6] One of the most important arguments in the book is that hate is really a form of fear, fear internalized and accumulated, bottled up, and then explosively vomited out, spewing in all directions. If fear is solid, hate is liquid, and he elsewhere describes the hate of the disinherited, when energized, as something "active, uncongealed, fluid, volatile and dynamic," flowing out of the deep place where we store our repressions.[7]

Black intellectuals, journalists, and activists forged a new understanding of Black fear in the middle decades of the twentieth century, and Thurman was very much a part of this. But all too often, religious intellectuals are treated as a class apart, isolated from their contemporaries. On this, a brief story from my stint as an associate editor of the *Papers of Howard Washington Thurman*: As part of our editing process, we came upon a writing in his papers titled "The Negro in the City," unsigned and undated. We weren't sure if Thurman was the author. It sort of sounded like him, but also seemed too angry, and too overtly political, to be a typical Thurman talk. So we did our research and determined that it was indeed written by Thurman and it was originally a lecture, delivered in May 1940, presumably before a largely white audience, at a meeting of the Chicago Roundtable of the National Conference of Christians and Jews.[8] Its thesis was that "the Negro in the northern city is not a citizen," and if things were somewhat better for Blacks in cities like Chicago than in Mississippi, the status of Blacks in the North was still "a perpetual threat and constant disgrace to democracy." The lecture was a warning. Just because many or most Blacks living in Chicago seem to have been intimidated into a sullen, fearful complacence, Thurman told his listeners, do not be surprised if, in the near future, their fear is transformed into rage, and northern urban Blacks will express their "wild resentment" of their situation through acts of aggression. And if Thurman, the lifelong pacifist, never approved of violence, he thought there was something, even if not admirable and necessary, in Blacks overcoming their emotional numbness and connecting to their oppression the way one connects to a sharp pain, by crying out in agony, uncensored in language, emotion, and action. Genuine interracial cooperation, Thurman closed, could avert this, but if not, you have been given notice.

His lecture was published under his name shortly after it was delivered, by a Jewish weekly newspaper in Chicago. But it had a different title, one that I am sure he had nothing to do with: "A 'Native Son' Speaks." When we discovered this, I remember thinking how odd that the editors had linked the hyperarticulate

---

[6] HT, *Jesus and the Disinherited*, 58.
[7] HT, *The Luminous Darkness: A Personal Interpretation of the Anatomy of Segregation and the Ground of Hope* (New York: Harper and Row, 1964), 84.
[8] HT, "A 'Native Son' Speaks," in PHWT 2:246–52.

Thurman to Bigger Thomas, Richard Wright's mumbling, murderous antihero in his novel *Native Son*.[9] That *Native Son* was being referenced in May 1940, is not, however, surprising. This foundational work of modern Black fiction had been published a few months earlier, the first work by a Black novelist to be a main selection of the Book-of-the-Month Club, and was a huge bestseller. Ever since, *Native Son* has been mired in controversy, with criticism from whites, Blacks, the right, and the left, with many taking issue with Wright's choice of his main character, Bigger Thomas, and the ways in which he was depicted.[10] Shortly after the appearance of *Native Son*, Wright responded to critics who felt the novel and its main character were too unremittingly scabrous. He said that his task in his novel had been "to weigh the effects of our civilization upon the personality of the Negro as it affects us here and now. If, in my weighing of those effects, I reveal rot, pus, filth, hate, fear, guilt, and degenerate forms of life, must I be consigned to hell? Yes, Bigger Thomas hated but he hated because he feared."[11] And in that way, perhaps, Thurman was indeed a native son, speaking uncomfortable truths about Black fear and hate.

A few years later, reviewing Wright's autobiography, *Black Boy*,[12] the distinguished Black sociologist Horace Cayton—like Wright, a cataloguer of Black hate and fear in Chicago—wrote that one of Wright's real contributions was that he "had the courage to say that he was afraid of white people and that he hated them." Cayton went on to describe what he called the "fear-hate-fear" complex. That is, Black people are afraid to "give vent of their hate toward white people," and when they do, they are afraid of their "own aggressiveness and of possible retaliations." So, in a vicious cycle, Black hate just intensifies Black fear.[13] In 1946 Benjamin Mays, Thurman's close friend, in his regular column in the *Pittsburgh Courier* claimed that "Fear is the greatest enemy of mankind. It is the foundation of many wars.... It is at the root of the hatred and ill will that exist between men of different races. It is the one element that makes all men, in some form or the other, cowards. Man is free in proportion as he able to get rid of his fears."[14]

---

[9] Richard Wright, "Native Son," in *Early Writings* (New York: Library of America, 1991), 443–850. The first of the three sections of the novel is titled "Fear."

[10] For contemporary responses to *Native Son*, see John M. Reilly, ed., *Richard Wright: The Critical Reception* (New York: Burt Franklin, 1978), 39–100. See also Lawrence P. Jackson, *The Indignant Generation: A Narrative History of African American Writers and Critics, 1934–1960* (Princeton, NJ: Princeton University Press, 2011), 123–48; Houston A. Baker Jr., ed., *Twentieth-Century Interpretations of Native Son* (Englewood Cliffs, NJ: Prentice-Hall, 1972).

[11] Richard Wright, "Author of 'Native Son' Replies to Atlantic Monthly Critic," *New Journal and Guide* (Norfolk), July 8, 1940.

[12] Richard Wright, "Black Boy," in *Later Writings* (New York: Library of America, 1991), 1–366.

[13] Horace R. Cayton, "Black Boy," *Pittsburgh Courier*, March 10, 1945.

[14] Benjamin Mays, "Two Fears," *Pittsburgh Courier*, July 20, 1946.

So let me suggest, without claiming any particular influence in either direction, that progressive Black religious thinkers like Thurman and Mays were the intellectual and spiritual companions of their contemporaries such as Wright, Cayton, Ralph Ellison, James Baldwin, and Gwendolyn Brooks, dealing with similar problems, and arriving at similar, if not identical answers. The message for Blacks was that the era of stiff-upper-lip stoicism in the face of racial atrocity was over, and for whites the time was long past to recognize the extent to which life was a living hell for Black Americans, a hell that had been built and maintained by whites and white fears.

For Thurman, for many of these authors, and for Black Americans in general, the war years saw an intensification of both Black fear and Black anger. Against a new official wartime agenda of racial inclusion, albeit a halting and inadequate one, there was, on the other side, a huge unofficial intensification of white rage. Black efforts to seek their full rights as citizens met with a fierce determination to maintain the racial status quo at all costs. Thurman wrote about the so-called Eleanor Clubs, the supposed secret revolutionary organization of Black maids dedicated to the violent overthrow of their employers, sponsored by Eleanor Roosevelt.[15] In 1943 Thurman wrote that wartime efforts by African Americans to establish what he called a "new civic character" were being met by a feeling on the part of many white Americans, that, as Thurman ventriloquized, "Negroes do not know what to do with their new sense of significance. They are flippant, arrogant, bigoted, overbearing. Therefore, they must be curbed, held in check," so that their new sense of significance must be blotted out as a wartime anomaly. To the extent that Black fears were being overcome, white fears were only increasing. Thurman noted that the perception of the war against Japan was a race war has given "excellent justification for the expression of the prejudices against non-white peoples just under the surface of the American consciousness."[16] One of the main reasons for the creation of Fellowship Church, though it was not Thurman's primary motivation, was the concern of Alfred Fisk and the San Francisco Presbytery that the accumulated racial kindling in San Francisco needed only a spark to violently combust and set the city ablaze.[17]

During the war years Black Americans were in the forefront of what amounted to a fundamental rethinking of the very nature of American democracy. The democratic ideal was not just a parcel of rights and civic responsibilities, but was a commitment to allowing and aiding people to live rich and fulfilling

---

[15] See PHWT 2:151–52. For the Eleanor Clubs rumor, see Howard Odum, *Race and Rumors of Race: Challenge to the American Crisis* (Chapel Hill: University of North Carolina Press, 1943), 73–89.

[16] HT, "The Will to Segregation," August 1943, in PHWT 2:337–43.

[17] Eisenstadt, *Against the Hounds of Hell,* 211–12.

emotional lives. As long as anyone was condemned to live a life of fear, American democracy would remain radically imperfect. Black Americans had to learn to live without fear, and white Americans had to learn to accommodate Black fearlessness. As the Black novelist Chester Himes titled an article he wrote in 1944 for a journal with the very Thurmanesque title of *Common Ground*, "Democracy Is for the Unafraid."[18]

The connection between fear, modern life, and democracy was a central theme in American culture and politics in the 1930s and 1940s. The study of emotions had been transformed by evolutionary psychologists such as Charles Darwin and William James. In the new psychology of fear, fear was seen as a primitive and visceral emotion, necessary in an earlier stage of evolution, perhaps appropriate when being chased by a saber-toothed tiger, but an out-of-place atavism in the twentieth century, and perhaps something modern civilization could ameliorate.[19] William James wrote in his *Principles of Psychology* (1890) that "the progress from brute to man is characterized as nothing so much by the decrease in frequency in proper occasions for fear. In civilized life, in particular, it has become possible for large numbers of people to pass from the cradle to the grave without ever having had a pang of genuine fear."[20] Fear, extreme fear, which had once been a rational response to danger, was now largely seen as irrational. In part because of this, discussion of fear, both popular and scholarly, was ubiquitous in 1930s and 1940s America. One example is the so-called caste and class school of (primarily white) psychologists, sociologists, and anthropologists who analyzed the emotional irrationalities of southern race relations in great detail.[21] John Dollard, a Harvard psychologist and one of the most prominent caste and class authors, wrote in 1937 that a key to southern race relations was "that white people fear Negroes," especially "when the Negro attempts to claim any of the white prerogatives or gains."[22]

---

[18] Chester Himes, "Democracy Is for the Unafraid," *Common Ground* 4, no. 2 (1944): 53–56.

[19] For a brief overview of the development of the modern psychology of fear, see Barbara H. Rosenwein and Riccardo Christiani, *What Is the History of Emotions?* (Cambridge: Polity Press, 2017), 9–16.

[20] William James, *Principles of Psychology* (1890; repr., Cambridge, MA: Harvard University Press, 1981), 1033–34.

[21] For typical works of the caste and class school, see John Dollard, *Caste and Class in a Southern Town* (New Haven, CT: Yale University Press, 1937); Hortense Powdermaker, *After Freedom: A Cultural Study of the Deep South* (New York: Russell and Russell, 1939); Allison Davis et al., *Deep South: A Southern Anthropological Study of Caste and Class* (Chicago: University of Chicago Press, 1941). Most of these authors were white, with the prominent exception of Allison Davis, who in 1942 became the first Black scholar tenured at a major white mainstream university (the University of Chicago).

[22] Dollard, *Caste and Class in a Southern Town*, 318.

Perhaps no one in the country was more identified with the fight against fear than the president of the United States himself. A few minutes after becoming president, on March 4, 1933, Franklin Delano Roosevelt told America, with the ravages of the Depression in mind, "Let me assert my firm belief that the only thing we have to fear is fear itself—nameless, unreasoning, unjustified terror which paralyzes needed efforts to convert retreat into advance."[23] The New Deal, like much progressive thought, was premised on the belief that one of the main functions of governments was the alleviation of preventable social fears such as bank failures, unemployment, and penurious old age, and that maintaining the psychological health of its citizens was a legitimate function of government. No society has ever been committed to the eradication of fear as was 1930s and 1940s America. Ira Katznelson has argued that three main fears animated the Roosevelt administration; fear that democracy was being superseded by fascism or communism; global warfare; and fear of the "backwardness," racially and otherwise, of the South. (And for white segregationists, the opposite fear held that the structures of white supremacy were under attack.) Over time these three fears became increasingly entangled.[24]

By the end of the decade, fears of another war had supplanted the economic fears originating from the Depression. In June 1940, Thurman spoke of the pervading darkness of the times, when "enraged power and madness seem at this moment to be sweeping over the world," while "a thousand fears paralyze our actions and render us impotent and vain."[25] The same year one of Thurman's favorite authors, Lewis Mumford, opened his book *Faith for Living*—Thurman would later use the title for a sermon series—as gloomily as possible: "Every human being is living through an apocalypse of violence. Fear enters the door with the daily newspaper, and the last radio report in the evening creates a waking nightmare which slips unnoticed into the horrors of sleep."[26] Meanwhile, the caste and class author John Dollard, trying his hand at pop psychology, wrote in *Victory over Fear* (1942) that while "everyone is more afraid today than he

---

[23] See David W. Houck, *FDR and Fear Itself: The First Inaugural Address* (College Station: Texas A&M Press, 2002). Perhaps Louis Howe, the FDR aide and speechwriter who added the famous phrase to the text, was familiar with William James's article, "What Is an Emotion?," *Mind* 9, no. 34 (April 1884), where he writes, "I am told of morbid terror of which the subject confessed that what possessed her, seemed, more than anything fear of fear itself" (197).

[24] For the role fear played in American politics in the 1930s and 1940s, see Ira Katznelson, *Fear Itself: The New Deal and the Origins of Our Times* (New York: Liveright, 2013), 11–18.

[25] HT, "The Light That Is Darkness," in PHWT 2:253–57.

[26] Lewis Mumford, *Faith for Living* (New York: Harcourt, Brace, 1940), 3. In 1952 Thurman delivered seven sermons under the title "Faith for Living." For Thurman on Mumford, see PHWT 1:37; 3:87.

was a year ago … you can use fear or fear can rule you. This is the choice that every one of us faces."[27] In early 1941, FDR, recognizing the global nature of this war-induced panic, told Congress of the need for the United States to engage in a worldwide campaign to realize what he called the "four essential human freedoms," of which the last and most basic of which, grounding them all, was "freedom from fear."[28] Many at the time, like FDR, saw one of the causes of totalitarianism and fascism as a fear of freedom.[29]

Black Americans on the whole approved of FDR's campaigns against fear but insisted that only by attacking the roots of Black fear could the broader question of fear be addressed. As the *Chicago Defender* wrote shortly after FDR's freedom-from-fear speech, "Mr. Roosevelt's party has refused to vote an anti-lynching law, and Mr. Roosevelt himself has been submissively accepting the verdict of the southern wing of his party on this issue. The place to first establish freedom from fear is the United States. Until that is done, it is absurd to talk of establishing it all over the world."[30]

Amid all the literature on Black fear in the 1930s and 1940s, *Jesus and the Disinherited* stands out as one of the subtlest and most profound contributions. It acknowledges the environmental explanation of Black behavior present in the work of Richard Wright or in Gunnar Myrdal's vastly influential 1944 sociological study, *An American Dilemma*, without reducing Black people to their troubled environment.[31] Thurman provides an unsparing account of how the fears of the disinherited could distort and wither their lives, along with a refusal either to sentimentalize or pathologize the impact of oppression. And while the work of contemporary psychology and sociology is distilled in the pages of *Jesus and the Disinherited,* the book at its core is a work of spiritual reflection, which

---

[27] John Dollard, *Victory over Fear* (New York: Reynal and Hitchcock, 1942), 1.

[28] For the "Four Freedoms" speech, delivered as FDR's State of the Union Address on January 6, 1941, see https://www.gilderlehrman.org/sites/default/files/inline-pdfs/Four%20Freedoms%20Speech%201941.pdf.

[29] This was the main theme of the émigré ex–Frankfurt School social psychologist Erich Fromm, whose bestselling book *Escape from Freedom* (New York: Farrar and Rinehart, 1941), was published in Britain under the title *Fear of Freedom*.

[30] "Other Papers Say," *Chicago Defender*, September 20, 1941.

[31] The Book-of-the-Month Club edition had an introduction that claimed that "our society puts Negro youth in the situation of the animal in the laboratory in which a neurosis is to be caused," and often reacts with "the same bewildered, senseless tangle of nerve reactions associated with lab rats." Dorothy Canfield Fisher, "Introduction to the First Edition," in Baker, *Twentieth-Century Interpretations of Native Son*, 110. Among the statements on fear in Gunnar Myrdal, *An American Dilemma: The Negro Problem and American Democracy* (New York: Harper and Brothers, 1944), is "the good humor that is associated with the Negro's emotionalism is the outcome, not only of the attempt to live life to the fullest, but of stark fear of the white man" (960).

enabled Thurman to avoid the limitations of either psychological or sociological determinism. The three conjoined fears of fascism, militarism, and white supremacy form the book's background, which foregrounds Thurman's belief that no psyche is damaged beyond repair, no life shattered beyond recovery, no one need be resigned to their abjectness. To Thurman, "awareness of being a child of God" can overcome this powerlessness and can lift a person to find "a new courage, fearlessness, and power." He knew "communities that were completely barren, with no apparent growing edge, without any point to provide light for the disadvantaged," yet he had seen "children grow up without fear."[32]

But if *Jesus and the Disinherited* was very much a product of the 1940s, one of its great strengths is its reinterpretation, in Thurman's own language and perspective, of a much older African American discourse on the connection between fear and religion, one that he internalized in his boyhood, rooted in the experiences of Jim Crow and memories of slavery. Barbara Rosenwein has popularized the idea of "emotional communities" in which people share the same norms of emotional expression and value or devalue the same emotions.[33] Thurman grew up in one emotional community, that of Black Daytona, one that he never entirely left, whatever other "emotional communities" he participated in and joined in later life.

Thurman, as far as one can tell from his autobiography and other sources, had a relatively happy childhood, even though he tends to describe himself as a morose loner. But he was also a child of fear, like almost all Black Americans raised at his time and in his place. As he wrote in 1963, on a return trip to his hometown of Daytona Beach, "The first fifteen years of my life were spent there. It was in that small Florida town that I was introduced to the terror and trauma of being born a Negro. During the years since, and after much living and experiencing, scar tissue marks the place where early blows made their mark and the searing pain invaded body and spirit."[34]

Thurman was generally reticent in discussing the particular incidents that frightened and scarred him, although one can, by looking carefully, find some hints. In this way his autobiography is unlike most first-person accounts of growing up in the Jim Crow South in the early years of the last century, so many of which are seared by a primal scene in which their authors first realized the full horror and power of white terror and supremacy. Perhaps Thurman took after his grandmother Nancy Ambrose, who told her grandson very little about the

---

[32] HT, *Jesus and the Disinherited*, 50–51, 55.
[33] For an overview of the idea of emotional communities, see Barbara H. Rosenwein, *Emotional Communities in the Early Middle Ages* (Ithaca, NY: Cornell University Press, 2006), 1–31.
[34] HT, "Annual Report: The Wider Ministry, 1962–1963," in PHWT 5:25.

first eighteen years of her life, spent enslaved in North Florida, and maybe both grandmother and grandson felt that the greatest victory over fear consisted in not giving further advertisement to their oppressors or the power of oppression. In any event, I believe Thurman was less interested in acute fear, the pure fright and adrenalin-fueled palpitations of panic, where one's options are often limited to the familiar dichotomy of fight or flee, than in the moral ambiguities of living with chronic fear, an emotion that tends to dull rather than heighten the senses and harden one's responsivity to others.[35]

In Daytona, during Thurman's childhood, fear, as it always does, created borders and built walls. It was a place defined by the symmetries of Black and white fear, hate, and mistrust, and the asymmetries of Black and white power. Black Daytona was a community in which, as he wrote in his autobiography, were shared "sorrows, joys, good times and bad, this was the way we lived. We helped each other and survived."[36] But it was a strictly bounded life. White Daytona was "a world apart, in another universe of discourse," and those within it "were simply out of bounds." Dealing with the white world was an unavoidable necessity, but whether interactions with it were malign, indifferent, or even occasionally benign, white people, for all the power they had over Black lives, were in the deepest sense unimportant. Toward those not in your group, there could only be "amorality," with its "cold, hard, minute, and devastating understanding of the other," the "kind of understanding one gives an enemy."[37] Thurman accepted this bifurcated and fragmented world as his social reality, but early on he also loathed it and found it contrary to his deep belief in the unity of nature, humanity, and God. He spent his life trying to live within, and to create, strong, intimate communities that did not need to use fear as their mortar.

Thurman found in many places the strength to fight the fears wrought by his childhood. He could find it within segregated institutions, at Morehouse College, where, as he wrote in his autobiography, every time college president John Hope called him and his classmates "young gentlemen" it provided protection against the other names they were regularly called.[38] He fought fear by going beyond the boundaries of segregation, as when, while still a Morehouse undergraduate, he joined the Christian pacifist organization the Fellowship of Reconciliation, connecting to his life's cause as well as making his first white friends, thereby finding "a place to stand in my own spirit—a place so profoundly affirming that I was strengthened by a sense of immunity to the assaults of the white world of

---

[35] For the distinction between acute and chronic fear, see John Hollander, "Fear: Its Political Uses and Abuses," *Social Research* 71, no. 4 (Winter 2004): 865–86.
[36] HT, WHAH, 5.
[37] HT, *The Luminous Darkness*, 63.
[38] HT, WHAH, 36.

Atlanta, Georgia."[39] And he could also fight fear by creating what was in effect a community of one, an imaginary community of like-minded souls, as when Rufus Jones at Haverford College in 1929 introduced him to the great mystic writers and he felt at home and bolstered by them. "It was as if," he wrote, "I was surrounded by a cloud of witnesses which gave to me a sense of belonging that the madness and terror to which I was exposed in America could not undermine."[40]

The model for Thurman in fighting fear had been provided by the enslaved creators and singers of the spirituals, which for him was always the most important of African American musical genres. The spirituals were at the center of his religious worldview, providing the blueprint for how to live a life without fear despite living in circumstances expressly designed to maximize fear. One of his earliest sermons on the spirituals, and representative of many that would follow, was delivered at Spelman College in 1928 on the spiritual "We Are Climbing Jacob's Ladder." As Thurman tells it, Jacob, on the run from his brother Esau, was living a life filled with tragedy and horror, and without a "redemptive element." Thurman adds, "How true was this of the slaves!" Enslaved people had been "driven and herded together like cattle, felled in their own blood if they resisted, these panic-stricken souls found their present cruel and demoralizing," with a brutal past and prospects of an equally brutal future. The message of the spiritual for Thurman was that "there are no situations which are so depressing, so devoid of hope, that the human spirit cannot throw itself into a realm in which these conditions do not exist." Thurman cautioned about using one's dreams as what he calls an "escape mechanism," as a way of avoiding harsh realities. But the point of Jacob's ladder was not to climb to heaven or to avoid living in the present, but rather to survive one's circumstances and not be trampled or destroyed by them. Its message was to affirm that "I am beaten and brutalized by power-maddened men, but I shall see to it that my experiences and my environment do not crush me."[41] This was not only central to Thurman's understanding of the spirituals, but of democracy. A society in which no person, ever again, would be crushed by their environment and then discarded—a society that works to preserve and protect the personal and spiritual intactness of every individual—could only be a society that does not use fear as its primary social fuel. This is what Thurman hoped the United States might become.

Some twenty-five years after his Spelman sermon, Thurman said much the same in his most extended consideration of democracy, four sermons on the Declaration of Independence from 1951. In a sermon that explores the phrase "all

---

[39] Ibid., 265.
[40] HT to Elizabeth Vining, April 18, 1956, HTC, 35:8.
[41] HT, "The Message of the Spirituals," October 1928, in PHWT 1:127–29.

men are created equal," he stated, as he often did, that the only type of equality that mattered was the equality of infinite worth.[42] However, some members of Fellowship Church challenged him. The "equality of infinite worth" sounded too mystical. What did it really mean?[43] So Thurman tried to explain the phrase in more down-to-earth language. It meant who you are can never be taken from you, or in Thurman's words, "My life is rooted in a kind of awareness of my meaning that does not arise from your interpretation of my significance, that nothing, that no judgment that you impose upon me, no order of society into which you seek to have me regimented, can sever my roots from the dimension of awareness that gives to me my inner significance."[44]

This was democracy understood from the vantage of the disinherited. But in 1950s and 1960s America, the fight against fear was an issue for all Americans. In March 1954, when Senator Joseph McCarthy was the most talked-about person in the United States, Thurman wrote that Americans "are surrounded by a climate of fear; fear of communism; fear of democracy; fear of one another; fear of tomorrow."[45] In a sermon delivered in 1961 at Boston University on nuclear weapons, "Community of Fear," he passionately inveighed against the arms race.[46] His fight against fear was a lifelong struggle.

For Thurman, the surest alternative and antidote to the climate of fear was the cause of radical nonviolence. It was the insistence, against all around him, that a life lived without fear was still possible. Radical nonviolence is the subject of the final chapter of *Jesus and the Disinherited,* a chapter Thurman titled "Love." Seeing radical nonviolence as a form of love has obvious Christian, as well as Hindu, roots, and much of great beauty has been written on this theme. However, thinking of radical nonviolence as love often leads people into misconceptions. It is a form of love that can be as penetrating and painful as a dentist's drill, but a drill that can hurt the dentist as much as the patient. Let me suggest another way to think about Thurman's understanding: nonviolence is a discipline of structured fearlessness. This is certainly how Black Americans saw Gandhi. Benjamin Mays, who visited with Gandhi a year after Thurman, wrote in 1937 that "the cardinal principles of nonviolence are love and fearlessness," and claimed

---

[42] Eisenstadt, *Against the Hounds of Hell,* 250–51.

[43] The medieval German mystic Meister Eckhart was indeed an inspiration for Thurman's views on democracy. See HT, *The Way of the Mystics,* 82–90.

[44] HT, "The Declaration of Independence I: Created Equal," July 29, 1951, in HT, *Democracy and the Soul of America,* ed. Peter Eisenstadt and Walter Earl Fluker (Maryknoll, NY: Orbis Books, 2022), 33–42.

[45] HT, *The Creative Encounter: An Interpretation of Religion and the Social Witness* (New York: Harper and Row, 1954), 133.

[46] HT, "Community of Fear," May 7, 1961, HTC.

that Gandhi "did more than any other man to dispel fear from the Indian mind and make Indians proud to be Indians ... [for] when an oppressed race ceases to be afraid, it is free."[47]

This was the message of Gandhi that Black America took to its heart. In the summer of 1963, Thurman wrote that "perhaps the most significant thing that has happened in the last few stirring years of the vast struggle for civil rights in the South and the North has been the dramatic loss of fear on the part of the masses of Negroes," with "the sense of direct, conscious, and collective participation in a joint destiny," generating "a strange and wonderful courage." He went on to describe a few instances of how this worked on an individual level, and how this sort of fearlessness was, to use one of Thurman's favorite words, contagious. The second stanza of the civil rights anthem "We Shall Overcome" begins, "We are not afraid."[48] As Dr. King once said to a frightened protester, the words are not, "I am not afraid," but "We are not afraid."[49]

But for the disinherited to overcome fear is only half of the discipline of radical nonviolence. The great challenge and its supreme difficulty are to do this in such a way that somehow transcends the fear of their dominators or oppressors. At the spiritual basis of radical nonviolence is the belief that it is possible to break the vicious cycles of fear and hate that endlessly circulate between the oppressed and their oppressors. And this task, as Thurman recognized, was in many ways more difficult in the United States than in India. Gandhi wanted to take his country back from the relative handful of Britons who were ruling the lives of the over three hundred million people living in British India, and this was accomplished, albeit rather messily, in 1947. In the United States, there could be no getting rid of white people. Rather the goal was to achieve the sort of genuine equality and citizenship that is only possible when, because the disinherited have overcome their fears, everyone in society realizes that fear has lost its dominion.[50]

Thurman late in life contemplated writing a book about Jesus and the so-called inherited, the advantaged, comfortable, and powerful.[51] It is a pity this didn't happen. The closest he ever came to a full exploration of this topic was his 1946 article "The Fascist Masquerade," which I urge people to read in

---

[47] Benjamin E. Mays, "The Color Line around the World," *Journal of Negro History* 6, no. 2 (April 1937): 141.
[48] HT, "Non-Violence and the Art of Reconciliation," in PHWT 5:5.
[49] I do not know if this story is apocryphal or not. A friend of mine told me that one of his college professors, on a protest march in the South that was being menaced by white thugs on the sideline, told King that he was scared and this was King's response. In any event, it is far too good a story not to retell.
[50] See "What We May Learn from India," in HT, SF, 207–8.
[51] Eisenstadt, *Against the Hounds of Hell*, 267.

conjunction with *Jesus and the Disinherited*. It is an article about how white fears of Blacks, Jews, labor unions, and liberals and leftists of all kinds were channeled and exacerbated by a pernicious combination of evangelical Christianity and xenophobic American nationalism, ideologies of exclusion and inequality. American fascism may assume many forms or names—or, in Thurman's term, masquerades—but it is always rooted in the same cardinal principles, and is still very much with us.[52]

One problem with the word "nonviolence," as Gandhi told Thurman, is that it describes what it is not.[53] For many, nonviolence is one of those old-fashioned 1960s words, like groovy, that just sounds hopelessly dated. What is in fashion in the historiography of the civil rights movement are books that explore the so-called myth of nonviolence, and argue that the civil rights movement was more than just people with linked arms singing songs.[54] This is a caricature of the role of nonviolence in the civil rights movement. I wish there was more space to go into this, but let me just say radical nonviolence is a collective rather than a personal response to the violence of oppression, and no great movement of civil disobedience, including the Indian, American, or South African varieties, is ever going to be completely peaceful. Thurman once wrote, "I am a Pacifist but I am also a human being. I am not an absolutist because I do not have the wisdom to be that."[55] At least once in his life, in Arkansas in 1947, Thurman spent an evening with a shotgun in his lap, after there were reports of possible violence by night riders.[56] If we get too hung up on debating the fine points of the tactics of the violence/nonviolence dichotomy, we can easily lose sight of the broader strategy. The goal of nonviolence is to build communities and polities not organized by fear.

But if Thurman was a passionate defender of nonviolence, he also understood the limits of its appeal. "For many years," Thurman wrote in 1942, "Negroes for various reasons have tended to be far too docile," but "so deep is the resentment of many Negroes to this overall picture that the technique of nonviolence is regarded by them as being an expression of cowardice," rather than requiring "an increment of courage," that is, overcoming fear.[57] As Thurman often stressed,

---

[52] HT, "The Fascist Masquerade," in PHWT 3:145–61.
[53] HT, "With Our Negro Guests," in PHWT 1:335.
[54] The best of these books is Charles E. Cobb Jr., *This Nonviolence Stuff'll Get You Killed: How Guns Made the Civil Rights Movement Possible* (Durham, NC: Duke University Press, 2014), which somewhat surprisingly gives the last word in the book to Thurman, quoting him eulogizing Juliette Derricotte in 1931: "There is work to be done … and ghosts will drive us on" (180).
[55] HT, "San Francisco Journal," in PHWT 3:85.
[56] Eisenstadt, *Against the Hounds of Hell*, 120.
[57] HT to Kay H. Beach, September 4, 1942, in PHWT 2:313–15.

overcoming the ultimate fear, the fear of death, was at the heart of the discipline of nonviolence. As early as 1938 he had written in praise of "the freedom of mind that comes with a great commitment," one that "robs a man of the fear of death." This path is reserved "for fanatics" because it requires a degree of fanaticism to confront "the kingdom of evil."[58]

The 1960s revealed another problem with nonviolence: what Thurman, speaking in 1969, called "the danger moment." The discipline of nonviolence can lead its followers to a growing awareness of the ways in which their world and their lives had been structured by fear, and "when I become aware of my predicament in a way of which I was not aware before, now I see the anatomy of injustice in a brand new way. And my first response to that is to renounce the thing that made it possible for me to become aware of it in the first place."[59] In other words, if one, through the discipline of nonviolence, becomes fully sensitive to the ways in which fear and terror rule the disinherited, nonviolence can seem like a puny and inadequate response to the brutal, hammering blows arrayed against it. The working of nonviolence, Thurman said in 1969, "often is slow," and "its most creative dimension is the way in which it activates the imagination" and allows people to project themselves into their enemy's "situation and place." This takes considerable time and effort, and even if this is accomplished it carries "no guarantee ... [that it] will make for social change."[60] The attraction of violence is its promise of providing for quick, unambiguous, and final resolutions of difficult problems. But victories over complexity are always temporary and illusory. As Thurman knew well, the debate over nonviolence and violence was central to Black politics in the 1960s. What united Black America in the 1960s was a shared conviction on the need for a fight, a fight to the death, if necessary, against Black fear and the institutions that created and fostered it. The division was over how best to achieve this. If Thurman's belief in integration and nonviolence never wavered, he was always willing to listen and try to find common ground with its critics.

One such critic was Derrick Bell. Recently, Bell, the late legal theorist, has been in the news. In the 1970s he was one of the creators of critical race theory, which has become the target of an unprecedented campaign of defamation by ignorant critics.[61] We do not have space to explore the tenets of critical race

---

[58] HT, "Christian, Who Calls Me Christian?," in PHWT 2:110–11.

[59] HT, "Man and Social Change, Part 2: Man and the Experience of Community (continued), 1969 March 20," PITTS, https://thurman.pitts.emory.edu/items/show/56.

[60] Ibid.

[61] On Bell, see Jelani Cobb, "The Man behind Critical Race Theory," *New Yorker*, September 13, 2021.

theory, but it was part of the broader turn toward nationalism and skepticism toward integration in the Black politics of the late 1960s and 1970s.[62] Bell was only one of several Black intellectuals—among them the historians Lerone Bennett Jr. and Vincent Harding—who were at once both deeply influenced by Thurman and committed to versions of Black nationalism.[63] What Thurman shared with these thinkers was a commitment to understanding how the disinherited can, whatever their external circumstances, live lives without fear, without aggression, and remain spiritually whole.[64]

After my biography of Howard Thurman, *Against the Hounds of Hell*, was published, I was contacted by a former student of Bell, who told me he had invited Bell to his wedding in 1982, and when Bell couldn't attend, he instead sent a copy of Thurman's autobiography, *With Head and Heart,* accompanied by the following letter: "As wedding gifts go, we hope you will consider this a combination toaster-oven, silver platter, crystal goblet for your soul. Howard Thurman was a great man whose greatness grew out of life experiences that with his abiding faith in God, he translated into sermons and writings that offered insight and provided uplift to all who came into contact with him."[65]

Bell was a great admirer of Thurman's writings on the spirituals. Bell suggested that the essence of critical race theory and the spirituals were "quite similar." Both "communicate understanding and reassurance to needy souls trapped in a hostile world."[66] Bell often quoted Thurman on the spirituals and Black religion.[67] For both Bell and Thurman, the spirituals were the first and

---

[62] See Richard Delgado and Jean Stefanic, *Critical Race Theory: An Introduction* (New York: New York University Press, 2001).

[63] I discuss Bell, Bennett, and Harding in more detail—as well as another historian, closer to Thurman's own views, Nathan I. Huggins—in "Three Historians and a Theologian: Howard Thurman's Impact on the Writing of African American History," in *Reconstruction at 150: Reassessing the Revolutionary "New Birth of Freedom,"* ed. Orville Vernon Burton and Brent Morris (Charlottesville: University of Virginia Press, 2023). For a more abbreviated discussion, see Eisenstadt, *Against the Hounds of Hell*, 369–75.

[64] See Derrick A. Bell Jr. to HT, February 27, 1978, in PHWT 5:286–90.

[65] Derrick and Jewel Bell to Cleophus and Carla, July 1982, letter in the author's possession. I would like to thank Cleophus Thomas Jr. for sharing this letter with me and allowing me to quote it for publication.

[66] Derrick Bell, "Who's Afraid of Critical Race Theory?" (1995), in Derrick Bell, *The Derrick Bell Reader*, ed. Richard Delgado and Jean Stefanic (New York: New York University Press, 2005), 81–83.

[67] Derrick Bell, *And We Are Not Saved: The Elusive Quest for Racial Justice* (New York: Basic Books, 1987), 215–17, quoting in full Thurman's "On Viewing the Coast of Africa," his meditation on African bodies in slave ships; see PHWT 5:49–50, 91n51. Bell quotes Thurman's book of meditations *Deep Is the Hunger* (New York: Harper and Brothers, 1951), in *Ethical Ambition: Living a Life of Meaning and Worth* (New York: Bloomsbury, 2002), 61–62.

most enduring example of how persons of African descent in American captivity, during and after legal slavery, were able to "make something out of nothing," carving out "a humanity for themselves with absolutely nothing to help—save imagination, will, and unbelievable strength and courage."[68]

For both men, what was radical about the composers and singers of the spirituals is that they insisted on their common humanity with their captors, because this challenged their enslavers' most fundamental belief, that between themselves and their human property was an unbridgeable social and spiritual chasm. The deepest belief of the spirituals was that everyone was an equal child of God, and that God did not and could not create any person or people to be perpetual slaves. The singers of the spirituals were clear-eyed about a future they did not really control. They did not seek spiritual panaceas. They might be in bondage, but they had found their freedom, the freedom of self-knowledge. For Thurman and for Bell, it was this freedom, the fearlessness of the disinherited, a freedom not to be confused with rashness, that could not be taken from them, and a model of spiritual survival amid the vicissitudes of life within a so-called democracy. And for both men, racial reconciliation can only occur when oppressors recognize that they ultimately have nothing to fear from the fearlessness of the disinherited. When this happens, Thurman writes in *Jesus and the Disinherited*, white Americans can abandon their "white necessity," which perhaps is a more psychologically precise and acute term than "white privilege." If this happens, they can begin to take "their place alongside all the rest of humanity," mingling their "desires with the longing of all the desperate people of all the ages."[69]

The fight against fear, against the hounds of hell, is not going well. Rather than conquering fear, we are currently sated with it, between COVID, the possibility of a new cold war, and the hateful rantings of politicians who will remain nameless. Rather than freedom from fear, America's motto today seems to be freedom with fear, with the assumption that the more that you fear, the freer you are. Radical nonviolence has always been a wager that fear need not be humanity's most constant and intimate companion. Those who wish this should not be daunted by long odds. Thurman was not. Vincent Harding said of him that he was dedicated to "exploring and experiencing those crucial life points where personal and social transformation are creatively joined."[70] These are moments when our heads meet our hearts, when we can experience what Thurman once

---

[68] Bell, *Ethical Ambition*, 172–73.
[69] HT, *Jesus and the Disinherited*, 100.
[70] Vincent Harding, foreword to *Jesus and the Disinherited* (1949; repr., Boston: Beacon, 1996), xii.

called the "orderly recklessness" of nonviolence, transcending the world while remaining fully a part of it.[71] Thurman always cherished these rare instances of action and illumination, when the heat of cast-out fears can begin to thaw and melt what had seemed to be imperviously frozen solid, and the structures of oppression begin to buckle, sag, and give way—while on the horizon glimpses appear of a new common ground.

---

[71] HT, "Christian, Who Calls Me Christian?," in PHWT 2:110–11.

11

HOWARD THURMAN, DEMOCRATIC LIFE, AND THE UNFINISHED SEARCH FOR COMMON GROUND

Paul Harvey

Howard Thurman spent his life trying to answer the question "What could religion mean to the man whose back is against the wall?" What could a Christianity that had historically been aligned with forces of power and authority say to the disinherited, the dispossessed? His form of dissent against Christianity as it was actually practiced harkened back to Frederick Douglass and other critics of institutional Christianity of the nineteenth century. Thurman explored "the religion of Jesus" (and religion as a general philosophical expression), in distinction to the Christianity he had seen practiced in the United States. The most material form of this dissent took place with his establishment of the Fellowship of the Church of All Peoples in San Francisco, which he cofounded and then pastored from 1944 to 1953. Thurman moved on to other endeavors from there, but he always saw that church as the deepest expression of his ideals, and considered it the work of his life.

Thurman the private mystic and Thurman the public activist found common ground in understanding that spirituality is necessarily linked to social transformation. Private spiritual cultivation could prepare the way for deeper public commitments for social change. His lifelong experience with, and protest against, the "psychic wounds" of racism took shape in his espousal of ideals of a universalist cosmopolitanism, one where humans could gather peacefully and worship with souls attuned to the divine and shed of the conflicts and blocks that human life presented.

He was a private man and an intellectual. He was not (usually) a public activist, as his informal mentee at Boston University, Martin Luther King Jr., became, nor one to take up specific social and political causes to transform a country. And in some sense, he did not see himself as trying to serve the church; rather, he wanted to transform the very idea of what church was. Thurman's lesson was that the cultivation of the self feeds and enriches the struggle for social justice. In a larger sense, the discipline of nonviolence required a spiritual commitment and discipline that came, for many, through self-examination, meditation, and prayer.

Thurman served as one of the most influential philosophers and religious leaders of twentieth-century Black America, a fact that only recently has become well understood. He was a mentor of the civil rights movement, but he was not a movement man. That is, he educated a generation in precepts of nonviolence and a kind of internal transformation that would lead to a societal revolution, but he himself stayed in the background. As he wrote to a young Jesse Jackson in 1973, "All of my life I have shunned publicity and the limelight; it is not my way of working."[1]

Walter Fluker and Peter Eisenstadt have correctly referred to Thurman as fundamentally an optimist. His optimism suffuses his work even in explorations such as come in *Jesus and the Disinherited*, a profound investigation into the psychology of dispossession. For that reason, one of Thurman's sermons intrigues and continues to trouble me. In what was his last public sermon, given to the Fellowship Church late in 1980 (about five months before his death), Thurman reflected on the meaning of what he and the congregants had tried to accomplish in the 1940s, in the midst of a war where people had been trained to hate, and in the height of the Cold War afterward. That was a most inopportune time to found a church that drew no lines of race or color, demonstrating that human beings could "come together ... to worship as the experience of celebration of the communal life they had lived during the week." The miracle was that "a remnant of the church has survived." And Thurman concluded with some rather dark reflections on the meaning of this entire experience: "whether it is possible to develop a caring, sensitive, loving community in a world organized on violence and brutality and hate, and until religion learns how to deal with the dynamism ... generating in the hearts of men and women that make for survival that is created by the idiom of hate and bitterness." Hate gave an individual a ground to stand on, even while it destroyed that same ground, but "he goes down to the grave with a shout, and religion has to learn how to deal with that at the level that makes for survival on this planet for man.... The burden of proof is on our weary shoulders."[2]

Thurman concluded ominously, quoting a favorite anonymous poet, that man was "God-like in image," and "if you don't believe it just pray to die before nightfall." In this surprisingly dark valedictory sermon, he thought hard on the

---

[1] HT to Jesse Jackson, January 17, 1973, in PHWT 5:234.
[2] HT, "The Growing Edge," sermon from October 26, 1980, in PHWT 5:317.

lessons of his long witness for peace, nonviolence, and human community in a world organized on principles of hate, violence, and human separation. The answer, he implied, was not yet evident. Thurman was indeed an optimist, but one with a keen sense of human evil: the evil he saw growing up, the evil he saw just in the ordinary everyday experiences of living while Black, the evil he saw and depicted in essays such as "The Fascist Masquerade," and in the assassinations of his heroes in the 1960s. His was an optimism acutely aware of the psychic wounds of American history.

Would Thurman preach that sort of sermon today, and would he continue to believe that the search for common ground would yield fruit? I believe he would have, but that he would continue to call us back to our internal spiritual reflections and quests to help us find the resources necessary to deal with the depth of human division and conflict so evident in today's politics and religious life. Thurman had seen that in his life. In fact, he had seen much worse. And so, he might lightly mock our own pessimism derived from briefly doomscrolling on Twitter or reading too many historically challenged pundits who assure us we've never been as close to a civil war as we are now. Thurman saw, and lived through, much worse. What he saw and lived through surely contributed to bouts of depression that sometimes paralyzed him, and to his lifelong emphasis on "relaxation"—those periods of rest spiritually necessary to prepare one's self for the quest of a just world. He knew better than we do the rigors involved in looking for a common ground. I think he might have told us to stop doomscrolling, pick up a clarinet (or whatever) and play a while, paint a penguin, walk up and down escalators, pray, meditate, memorize some beautiful poetry, listen to one of Beethoven's later quartets, take a nap, and then reenter the struggle with a fresh frame of mind, always conscious of evil but never giving in to hating the haters, since if we do so we simply become one of them. And surely, he would put a crown on our heads, hoping against hope that eventually we would grow to the point that we would be capable of wearing that crown together with others living together under a friendly sky.

The Search for Common Ground: Thurman's Life and Work

His life work brought together his southern African American Baptist upbringing, his training in Quakerism, a natural propensity to nature mysticism, and an encounter with religions in a global and cosmopolitan context. His message about the democratic soul to be found in searching for common ground drew from all these roots. He profoundly explored the psychology of relations between the powerful and the powerless, but also the very fragility of the power held by authorities. It came, he suggested, with just a thin veneer covering over it:

> The experience of power has no meaning aside from the other-than-self-reference which sustains it. If the position of ascendance is not acknowledged tacitly and actively by those over whom the ascendance is exercised, then it falls flat. Hypocrisy on the part of the disinherited in dealing with the dominant group is a tribute yielded by those who are weak. But if this attitude is lacking, or is supplanted by a simple sincerity and genuineness, then it follows that advantage due to the accident of birth or position is reduced to zero. Instead of relation between the weak and the strong there is merely a relationship between human beings. A man is a man, no more, no less. The awareness of this fact marks the supreme moment of human dignity.[3]

We may begin with his recovery of the meaning of the spirituals—one of Thurman's most original scholarly contributions, and something for which he is underappreciated. Not that he was first, or alone, in this, but he brought to the task a particular understanding of their meaning that differed from many others offered. Only W. E. B. DuBois wrote about them with greater eloquence. Many in Thurman's era, who struggled to fit the spirituals into a social protest framework, could not hear their poetry. Thurman could. Of the spirituals he wrote, "There is no attempt to cast a false glow over the stark ruggedness of the journey. The facts of experience are seen for what they are—difficult, often even unyielding." What others saw as otherworldly or escapist, he saw as precisely the point. The spirituals, he said, "made a worthless life, the life of a chattel property, a mere thing, a body, *worth living!* They yielded with abiding enthusiasm to a view of life which included all the events of their experience without exhausting themselves in those experiences. To them this quality of life was insistent fact because of that which was deep within them, they discovered of God."[4]

Much writing from that era cast the spirituals as a sort of protest music and overread specific directives into them. The so-called escapism, or otherworldliness, of the songs was in reality a "precious bane," he said, because "it taught people how to ride high to life, to look squarely in the face [of] those facts that argue most dramatically against all hope and to use those facts as raw material out of which they fashioned a hope that the environment, with all of its cruelty,

---

[3] HT, *Jesus and the Disinherited* (Nashville: Abingdon, 1949), 73.
[4] HT, SF, 68.

could not crush. With untutored hands—with a sure artistry and genius created out of a vast vitality, a concept of God was wrenched from the Sacred Book, the Bible, the chronicle of a people who had learned through great necessity the secret meaning of suffering. This total experience enabled them to reject annihilation and affirm a terrible right to live." The slave authors "made a worthless life, the life of chattel property, a mere thing, a body, *worth living!*" The songs were a "monument to one of the most striking instances on record in which a people forged a weapon of offense and defense out of a psychological shackle. By some amazing but vastly creative spiritual insight the slave understood the redemption of a religion that the master had profaned in his midst."[5]

Thurman's writing on the spirituals contrast but also pair with his reflections on mysticism. For Thurman, the root of human spirituality lay in a personal connection with God achieved through mystical experience—but such experiences made believers more, not less, connected to the everyday realities of the world. Thurman always attempted to balance his mysticism with activism, his reveries toward God with an emphasis on what should happen in this world because of that connection to God. This may be seen in his influence on what became the civil rights movement. He was, in many senses, the mentor of the movement. He spread the Gandhian gospel and planted the seeds of what would become the ethic of nonviolent resistance to white supremacy in America.

He worked out his ideas, expressed later in *Jesus and the Disinherited*, that Jesus represented the oppressed in American society. This book was Thurman's most succinct expression of the fundamental idea he pursued throughout his writings and sermons: that the meaning of Jesus could be found in his status as a poor, disinherited Jew living under an oppressive Roman regime. In this work, too, Thurman explored how the "hounds of hell" pursued the disinherited, and how the same fear and hate that shaped the rules of the dominant regimes also deformed the psychology of the dispossessed. The very religious iconography of American Christianity, symbolized by images of a white Jesus, imprinted the sacralization of whiteness and demonization of blackness. Thurman reasoned that if segregation was considered "normal, it was then correct; if correct, then moral; if moral, then religious." And thus, God was "imaged as an elderly, benign white man," Satan as "red with the glow of fire," and the "imps, the messengers of the devil are black." The implications of such a view were "simply fantastic in the intensity of their tragedy. Doomed on earth to a fixed and unremitting status of inferiority ... and at the same time cut off from the hope that the Creator intended it to be otherwise, those who are thus victimized are stripped of all

---

[5] HT, *For the Inward Journey* (Richmond, IN: Friends United Press, 1994), 215, 223, 230.

social protection.... Under such circumstances, there is but a step from being despised to despising oneself."[6]

A generation later, Black theology pushed these insights further, but Thurman from the 1930s forward already had fastened on the key insight. He had come to see, during the war, that segregation was in effect a will to dominate, and that it could only be defeated through powerful forces of resistance. Full preparation to do nonviolent battle with Jim Crow, he said, would require "great discipline of mind, emotions, and body to the end that forces may not be released that will do complete violence both to one's ideals and to one's purpose."[7]

Sitting in his class at Howard in the late 1930s, a divinity school student under Thurman's tutelage was James Farmer, soon to become one of the founding members of the Committee (later Congress) of Racial Equality (CORE) in Chicago in 1942. Farmer remembered penetrating philosophical questions, the point of which was to challenge students to think beyond becoming complicit in the American racial system of oppression. From its beginnings, Farmer also later remembered, CORE determined that people, not experts or professionals, should lead the struggle for racial justice based on the principles of nonviolent direct action.

One of Thurman's most prominent intellectual mentees was Martin Luther King Jr., who quoted Thurman frequently in his sermons. King also frequently turned to Thurman's *Jesus and the Disinherited*. In December 1955, at the beginning of the Montgomery bus boycott, King urged the crowd that the protests should be shaped by "the teachings of Jesus," that they must love their enemies, and concluded, "We, the disinherited of this land, we who have been oppressed so long, are tired of going through the long night of captivity. And now we are reaching out for the daybreak of freedom and justice and equality."[8] King was channeling Thurman, who spent much of his working life answering the question of what religion might mean for the dispossessed. "The masses of men live with their backs constantly against the wall. They are the poor, the disinherited, the dispossessed." And what did religion say to them? The answer to that question "is perhaps the most important religious quest of modern life." He answered it most fully in *Jesus and the Disinherited*: "The basic fact is that Christianity as it was born in the mind of this Jewish teacher and thinker appears as a technique of survival for the oppressed. That it became, through the inter-

---

[6] HT, *Jesus and the Disinherited*, 43.
[7] HT, "The Will to Segregation," 1943, in SF, 211–19 (quote on 219).
[8] King's speech of December 4, 1955, is reproduced at http://www.digitalhistory.uh.edu/disp_textbook.cfm?smtid=3&psid=3625.

vening years, a religion of the powerful and the dominant, used sometimes as an instrument of oppression, must not tempt us into believing that it was thus in the mind and life of Jesus.... Wherever his spirit appears, the oppressed gather fresh courage; for he announced the good news that fear, hypocrisy, and hatred, the three hounds of hell that track the trail of the disinherited, need have no dominion over them."[9]

Thurman remained a critic of Christianity. He wrote, "I belong to a generation that finds very little that is meaningful or intelligent in the teachings of the Church concerning Jesus Christ.... The desperate opposition to Christianity rests in the fact it seems, in the last analysis, to be a betrayal of the Negro into the hands of his enemies by focusing his attention upon heaven, forgiveness, love, and the like.... For years it has been a part of my own quest so to understand the religion of Jesus that interest in his way of life could be developed and sustained by the intelligent men and women who were at the same time deeply victimized by the Christian Church's betrayal of his faith." He often retold the story of the slave minister who preached to the congregation including his grandmother, "'You—you are not niggers. You—you are not slaves. You are God's children.' This established for them the ground of personal dignity, so that a profound sense of personal worth could absorb the fear reaction. This alone is not enough, but without it, nothing else is of value."[10]

Thurman's background as a Black southern Christian formed the fundamental root of his philosophy, even when he had left behind that background. "A profound piece of surgery has to take place in the very psyche of the disinherited before the great claim of the religion of Jesus can be presented," he wrote. "Tremendous skill and power must be exercised to show to the disinherited the awful results of the role of negative deception into which their lives have been cast. How to do this is perhaps the greatest challenge that the religion of Jesus faces in modern life." Those in power attempt to keep the disinherited in fear for their lives and livelihood, because if they are able to get a greater vision, that of true liberty, then the "aim of *not being killed* is swallowed up by a larger and more transcendent goal." That is why it was so important to make the dispossessed feel like aliens, without any place in the social order.[11]

Thurman applied his theology directly to the effects of segregation. For him, any structure that prevented the free flow of human beings into one another stifled the love ethic. Thus, segregation or other means of separating humans were

---

[9] HT, *Inward Journey*, 122; *Jesus and the Disinherited*, 29–31.
[10] HT, *Inward Journey*, 147.
[11] Ibid., 159.

a "disease of the human spirit and the body politic," for the very existence of that separation "precludes the possibility of the experience of love as a part of the necessity of man's life."[12] And love took work, because love for humanity as such did not exist: "There is no such thing as humanity. What we call humanity has a name, was born, lives on a street, gets hungry, needs all the particular things we need. As an abstract, it has no reality whatsoever."[13] That meant loving whole people, good and bad, including enemies. The key was to meet the person where they were, but to then treat the person as if they were already at the point where they could reach.

For Thurman, the "true purpose" of spiritual discipline was to "clear away whatever may block our awareness of that which is God in us. The aim is to get rid of whatever may so distract the mind and encumber the life that we function without this awareness, or as if it were not possible."[14] The hunger can take many forms and can be distorted and twisted, and yet it never disappears. And "Prayer is the experience of the individual as he seeks to make the hunger dominant and controlling in his life. It has to move more and more to the central place until the hunger becomes the core of the individual's consciousness."[15] As well, he emphasized the importance of the "moral essence of vital religious experience" in preparing "those most engaged in sustaining democracy." Love of God and working to him would strengthen congregants to understand others; they would become "apostles of sensitiveness."[16]

Thurman sought to recover the essential religious core of the human experience and inculcate democratic habits of spiritually grounded self-reliance. He saw the church as a key resource for those engaged in the creation of a just and loving society. For his critics, Thurman's church was like a lemonade stand, where people would pause to refresh themselves while on their way to somewhere else. For Thurman, those people would not get to that "somewhere else"—nor would society at large—without those moments of spiritual nourishment, those cool drinks on a hot day.

Perhaps adding another ironic twist to Thurman's legacy, he did change America, less through his creation of interracial visions such as the Church of the Fellowship of All Peoples, and more through his translation of universalist ideas to an American religious idiom. He was a "seeker" before we had such a term and paved the way for contemporary ideas of religious pluralism. He labored under anonymity, but ultimately the arc of history is bending his way.

---

[12] HT, SF, 184.
[13] HT, *Mysticism and the Experience of Love* (Wallingford, PA: Pendle Hill, 1961), 15.
[14] HT, *Inward Journey*, 280.
[15] HT, SF, 90.
[16] Ibid., 12.

Thurman and the Spiritual Disciplines of the Now

At the height of the nonviolent civil rights movement, Thurman continued his philosophical explorations into the ideas he had been so important in fostering and spreading. In 1963 he published *Disciplines of the Spirit*, parts of which explored the history and purpose of nonviolence. Like others, he insisted that "non-violence is not a negative attitude—it is a positive act of resistance. It is not passive; it is positive and creative."[17] It once was considered weak and cowardly, but no longer was so after the life of Gandhi and the dramatic developments within the United States during the civil rights years.

Nonviolence, Thurman insisted, was not "merely a mood or a climate, or even an attitude," but a "particular kind of art or technique." It was not just the only available tool, because, if so, it simply participated in the very order it was struggling against. In this case, it would have "the same moral basis as violence and cannot be separated from it in essence." Rather, nonviolence could be one of the "great vehicles of reconciliation because it tends always to create and to maintain a climate in which the need to be understood and cared for can be honored." Those practicing nonviolence could be full of rage, of an internal will to violence, but nonviolence was a rejection of both the physical and the psychological tools of violence. The tools of nonviolence were those aimed not merely at changing a situation but requiring "a man to face *himself* in his action—to see how he looks to himself in the violent act itself without regard to what he hopes the violent act will accomplish." The tools of nonviolence placed upon people "the demand to absorb violence rather than to counteract it in kind," something that profoundly challenged people to face naked fear: "There is rioting in the streets of the spirit, and the price of tranquility comes terribly high. Order and reconciliation must be restored within—it is here that the major conquest must be achieved." As with Dr. King, Thurman saw nonviolence as a fundamental philosophical principle, not just a stratagem.

That spirit had become apparent in recent years, he said, and was evident in Supreme Court decisions, in the quiet tramping of feet on the streets, and in every place where people sought justice where "injustice abounds, to make peace where chaos is rampant, and to make the voice heard on behalf of the helpless and the weak. It is the voice of God and the voice of man; it is the meaning of all the strivings of the whole human race toward a world of friendly men underneath a friendly sky."

---

[17] Paul Harvey, "The Fierce Urgency of Now and the Disciplines of the Spirit: Life Lessons from Martin Luther King Jr. and Howard Thurman," *Word & World* 41S (Racial Justice Now 2021): 84. https://wordandworld.luthersem.edu/content/pdfs/41-3_Racial_Justice_Now/41-3_Harvey.pdf.

Some of his contemporaries, and nearly all scholars since his time, have pondered the paradox that Thurman was a mentor of the movement without being deeply involved in its everyday workings. He was not a movement man. That is, he educated a generation in precepts of nonviolence and a kind of internal transformation that would lead to a societal revolution, but stayed himself in the background. As he told the *Christian Century* in 1973, "I didn't have to wait for the revolution. I have never been in search for identity, and I think that [all] I've ever felt and worked on and believed in was founded in a kind of private, almost unconscious autonomy that did not seek vindication in my environment because it was in me."[18] His vision of the church emanated from that. As Thurman saw it, individuals in the thick of the struggle should have a place to "be able to find renewal and fresh courage in the spiritual resources of the church.... The true genius of the church was revealed by what it symbolized as a beachhead in society in terms of community, and as an inspiration to the solitary individual to put his weight on the side of a society in which no person need be afraid." As his wife and pioneering African American historian Sue Bailey Thurman later expressed it, "We had a feeling that those who were leading in the civil rights movement had to have some place to rest their hearts at night. They had to fight all day, all day long. And then at night, they had to go somewhere and find their rest, or find their peace that the next morning would bring renewed energy. So he pastored to civil rights people."[19]

Thurman reflected on his relationship with Dr. King, relatively distant as it was, at Boston University and afterward. Toward the end of his life, Martin Luther King Jr. most personally and existentially confronted questions about the future of the freedom movement in the midst of the advance of the Vietnam War and the retreat from the war on poverty. Of the latter, he said, it had not even been a skirmish. Meanwhile, Thurman contemplated what was necessary on the "search for common ground," as he titled his last theological work. Considering these two giants of African American religious history together provides important spiritual food for thought. King's hallmark phrase in later years looked to the "fierce urgency of now." Thurman's, by contrast, was the "apostle of sensitiveness," ever looking to expand our capacities for spiritual reflection and growth even in the midst of sometimes tumultuous social struggles.

Neither social justice and spiritual leader serves as a complete model, without considering the other, and both moved significantly in their own thinking about

---

[18] Mary Goodwin, "Racial Roots and Religion: An Interview with Howard Thurman," *Christian Century* 90 (May 9, 1973): 533–35.

[19] HT, WHAH, 160–61; Beth Rhude, "A Biography of a Free Spirit," manuscript in Sue Bailey Thurman papers, HTC, Box 1, Folder 1.

the purpose of role of anger and passion in confronting injustice. In considering the two together, we may productively contemplate how to respond to the prophetic urgency of the now while attending to individual and communal spiritual lives. King spoke eloquently and famously of the "fierce urgency of now." For King, that social struggle grew ever broader and more urgent as he pressed some of his former allies in the US government about the connections between racism and militarism evident in the Vietnam War era. King also had learned via some important mentors from Thurman how to integrate spiritual growth and social transformation. Yet as one observes King's last few years of frantic activity, and his frequently expressed desire for a moment of peace and reflection, it appears painfully obvious how much he sought moments of peace and spiritual rest that forever eluded him.[20]

Thurman's primary concern for King was the state of King's spiritual life. For Thurman, what was most profound about King was that he saw how nonviolence "could not become for him a technique merely for social change." It was possible to embrace the techniques of nonviolence as a manipulative force and to remain personally uninvolved. King saw this and "insisted that always coupled with nonviolence there must be the other words: direct action. There must be confrontation; there must be always the test, the checking out so that nonviolence would not degenerate either into a philosophy merely or into a metaphysic or even into a manipulating ethic." Then, in the face of King's assassination, it was easy to think that "what you experienced in the light is no longer true because you are in the darkness. What you experienced in the light remains true and you must hold this until the light breaks again. And if you do that, you will discover … that it is the intent of life that we shall all be one people." These are words of Thurman's for King delivered on April 7, 1968.[21]

Thurman was part of a generation that had introduced ideas of nonviolence and civil disobedience to twentieth-century Americans. His students, including James Farmer and Pauli Murray, brought that message out into the world, through CORE and many other efforts. But Thurman was more of a spiritual elite carrying that message, a bit purer in Gandhianism than King, who took the unadulterated message of nonviolence to the masses. In doing so, King became a symbol of a movement that transformed America. Thurman had been called the American Gandhi, but he wasn't; he was the American Gandhi's mentor. His depth of vision and stillness of spirit were just what the young celebrity preacher needed as he became, at twenty-five years old, the symbol of a movement that

---

[20] Harvey, "The Fierce Urgency of Now and the Disciplines of the Spirit," 80.
[21] HT, "Martin Luther King, Jr.: Litany and Words in Memoriam," April 7, 1968, in PHWT 5:183.

would soon swallow him up. King felt compelled to be relentlessly active; he could have used more of Thurman's stillness of spirit. And Thurman needed someone like King to make his message something that would go beyond the poetic sermon delivered to thoughtful middle-class intellectuals. The two needed each other to make America closer to what it could be. Through them together, the unadulterated message of nonviolence, for a brief moment, seemed to have transformed America.

To put it another way: neither King nor Thurman were sufficient, but both were necessary. Neither one could have fulfilled the role that the other did. Thurman had wisdom enough to know that as early as the 1940s when people tried to cast him as the American Gandhi. He knew he was no such thing. He had the wisdom too to see what King was about, to move beyond his own more purified ideas of a spiritual elite, and to move in accord with the tempo of the times. He was not a drum major for justice, but he wrote some of that music. Thurman's life message was about spiritually preparing one's self for the now, such that the exigencies of the now would not consume a person's soul, because that person's soul would be strengthened and disciplined through spiritual practices. King's message—at least one of them—was that the evils of the now had to be dramatized through civil disobedience and confronted politically and socially. For a person of spirit seeking discernment on how to conceive of and act in our now, both parts of these messages can inform, sustain, and empower.

Following his Quaker mentor in mysticism, Rufus Jones, Thurman declared himself an affirmation mystic, one who searched spiritual experience in order to engage with the world more fully, not to withdraw from it. Jones had said that the "mystic is always more than any finite task declares," and yet accepted the task because "he has discovered that only through the finite is the Infinite to be found."[22] The finite could be an ordinary event of the day, the beauty in nature, the deep engagement with another human being, the pleasure of a well-cooked meal—any of it. Thurman advised, "Do not wait to hear His spirit winging near in moments of great crisis, do not expect Him riding on the crest of a wave of deep emotional excitement—do not look to see Him at the dramatic moment when something abnormal or spectacular is at hand. Rather find Him in the simple experiences of daily living, in the normal ebb and flow of life as you live it."[23]

Another important truth of Thurman's was his ability to bring together different strands of the American religious tradition, between individual trans-

---

[22] Rufus M. Jones, *Social Law in the Spiritual World: Studies in Human and Divine Inter-Relationship* (Philadelphia: J. C. Winston, 1904), 154. See also Walter E. Fluker, *They Looked for a City: A Comparative Analysis of the Ideal of Community in the Thought of Howard Thurman and Martin Luther King Jr.* (Lanham, MD: University Press of America, 1988), 27.

[23] HT, "Barren or Fruitful," sermon preached in Washington, DC, 1932, in SF, 28.

formation and social transformation. He connected the two in ways that deeply informed the movement of the 1960s. His quiet counsel to many provided that. "The greatest mystic-ascetics in the Christian tradition have turned the whole stream of Christian thought and achievement into new and powerful channels of practical living. It is basic to the Christian tradition that social sin and personal sin are bound up together in an inexorable relationship so that it is literally true that no man can expect to have his soul saved alone," he wrote.[24] At another place, he stated,

> It seems to me that experience reveals a potent half-truth; namely, that the world can be made good if all the men in the world as individuals become good men. After the souls of men are saved, the society in which they function will be a good society. This is only a half-truth. Many men have found that they are caught in a framework of relationships evil in design, and their very good deeds have developed into instrumentalities for evil. It is not enough to save the souls of men; the relationships that exist between men must be saved also. To approach the problem from the other angle is to assume that once the relationships between men are saved, the individual men will thereby become instruments of positive weal. This is also a half-truth.... We must, therefore, even as we purify our hearts and live our individual lives under the divine scrutiny, so order the framework of our relationships that good men can function in it to the glory of God.[25]

Thurman had a lifelong lover's quarrel with the church and various institutionalized forms of religious traditions. His early bitter experiences both with the racism that pervaded earlier twentieth-century America and with the unloving moralism he found in the Black Baptist church set him on a course of being a seeker. But he was a seeker with a center, a spiritual ballast that guided him. He sought always to answer the question of what religion meant to those whose backs were against the wall.

One may easily transfer the metaphor to the question: what does religion mean to the person whose body is crushed against the ground by an overweening police force in a state devoted to incarcerating petty criminality while allowing for grand theft and fascist-style organizing at the highest levels? Thurman would have been all too familiar with the irony of that question; it's what he saw and lived with his entire life, even while he continued on the search for common

---

[24] HT, "Mysticism and Social Change," lectures delivered to Eden Theological Seminary, 1939, reprinted in SF, 117.

[25] HT, "What Shall I Do with My Life," sermon from 1939, in SF, 33.

ground, as the title of his last work of philosophical reflections put it. For him, God was the last word, the end of all our strivings. And humans best cultivate that relationship through meditation and prayer, through an extended inward journey employing multiple spiritual resources. What could be learned through such inner explorations could prepare the way for a society based on love. This was a vision expressed well in the founding statement of the Student Nonviolent Coordinating Committee, from April 1960, authored by Thurman's friend and fellow minister and devotee of Gandhi, James Lawson:

> We affirm the philosophical or religious ideal of nonviolence as the foundation of our purpose, the presupposition of our belief, and the manner of our action. Nonviolence, as it grows from the Judeo-Christian tradition, seeks a social order of justice permeated by love. Integration of human endeavor represents the crucial first step toward such a society. Through nonviolence, courage displaces fear. Love transcends hate. Acceptance dissipates prejudice; hope ends despair. Faith reconciles doubt. Peace dominates war. Mutual regards cancel enmity. Justice for all overthrows injustice. The redemptive community supersedes immoral social systems.[26]

Little wonder, then, that Thurman thrilled at the rise of groups such as SNCC in the early 1960s. He saw the philosophy and theology he had taught his whole life put into action to combat the very forces of hatred that produced human separation and blocked human community. He translated his particular experiences and training into a universalist cosmopolitan idiom fully grounded in the painful and scarring experiences of African American life and history. His was an American spirituality full of wisdom drawn from sources as varied as his grandmother and early teachers, the trees and waterways where he grew up, his deep reading in religious texts, his training with Quaker mystics and social justice activists, and his experience in teaching students and preaching to congregants over decades of time. The paradoxes of his life made him only more aware that the larger contradictions of life were transitory, not ultimate.

His dissent against American Christianity as it was actually practiced helped empower the most important social movement in twentieth-century American history, and it can continue to compel a rejuvenation of contemporary religious practice. The first step, he would say (I think), is to turn off your devices, center yourself, meditate, pray, and then put your centered self squarely into some struggle to make the world a more just place.

---

[26] SNCC statement, The Sixties Project, http://www2.iath.virginia.edu/sixties/HTML_docs/Resources/Primary/Manifestos/SNCC_founding.html.

12

FREE-MINDEDNESS, LOVE, AND HOPE

Three Virtues for a Better Democratic Future

Anthony Sean Neal

Philosopher and theologian Howard Thurman would frequently quote Thomas Carlyle: "It once was and has always been a serious thing to live!"[1] He made this profound acknowledgment while describing the existential moment of human awareness that life is short and also fragile. Many of the things that we accumulate along the way are meaningless and valueless, particularly as pertaining to sustainability and happiness.

To better approximate the aim of such pronouncements, Thurman told the story of Mirabehn, the British-born activist who often accompanied Gandhi on his trips abroad.[2] The story goes that at a certain point in her journey with Gandhi she began to send home those possessions she no longer needed. So much was sent—or, better yet, discarded due to her no longer needing them—that when she died, she only possessed a hairbrush, a pair of sandals, and a cloth with which to keep warm. In spite of Mirabehn's moment of clarity, the rest of us are also confronted with the additional quandary "Why do we hold on so dearly to that which is meaningless and valueless?" I want to suggest that it is because we rarely ask ourselves, as Friedrich Nietzsche intimated, "What is the value of our values?"[3] It can be said that what we value, generally speaking, is at the core of our desired experience. And it is our desired experience that is inclusive of, but not limited to, the type of nation and national government we desire and what type of democracy will we work toward.

In 2016, Eddie Glaude, in an attempt to pose a similar question—"What is the real value of democracy in the United States?"—authored a book titled

---

[1] HT, "We Believe: Responsible Living," sermon series, June 30, 1961, HTC, 123:16.
[2] HT, *The Living Wisdom of Howard Thurman: A Visionary for Our Time*, audio CD (Boulder, CO: Sounds True, 2010), track 1.
[3] Friedrich Nietzsche, *The Antichrist* (New York: SoHo Books, 2010), 25.

Democracy in Black. Glaude launched the book through appearances on MSNBC, and during one of these conversations he quoted a political historian who said, "America has not developed the type of citizens she needs to have and maintain the type of democracy she desires."[4] This statement assumes much, but at a minimum, it assumes that Glaude knows what type of democracy America desired to have. A lot is at stake here, but I want to make a suppositional leap of logic by starting my philosophical quest from the junction where Glaude meets Thomas Jefferson, and I want to further suppose that Glaude took Jefferson seriously by acquiescing to the notion that the type of democracy America desired is grounded in the principles set forth by Jefferson in the Declaration of Independence. Here I am using "principle" in the Hegelian sense: a principle can neither be proven or disproven; it is the fundamental concept upon which a consciousness or philosophical endeavor begins. In this sense there would be no means to go beyond it. According to Hegel, "It refers to the nature of cognition and consequently is supposed to be only a criterion rather than an objective determination."[5] An early example is the definition the geometer Euclid used, attempting to build his whole system of geometry on the notion of a point, which he defines as that which has no part. It seems that he developed a brilliant way to put forward a rational conception of his principle without having to prove its existence. In other words, points are necessary and sufficient for the system, but beyond this, little can be argued in terms of their existence. In much the same manner, Jefferson balances the Declaration of Independence on the principle of unalienable rights when he asserts, "We hold these truths to be self-evident, that all men are created equal, that they are endowed by their Creator with certain unalienable Rights, that among these are Life, Liberty and the pursuit of happiness."[6] Proof to the claim that this can be seen as the principle for Jefferson lies in a later statement made by Abraham Lincoln that America was a test of sorts, to see "whether this nation or any nation so conceived can long endure."[7]

I want to say yes, but I also want to stipulate that Jefferson put forward a deficient document. His declaration needed at least one more statement. So I can't say yes to the deficient document; I can only say yes to the document with the

---

[4] Eddie Glaude Jr., *Democracy in Black: How Race Still Enslaves the American Soul* (New York: Crown, 2016), 46.

[5] Georg Wilhelm Friedrich Hegel, *Hegel's Science of Logic* (Amherst, NY: Humanity Books, 1969), 67.

[6] Declaration of Independence, https://www.archives.gov/founding-docs/declaration-transcript.

[7] Abraham Lincoln, "The Gettysburg Address," https://www.loc.gov/resource/rbpe.24404500/?st=text.

addition of the necessary adjustment. The adjustment to be made adds a conditional to the condition that Jefferson put forward. Jefferson's condition was "for this cause, governments are established to protect these rights."[8] He left vacant any mention of the types of people required to populate the institutions that are considered necessary for the sustainability purposes. I want to further extend his conditionals, as follows: *but, to ensure the sustainability of such a government, people who are committed to love, hope, and freedom (free-mindedness) are required.*

In what follows, I do not argue for the validity of this new conditional, except to say that institutions do not perform work—people do. I make the further claim that the addition of this adjustment to the original statement requires postulating the question "How do such people get created?" I am doubtful that anyone could do justice to such a question, but again, my goal is to gain insight and lay groundwork. To be clear, by doing so, I simply mean to prioritize and make necessary the reading and deep reflection upon Thurman as a contemplative thinker, over and against the writings of others whose works seem not to challenge oppression and sustain the weakening of our nation through its place as the status quo.

In *Disciplines of the Spirit*, Thurman used an Augustinian, humanistic frame to assist readers in finding what they really valued. In the section "Commitment," Thurman put forward three questions. The first two were posed by Augustine, and Thurman added the last. "Who am I?" "What do I want?" and "What will I do?"[9] Thurman saw that at the center of all three was the more intrusive query of, "For what will I live?" and "For what will I die?" Thurman put forward these questions to provide tools through which an individual can define and classify commitment for themselves. To this end he wrote,

> Commitment means that it is possible for a man to yield of his consent to a purpose or cause, a movement or an ideal, which may be more important to him than whether he lives or dies. The commitment is a self-conscious act of will by which he affirms his identification with what he is committed to. The character of his commitment is determined by that which the center core of his consent is given.[10]

Unspoken by Thurman, but implied, is that it is a serious thing to think about or to contemplate living. Thurman uses the term "consent"—which implies that intentionality is involved in any decision to give one's life to a particular formation and that the individual is responsible for whatever forms of life to

---

[8] "Preamble," the Declaration of Independence.
[9] HT, *Disciplines of the Spirit* (Richmond, IN: Friends United Press, 1963), 26.
[10] Ibid.

which they consent. Here, in the act of giving consent, the individual's freedom begins. Thurman focuses on people who find themselves living in deeply oppressive structures and who either resist or imitate their oppressor. It is not my aim to fully explicate Thurman's thoughts on oppression but suffice to say that even within the limited scope of the two options provided, the individual is provided space to give consent and to also commit to their decision with the understanding of its serious nature. It is my aim to work out the beginnings of what could lead to applicable insight and the groundwork for the development of an account of how the writings of Thurman—a Black, socially minded thinker from the modern era of the African American freedom struggle—might provide living virtues for all in this current American moment.

But first I want to shed light on the occasion that gave rise to my perceived need for such a discussion. Many questions concerning curricula and books are currently floating around the nation. A wall of resistance is swelling with the will to make certain that these books and curricula—used for discussing prior oppressions, horrors, and atrocities—should be illegal to teach. What is being missed, particularly as it applies to books written during or about the modern era of the African American freedom struggle (1896–1975),[11] is that they provide Americans with an understanding of how one group of people endured extremely harsh conditions and explore an understanding of the virtues this group developed such that they could withstand their existential crisis.

How Is Freedom Possible?

The possibility of freedom is contingent upon the existence of a common notion of it that reasonable people might accept as self-evident, similar to notions of life, liberty, and the pursuit of happiness. Offering such a distinction for freedom is essential on the same basis that dismissing the notion of freedom is flaccid. A notion of freedom is deeply and historically entrenched in every culture, even when it is not the intent of the culture to portray it. For example, there are many depictions in ancient art of people held in various forms of captivity, whether because of war or as action meant to resist unwanted intruders. If individuals or groups could be held in captivity, then there is justification to suppose that others meanwhile were not captives, or essentially, were free. Therefore, offering a definition to meet these preexistent notions of freedom is worthwhile and viable, since it's unlikely they were going to be jettisoned in the foreseeable future.

---

[11] Anthony Sean Neal, *Common Ground: A Comparison of the Ideas of Consciousness in the Writings of Howard Thurman and Huey P. Newton* (Trenton, NJ: Africa World Press, 2015), 1.

A conception of freedom is inherent in our humanity. We are feeling-thinking beings. Based on our judgments, we act. One definition that might account for freedom, then, is to describe it as the ability to move and think as one wills when one wills. The ability to will or the act of volition is what separates humans from other animals, and it is foundational to freedom. In other words, when we will an act, we will our freedom through our commitment to that act. Our commitment to act is also our commitment to freedom. So, then, bondage or restrictions on physical acts are attempts to break or hinder a person's will to act or will to be free.

Freedom thus requires commitment—to struggle against one's own oppression and a commitment on the collective level to create a sustainable space in which free-minded people may exist unhindered. A great part of the Black experience in America has been about that kind of struggle, and any philosophizing arising from that experience must account for its meaning and value. How is meaning captured from such an experience? Fundamental, particularly during the modern era, is the recognition of the role that struggle has played in shaping the hopes, dreams, and desires of Blacks in America. This is to say that Black people rose above their oppressed state through giving their consent and commitment to struggle against oppression. The object of this struggle has taken on many forms, including for physical freedom and for the ability to read and write. However, this struggle has always demonstrated that a commitment to freedom through free-mindedness, love, and hope was necessary to see the struggle through to the end. These virtues are revealed in Howard Thurman's thoughts and writings.

Thurman demonstrated great concern for the damage that oppression was doing to American society in general, and for its damaging effects on Black people in particular. In his 1965 book, *The Luminous Darkness*, he wrote, "The fact that the first twenty-three years of my life were spent in Florida and Georgia has left its scars deep in my spirit."[12] But his deepest and most well-known philosophizing on the matter came in his 1949 book, *Jesus and the Disinherited*. There he struggled with how he, as a Black man, could be a Christian in spite of Christianity's support of slavery and oppression.

Jesus and the Disinherited contains an overall disposition toward this question, but for our purposes here, a narrower concern will be used to demonstrate how Thurman answered oppression in general while standing within the African American tradition narrowly defined. He identifies three ancillary struggles for those who are the object of oppressors. First, fear is examined in its capacity to effect aspects of experience and detailed states of mind. Fear

---

[12] HT, *The Luminous Darkness: A Personal Interpretation of the Anatomy of Segregation and the Ground of Hope* (1965; repr., Richmond, IN: Friends United Press, 1989), x.

is a tactic used by imperialist forces to wage war on the consciousness of the oppressed, and Black people held captive in America fell victim to this oppressive tactic of their slave captors.[13]

Thurman saw free-mindedness—the ability to say yes or no and to also experience meaningful silence—as one of the most significant forms of struggle against fear. He put forward his thoughts on the matter using analogy instead of analysis or dialectics.[14] He reflected on a quote from his grandmother, "You are not niggers. You, you are not slaves. You are God's children."[15] This was intended to apply to a particular moment in time and for a specific people, and then Thurman's intent in its reuse was as a principle understood this way: In the face of great oppression, freedom equals choice. Sometimes the choice is as simple as saying yes or no, or maintaining a meaningful silence. No, to hurled epithets. Yes, to being equal to your greatest ideals. And then, in the maintenance of a meaningful silence, the notion that the oppressor cannot own the thoughts of the oppressed without their consent.

Why Struggle for Others to Be Free?

Some notion of freedom has probably existed in the minds of humans since the beginning, whether explicitly or implicitly. Explicit freedom is understood as a verbal representation coming together with symbolic representation in the form of written words or pictures, created to meet sensory experience. Implicit freedom is understood in the sense that verbal representations have often distinguished those who were servants, prisoners or in bondage, and even slaves from others who were not. Those who were not in these senses "bound" might be understood to be implicitly free. Still, what do humans really mean when they speak of freedom?

It seems that we are not describing freedom as something we become but something we are. In other words, to be human is to be free qualitatively. Therefore, we might come to understand that limiting freedom limits life such that the individual experiences a type of death. So, then, to struggle for someone else's freedom is an attempt to save their life, and not just figuratively, but in a real and existential sense. In other words, struggling against oppression, any oppression,

---

[13] HT, *Jesus and the Disinherited* (Boston: Beacon Press, 1996), 29.

[14] Analysis separates the elements of an argument in order to demonstrate the role of each part. Dialectics contrasts certain elements with their alternatives in order to demonstrate flaws. Analogy forms a generalization by selecting a root metaphor so that the move from part to whole or whole to part can be seen in terms familiar to the audience.

[15] HT, *Deep River and The Negro Spiritual Speaks of Life and Death* (Richmond, IN: Friends United Press, 1975), 12.

is necessitated by a deep understanding of what it is to be human and a thorough desire to not see the human experience limited for anyone else. One simply cannot be for life without being against oppression.

But what about self-interest? Thurman rejects self-interest as being against community development, and therefore against life.[16] For him, true community nurtures life and is life sustaining. Love as the foundation of community is established when human beings have an intrinsic interest in each another. Thurman intimates further that there exists an impossibility of this interest without definite knowledge of the other person, which he calls "the fact" of the other. In this sense, love becomes a type of consciousness or awareness, and it also becomes the very desire to be aware of the other. So anything that causes communal separation or fragmentation works against, and is not an action of love. Even inaction, or a passive posture toward the other, becomes a work against community—a violation of wholeness, or a violent act toward the very notion of community.[17] Accordingly, Thurman wrote, "This serves as a corrective against doing violence against those for whom we have lost a sense of caring because of great gaps in our knowledge of their fact."[18]

The moral nature of love as knowledge of the other in action, as Thurman conceived it, can be found in *The Search for Common Ground*.[19] It stems from his notion of the basic community, which he termed the primary social unit or family. Thurman's analysis of the family as a primary human community is rooted in the assumption of human life having an urgent need for care at the very beginning. Without a particular kind of care, there is the strong possibility for the development in the individual of a maladjusted personality type or even death. In this community, through necessity, full actualization of human potential rests within the constraints of the interdependent nature of the community. Full actualization of human potential is referred to by Thurman as whole-making or becoming whole, which is the aim of human life, aided by the active participation of others in the form of caring or love.

Thurman considers love, or simply proper treatment of others, as normative or moral behavior. The interdependent nature of the human reality never dissipates. Certainly, an argument can be made that some have fared well even after such actions as taking to the wilderness and going it alone, but even in such cases, we mustn't discount the initial necessity of care, such as the mother-child

---

[16] HT, *Mysticism and the Experience of Love* (Wallingford, PA: Pendle Hill, 1961), 12–14.

[17] Anthony Sean Neal, *Howard Thurman's Philosophical Mysticism: Love against Fragmentation* (Lanham, MD: Lexington Books, 2019).

[18] HT, *Mysticism and the Experience of Love*, 3.

[19] HT, SCG, 81–82.

relationship, as requisite in all human life. In this sense, love as knowledge, or constitutive in knowledge, is always somehow an active process in community development.

Freedom as being alive, freedom as love, freedom as knowledge, and freedom as being human—when these are understood as necessary elements of the same equation it becomes clear why we would and must struggle for others to be free as well. To do so is the ultimate demonstration of our recognition of what it means to be human. Humans will always struggle to be free, and the more an understanding is gained about what freedom contains, humans will begin to struggle more for others to be free too. It is automatic.

One explanation for this is the recognition of what freedom really is and of how it is constituted. The presence of freedom creates what can be called free spaces, and there is innately within the occurrence of free spaces the ability to gain knowledge that reduces the need for anyone to struggle to be free. Where there is no oppression, or very little oppression, the elements of freedom create freedom itself. Understood as a mathematical or scientific equation, the harmony contains simplicity and elegance. Simplicity arises from the ease in which the necessity of each constituent part can be seen. Elegance arises from the vision of such a harmonious society.

The Value of Freedom

What about the value, rather than the meaning, of freedom? If freedom is inherent or fundamental to being human, then any attempt to restrict freedom is an attempt to restrict the humanity of others. An example of this can be seen whenever there are attempts to limit the freedom of individuals within a particular group in the form of oppression. The oppressor realizes it cannot reduce an individual's freedom, but through oppression hopes to convince the oppressed to act as if they were not free. This is usually done by focusing on the fears of the oppressed, particularly the fear of death. If the oppressed allow their fear of death to take control, they can sometimes lose their will to dream and possibly the will to live.

For Thurman, the value of freedom is consistent with his thoughts on hope. He wrote, "As long as a man has a dream in his heart, he cannot lose the significance of living."[20] Hope is portrayed as belief in a possibility. As a consequence of such hope, the individual is able to maintain a reasonable understanding of the value of life as well as a desire to live. This value may include the knowledge that a current moment of oppression is not permanent. This sentiment allowed

---

[20] HT, *Meditations of the Heart* (Boston: Beacon Press, 1999), 36–37.

Thurman to assert that the contradictions of life are not final. He thought this to be true because he took change as a constant—even as necessary to existence. In this sense, freedom or free-mindedness is contingent upon one's ability to dream, which is contiguous with our humanity. It operates through the imagination, giving us the ability to live in community and to love, and the desire to struggle to be free or become who we know ourselves to be.[21]

Thurman, however, provides a caution in conjunction with his encouragement to dream. The caution arises from his understanding that freedom cannot be taken from someone, but that each person can be convinced not to act or commit themselves to their freedom. Thurman urges each person to listen to "the sound of the genuine." In doing so, we ensure that through our dreams we won't "spend our days on the ends of strings that somebody else pulls."[22] This is a reminder that freedom is an intrinsic value contiguous with existence, and it requires commitment. Its value or virtue is always with us in spite of our recognizing its presence. The value of freedom is priceless and ineffable.

---

[21] HT, *Mysticism and the Experience of Love*, 17–18.
[22] HT, "The Sound of the Genuine: Baccalaureate Address, Spelman College, May 4, 1980," *Spelman Messenger* 96, no. 4 (Summer 1980).

13

Howard Thurman

Strange Forms of Freedom

Kipton Jensen

"Thurman is first and foremost a philosopher of freedom," suggested Mozella Mitchell many years ago.¹ As a moral psychologist and philosophical anthropologist, Thurman provides an array of profound insights into personal freedom and social if not also political liberation. Whether he was talking about individuals or communities, examining the conditions requisite to personal freedom, or in allegedly free and democratic societies, Thurman was convinced that the clue to freedom was found in the tendency in life itself toward "wholeness, harmony, and integration."

"There is a medley of confusion as to the meaning of personal freedom," Thurman wrote.² I aim to examine his philosophy of freedom alongside another Black liberation philosopher, Angela Davis's account of philosophical freedom in her 1969 "Lectures on Liberation."³ Thurman and Davis both sought to discover and delineate a philosophy of freedom construed as "a constant struggle" and an arduous "discipline of the mind and emotions," as well as an "achievement of the human spirit."

We should read Thurman for a better "understanding of the conditions of oppression and the possibility of abolishing these conditions,"⁴ but we should also recognize his thought as a vital resource for contemporary struggles for freedom, and a critical corrective to contorted conceptions of freedom associated with the Western philosophical canon. He was eager to discover the secret

---

[1] Mozella Mitchell, *Spiritual Dynamics of Howard Thurman's Theology* (Bristol, IN: Wyndham Hall Press, 1985), 24.

[2] HT, "Freedom Is a Discipline," 1953, in SF, 99–100; HT, *The Inward Journey: Meditations on a Spiritual Quest* (New York: Harper & Row, 1961), 63.

[3] Angela Davis, "Lectures on Liberation" (1969), in *Narrative of the Life of Frederick Douglass* (San Francisco: City Lights Books, 2010); also see *Freedom Is a Constant Struggle: Ferguson, Palestine, and the Foundations of a Movement* (Chicago, Haymarket Books, 2016).

[4] Davis, "Lectures," 49.

sources and mechanisms, methods of physical survival, and psychological resilience and spiritual renewal that emerge within the historical struggle for freedom by Black people in America.

Some observers have suggested that freedom and community are the two great philosophical themes in Thurman's thought, but ultimately, freedom and community are the warp and woof of a single fabric. This essay explores the thesis that freedom is to be found primarily if not exclusively at "the growing edges of social concern" and, moreover, that whatever undermines human potential or otherwise inhibits community construed as dynamic integration constitutes a pseudo concept of freedom.

A Philosopher of Freedom

While it makes sense to view Thurman as an early exemplar of Black liberation theology, I believe it is also possible to portray him as an early representative of what some would now call *Black liberation philosophy*. His spoken and literary corpus constitutes a comprehensive and compelling philosophical worldview as well as a strenuous yet tender way of finding meaning in life and death. The philosophical strands of Thurman's thought were informed by strange experiences of freedom and unfreedom. His philosophy of freedom is a useful lens through which to explore his philosophical anthropology and metaphysics, his philosophy of identity, as well as his ethical theories and social philosophy. There is an underlying logical integrity or soundness to Thurman's thought: "always there is the order; always there is the logic."[5] But his brilliance as a philosopher consists in his creative "plaiting of the strands" of logic and experience. He was tough-minded yet disarmingly tender-hearted. Regardless of how we wish to classify him, whether a theologian and a mystic or a philosopher, Thurman wrote for "those who are on the hunt—for life."[6] In ways reminiscent of Ralph Waldo Emerson, who believed that every natural fact doubled as a spiritual truth, Thurman claimed that the "underlying unity of life manifests itself in the basic structural patterns of nature and provides the precious clue" to understanding "that the interest in or concern for wholeness should be part of the intention of life, more basic than any particular tendency toward fragmentation."[7]

Thurman once claimed that he had "only one basic statement to make about the love of God and that is that it is always concerned with breaking the sense of isolation that the individual human spirit feels as it lives its way into

---

[5] HT, *The Negro Spiritual Speaks of Life and Death* (New York: Harper, 1974), 94.
[6] HT, *Disciplines of the Spirit* (New York: Harper & Row, 1963), 13.
[7] Ibid., 104.

life."[8] And in a 1956 sermon titled "Freedom," Thurman preached, "Jesus was convinced that the purpose of God in the creation of man is to establish community, to establish wholeness, to establish conscientious cooperation, freedom, equality."[9] Thurman thought that "when a person actualizes his own potential he becomes whole, harmonized, or fulfilled."[10] He was methodologically attentive to what Angela Davis considers to be "the crucial transformation of the concept of freedom as a static, given principle into the concept of liberation, the dynamic, active struggle for freedom."[11] The clue to the communal is sought within the individual, and the clue to the individual is sought in the communal. Although precedent can be found within the Western canon for Thurman's philosophy of freedom—for instance, in Plato and Plotinus, Aristotle and Aquinas—and while aspects of Thurman's thought admit of comparison to Augustine and Kierkegaard, Thurman should not be reduced to his philosophical or theological predecessors. Throughout his career he displayed a preoccupation with the meaning of freedom, which he occasionally distinguished from liberty, from his early *Deep River* (1945) and *Jesus and the Disinherited* (1949) to his later *Disciplines of the Spirit* (1963) and *Search for Common Ground* (1971).

Angela Davis notes that "one of the most acute paradoxes present in the history of Western society is that while on a philosophical plane freedom has been delineated in the most lofty and sublime fashion, concrete reality has always been permeated with the most brutal forms of unfreedom."[12] The strange and abstract freedom that emerged from this painful paradox and historical contradiction was little more than a self-proclaimed liberty[13]—or secretly sanctioned license granted by "a cult of inequality"—"to control the lives of others" and "suppress other human beings." In this strange conception, claims Davis, an individual is only "free at the expense of the freedom of another."[14]

---

[8] HT, *The Growing Edge* (Richmond, IN: Friends United Press, 1956), 65.

[9] "Freedom" (unpublished sermon, December 9, 1956). Thurman went on to say, "The second thing that follows is that this is the work of God, not merely in human history, but in the life of the individual man. This leads then to the statement that it is fundamental to the human spirit, to the nature of man to work for community. To work for a world in which it is not only reasonable but normal for men to be sharing their values, sharing their lives, sharing the living texture of their togetherness. Now this is fundamental to the nature of man in the thought of Jesus."

[10] HT, SCG, 80.

[11] Davis, "Lectures," 47.

[12] Ibid.

[13] In "America in Search of a Soul" (1976), Thurman describes "a true distinction between freedom and liberty" (PHWT 5:270). Whereas "liberty has to do primarily with elements of the social contract," which "can be altered by law, improved, destroyed, prostituted, or glorified," Thurman thought of freedom "as a quality of being" that "cannot be given and cannot be taken away" (270–71).

[14] Davis, "Lectures," 49.

Thurman was distraught by a similarly strange, albeit all-too-familiar, set of misconceptions—for example, "to function without limitations" and "to do what one wants with hindrance"—concerning the meaning and significance of personal freedom.[15] Both he and Davis emphasized the dialectical somersaults by which unfreedom was transformed into freedom, when "the roles were reversed." In her reading of Frederick Douglass's *Narrative*, Davis writes,

> The slave experiences the freedom of the master in its true light. He understands that the master's freedom is abstract freedom to suppress other human beings. The slave understands that this is a pseudo concept of freedom and at this point is more enlightened than his master for he realizes that the master is a slave of his own misconceptions, his own misdeeds, his own brutality, his own efforts to oppress.[16]

As a critical corrective to this "medley of confusion" apropos of personal freedom, Thurman sought to transform abstract ideas of freedom and essentialist definitions into a sensitive examination of the concrete struggles for freedom qua liberation among what he called "the disinherited."

Angela Davis encourages us to explore "the idea of freedom as it unfolded in the literary understanding of Black people" because "Black people have exposed, by their very experience, the inadequacies not only of the practice of freedom, but of its very theoretical formulation."[17] As a methodological corrective and a hermeneutical principle, Davis would have us read Hegel and Marx on freedom alongside Frederick Douglass as an illustration of "a physical voyage from slavery to freedom that is both the conclusion and reflection of a philosophical voyage from slavery to freedom."[18] For Davis, "Douglass existentially experiences what Marx theoretically formulates."[19] Similarly, the "struggle for recognition" of the so-called master-slave dialectic in Hegel should be read in tandem with Douglass's own account of his struggle with Edward Covey[20] if not also Fanon's chapter titled "Hegel and Recognition" in *Black Skin, White Masks*.[21] The nature of human freedom is disclosed within the struggle against

---

[15] HT, SF, 99.
[16] Ibid., 59.
[17] Ibid., 46.
[18] Ibid., 49.
[19] Ibid., 71.
[20] Edward Covey (1806–1875) was the notorious slave breaker and Douglass's nemesis in the *Narrative of the Life of Frederick Douglass*.
[21] Frantz Fanon, *Black Skin, White Masks*, trans. Richard Philcox (New York: Grove Press, 2008).

brutal forms of unfreedom. Anticipating this hermeneutical principle in Davis, several of Thurman's earliest publications focused on the emancipatory genius of the Negro spirituals.

The Melody of Freedom and Sorrow Songs

In *Deep River* (1945) and *The Negro Spiritual Speaks of Life and Death* (1947), Thurman explores a "reservoir of spiritual creativity and renewal" as well as "the ground of hope and self-respect in the idiom of the Spirituals."[22] In his foreword to *The Negro Spiritual*, "On Viewing the Coast of Africa," Thurman asks readers to consider the brutal forms of unfreedom experienced by those subjected to the infamous Middle Passage: "How does the human spirit accommodate itself to desolation? What tools of the spirit were in their hands with which to cut a path through the wilderness of their despair?"[23] Thurman was convinced that focusing on the slave's experience of unfreedom was crucial to understanding freedom construed as a sustained struggle for personal and collective liberation. He believed it was "important to examine what this literature revealed concerning the attitude toward death" from the standpoint of those who were confronted with death and violence. For Thurman, "the clue to the meaning of the spirituals is found in religious experience and spiritual discernment."[24] What he discovers in the spirituals, and what his ancestors discovered there, and what they wished to transmit to all their children, among other life lessons, was that "the bitter contradictions of life are not final, and that hope was built into the fabric of the struggle."[25]

Thurman believed that "the existence of these songs is in itself a monument to one of the most striking instances on record in which a people forged a weapon of offense and defense out of psychological shackles."[26] The "secret" of those who survived enslavement and the Middle Passage was that the ancestors "were unwilling to scale down the horizon of their demands to the level of their existential circumstances." When writing the preface to the revised edition of *Deep River and The Negro Spiritual Speaks of Life and Death*, Thurman suggested in retrospect—twenty years later—that the curious clues and salvific secrets contained within these "sorrow songs"[27] could, if only we would listen, provide what was needed to "redeem the times." *Deep River* and *The Negro Spiritual* provided an

---

[22] HT, *The Negro Spirituals*, 103.
[23] Ibid., 105.
[24] Ibid., 111.
[25] Ibid., 103.
[26] *Deep River and The Negro Spiritual Speaks of Life and Death* (Richmond, IN: Friends United Press, 1975), 39–40.
[27] Ibid., 31.

entire generation of freedom activists with a "powerful balm," and indeed "a timeless reservoir of spiritual creativity and renewal." Throughout his life, Thurman wrote for those "who needed profound succor and strength to enable them to live in the present with dignity and creativity."[28]

For Thurman, "meaning is inherent in life." The meaning that enslaved ancestors sought in life and the significance they found in death transcended the vicissitudes of their dire circumstances. Thurman draws our attention to "a strange moment"—when, in the hull of the slave ships, "stripped of all supports of life save the beating of the heart and the ebb and flow of the fetid air in the lungs," his ancestors discovered "some intimation from the future" and a "hint of promise."[29] He asks, "In the darkness did you hear the silent feet of your children beating a melody of freedom to words you would never know, in a land in which your bones would be warmed again in the depths of the cold earth in which you will sleep unknown, unrealized and alone?"[30]

The "melody of freedom" is intrinsic to all living creatures, thought Thurman, and this constitutes a crucial clue to personal freedom. The discovery of divinity, or the voice of the divine, bestows ultimate dignity. "In God's presence, at least, there would be freedom."[31] But where there is choice and a sense of alternatives, even "to be or not to be," Thurman would insist that there is a modicum of freedom. Thurman was convinced that "the silent feet of [their] children" provided hope to those engulfed in a hopeless situation. Despite the dehumanizing conditions to which the enslaved or otherwise disinherited were subjected, the spirituals affirmed "the ultimate dignity of the human spirit" and "the ultimate basis of self-respect."[32] And it was out of this crucible of the soul that the enslaved ancestors sought and found "the spark of the divine" that "rekindled the few expiring embers of freedom." Thurman insists that personal freedom was a distinct possibility despite the forms of unfreedom to which the enslaved ancestors were subjected. "Daring to believe that God cared for them despite the cruel vicissitudes of life meant giving of wings to life that nothing could destroy. This is a basic affirmation of all high religion."[33]

In his examination of the spirituals, Thurman focused on aspects of freedom or liberation as they arose from within what Davis calls the "dynamics of a real situation in which a slave meets his death in a fight for concrete freedom" rather than a concept of freedom deduced from "an abstract context."

---

[28] HT, *Jesus and the Disinherited* (Boston: Beacon Press, 1996), 11.
[29] HT, *The Negro Spiritual*, 106.
[30] Ibid.
[31] HT, *Deep River*, 48.
[32] HT, *The Negro Spiritual*, 113.
[33] HT, *Deep River*, 21.

In the struggle for freedom as expressed in the spirituals, Thurman explains how certain sorrow songs transmit the deep insight that "death was not regarded as life's worst offering":

> *Oh Freedom! Oh Freedom!*
> *Oh Freedom, I love thee!*
> *And before I'll be a slave,*
> *I'll be buried in my grave,*
> *And go home to my Lord and be free.*

He suggests that this refrain and others like it within the genre were "something more than a mere counsel of suicide."[34] The difference between "slavery or suicide" and "slavery or liberation at all costs" is also important to Davis's account of freedom.[35] Thurman disparaged the fact that "freedom from slavery and the freedom from life were often synonymous." Scattered throughout the genre, he finds that "there is always the growing edge of hope in the midst of the most barren and most tragic circumstances."[36]

Thurman would have us understand hope as an ultimate and abiding element of human life. But hope of this sort is not at all like "whistling in the dark," he says, nor is it "a shallow optimism covering a stark fear and panic."[37] Rather, it is a reliable guide and resource of renewal inherent in all human life. He was always seeking sources of "inspiration and courage in the spiritual insights that had provided a windbreak for our forefathers against the brutalities of slavery and the establishing of a ground of hope undimmed by the contradictions which held them in tight embrace."[38] Thurman recognizes that some will view hope and optimism as a mere defense mechanism, but he argues that "there would have been no survival in this philosophy for the Negro if it were merely a mechanism of sheer defense."[39] And while it may be true that hope, like religion itself, can sometimes seem otherworldly if not altogether counterrevolutionary, he believed that religion at its best provided just such a "windbreak"

---

[34] HT, *The Negro Spiritual*, 113, 32–34.

[35] In her analysis of freedom in "Lectures on Liberation," Davis comments on "one of the more notorious statements" and "extreme" assertions made by Sartre, viz., "that even the man in chains remains free" because "he is always at liberty to eliminate his condition of slave even if this means death." Davis dismisses Sartre's pseudo definition of freedom by removing it from "an abstract context" and examining instead, e.g., in the case of Douglass, "dynamics of a real situation in which a slave meets his death in the fight for concrete freedom" ("Lectures," 48).

[36] HT, *Deep River*, 64.

[37] Ibid., 93.

[38] Ibid., 5.

[39] Ibid., 63.

and "ground of hope." In his autobiography, *With Head and Heart*, he writes of the Fellowship Church,

> There are times when guidance as to techniques and strategy is urgent, when counsel, support, and collective direct action are mandatory. But there can never be a substitute for taking personal responsibility for social change. The word "personal" applies both to the individual and the organization—in this instance, the church. The true genius of the church was revealed by what it symbolized as a beachhead in our society in terms of community, and as an inspiration to the solitary individual to put his weight on the side of a society in which no man need be afraid.[40]

Rather than relegating religion to the opium of the masses, as a means of psychological escape, which is the Marxian depiction Davis explores in "Lectures on Liberation," Thurman—not unlike Douglass and Nat Turner or John Brown—understood Christianity, or the religion of Jesus, as reinforcing the equality of all persons before God. And while Davis "concur[s] with Marx that one must overcome religion in order to regain one's reason," she also concedes that "resistance was a lesson learned from the Bible":

> On this road to freedom, Frederick Douglass experiences religion as a reinforcement and justification for his desire to be free. Out of the Christian doctrine, he deduces the equality of all men before God. If this be true, he infers, then slave-masters must be defying God by suppressing the will of human beings and should be dealt with in accordance with God's anger. Freedom, the abolition of slavery, liberation, the destruction of alienation—these notions receive a metaphysical justification and impetus through religion.[41]

Thurman claims that "it was dangerous to let the slave understand that the life and teachings of Jesus meant freedom for the captive and release for those held in economic, social, and political chains."[42] Davis would view Thurman as one of those freedom fighters who, like Douglass and Nat Turner as well as Demark Vesey and Sojourner Truth, "turned Christianity against the missionaries."[43] In her own reflections on whether it is "possible for a man to be in chains and at the same time free," Davis claims that the "first phase of libera-

---

[40] HT, WHAH, 161.
[41] Davis, "Lectures," 72–73, 63, 59.
[42] HT, *Deep River*, 20.
[43] Davis, "Lectures," 63.

tion" consists in acts of resistance on all fronts, physical as well as psychological, both outward and inward, from violent resistance to the rejection of "the image of himself that the slave-owner has painted."[44] For both Davis and Thurman, "the problem of freedom leads us directly into the question of identity."[45]

Freedom and Identity

Thurman's philosophy of freedom includes his account of wholeness and actualized potential. As an identity theorist, he believed that the transformation from unfreedom to freedom was expressed in moments of individuation or self-determination. He was fascinated with transformative experiences that integrated the fragmented if not also conflicting aspects of one's personality. As illustrated in the case of Legion,[46] we become genuinely free when we are liberated from a crisis of multiple identities. And while Legion is an extreme case, Thurman claims, "It is a commonplace that each of us seems to have many selves"; at the very least, each and all of us are confronted with "so many claims and counterclaims that to honor the true self is not easy."[47] While the many voices that ran riot over Legion were harmonized or tamed by the sound of the genuine in the person of Jesus, Thurman thought it was possible for each of us to hear the "sound of the genuine" within ourselves, which, he added, "is the only guide we will ever have."[48] Legion could hear the voice of the genuine in himself because he heard the voice of the genuine in Jesus.[49]

Thurman tells a local version of the Legion story, the case of Ma Walker, back in Daytona Beach.[50] What the voice of the genuine in Jesus, or Ma Walker, accomplished was "to introduce harmony into another's life by sensing and honoring the need to be cared for and therefore understood." The liberation of Legion, similar to the prodigal son, is captured in that moment when "he came to himself."[51] Thurman adds, "Again and again, the testimony is that a man

---

[44] Ibid., 53.

[45] Ibid.

[46] See biblical references to Legion: Matthew 8:28–34, Mark 5:1–20, and Luke 8:26–39.

[47] HT, *Disciplines of the Spirit*, 26, 27. Thurman in 1977 uses Legion as an example of listening for the sound of the genuine; see PHWT 5:284. Also see *Sermons on the Parables*, ed. with an introduction by David Gowler and Kipton Jensen (Maryknoll, NY: Orbis Books, 2018), 30ff.

[48] HT, "The Sound of the Genuine: Baccalaureate Address, Spelman College, May 4, 1980," *Spelman Messenger* 96, no. 4 (Summer 1980).

[49] HT, *Disciplines of the Spirit*, 27.

[50] Ibid., 107.

[51] HT, *Sermons on the Parables*, 30.

did not know that he had been fragmented until he became whole."[52] Indeed, experiences of this sort are "infinitely more miraculous than walking on the water or turning water into wine."[53] Like Augustine,[54] Thurman often explained freedom in terms of surrendering of one's head and heart to God. In the *Inward Journey*, Thurman says that "there can be no personal freedom where there is not an initial personal surrender" that orders, organizes, and empowers.[55] He was interested in the "politics of conversion," borrowing a phrase from Cornel West, one that Walter Earl Fluker applies to Thurman,[56] and the psychosocial or spiritual process by which one becomes "a living 'for-instance' of the cause to which he or she is loyal." And while he sometimes described loyalty as "a willing and thoroughgoing devotion of the person to a cause," Thurman would also insist that "our loyalty to the individual is derivative because the thing that is primary is my devotion to the tie that unites me to you and you and you and you."[57] On this model of freedom, Thurman aims to convince us that "we were made for one another."[58]

When an individual surrenders his or her will—construed as the "nerve center of consent"—to a cause, Thurman thought that "the cause then gives him back his will in order that he might put at the disposal of the cause all that he is, worthily or unworthily."[59] Individuation qua internal integration could sometimes consist in expressions of sincere loyalty or devotion to some communal cause—for example, the beloved community. "Commitment means that it is possible for a man to yield the nerve center of his consent to a purpose or a cause, a movement or an ideal, which may be more important to him than whether he lives or dies." In *Luminous Darkness*, he put it this way:

---

[52] HT, *Disciplines of the Spirit*, 29.

[53] Ibid.

[54] In *Deep River*, Thurman plaits these strands of influence on his thought:

"Thou has made us for thyself, and our souls are restless till they find their rest in thee," says Augustine. Life is like a river:

Deep River, my home is over Jordan—
Deep River, I want to cross over into campground. (78)

[55] In more philosophical and less religious terms one could describe Thurman as a "deep-self compatibilist" (see Kipton Jensen, *Howard Thurman: Philosophy, Civil Rights, and the Search for Common Ground* [Columbia: University of South Carolina Press, 2019], 81–85).

[56] Walter Earl Fluker, "The Politics of Conversion and the Civilization of Friday," in *Courage to Hope: From Black Suffering to Human Redemption* (Boston: Beacon Press, 1999), 103ff.

[57] HT, "The Meaning of the Philosophy of Loyalty," 1951A (audio).

[58] HT, *Common Ground*, 104.

[59] HT, "The Meaning of the Philosophy of Loyalty."

A strange and wonderful courage often comes into a man's life when he shares a commitment to something that is more important than whether he lives or dies. It is the discovery of the dynamic character of life itself. This may not be a conscious act as far as the rationale for it is concerned. It is a discovery of the conditions that generate fresh resources of energy.[60]

In the context of his analysis of the "structure-functional integrity" of living organisms, Thurman argues that "the intent [of life] is for integration, for wholeness, for community within the limits of the organism itself."[61] Following this fractal logic, he educes that "it is not unreasonable, then, to assume that as he seeks community within himself, with his fellows, and with his world, he may find that what he is seeking to do deliberately is but the logic of the meaning of all that has gone into his own creation."[62] According to Luther Smith, "Thurman not only ties integration to the demands of the love-ethic, but to the self-interest impulses of the personality. The self can only find fulfillment in a loving community, and a loving community is only possible when the individual selves are given the opportunity for their fullest possible nurture and expression."[63]

The connection between the search for community and the intent of God is expressed succinctly in an unpublished sermon titled "Freedom,"[64] which was part of his sermon series titled "The Religion of Jesus" at Marsh Chapel in Boston. Thurman preached,

> Now if the will to community is the purpose of God, as Jesus felt, then community becomes a necessity of history. If an individual is faced finally with necessity, then this means that he is no longer free to reject it. But if he rejects this intent of community, the rejection, since it is part of the necessity of history, the rejection becomes self-defeating, frustrating, destructive. When a man then is faced with the necessity and he wishes to maintain the dignity of his freedom, what does he do? He makes the necessity a part of his deliberate intention. Then he becomes free.[65]

---

[60] HT, *Luminous Darkness* (New York: Harper & Row, 1965), 58, 8, 106–7; see also HT, *Jesus and the Disinherited*, 75.

[61] HT, SCG, 39.

[62] Ibid., 41.

[63] Luther Smith, *Howard Thurman: The Mystic as Prophet* (Richmond, IN: Friends United Press, 1992), 128.

[64] HT, "The Religion of Jesus: Freedom" (1965); also see "Quest of Freedom" (1962), "Meaning of Human Freedom" (1962), and "What Do I Believe In?" (1973) in PHWT 5.

[65] HT, "The Religion of Jesus: Freedom." Thurman finds precedent for this insight in

The disciplines of the spirit could also be described as a set of techniques, if not "clinical procedures of analysis," aimed at "helping the individual to find his core" and "an authentic sense of self."[66] The search for authentic and unified self—what Angela Davis calls "the destruction of the alienated self"—is not for the faint of heart. And the process by which one recovers from an inauthentic identity, or from no real sense of self at all, is demanding because it "cannot be separated from the discipline of religious experience."

> In religious experience a man has a sense of being touched at his inmost center, at his very core, and this awareness sets in motion the process that makes for his integration, his wholeness. It is as if he saw into himself, beyond all his fragmentation, conflicts, divisiveness.[67]

"A sense of self is achieved, even in its most elementary aspect," Thurman adds, "by an arduous process."[68] But the result of not seeking one's authentic self, which is also an option he considers, is also foreboding: "when it comes time to die," wrote Thoreau, "let us not discover that we have never lived." Thurman believed that "if you cannot hear the sound of the genuine in you, you will all of your life spend your days on the ends of strings that somebody else pulls."[69]

He experimented throughout his life with various methods of readying the mind and calming the emotions for the purpose of "lending a listening ear" to the "sound of the genuine." This process of individuation and dynamic integration of personal identity can happen in a broad spectrum of ways: for example, in acts and rituals of commitment, in experiences of conversion, through prayer or meditation, amid suffering or experiences of unity, and "the gift of reconciliation."[70]

Thomistic thought, to be sure, but he was also familiar with Spinoza's pantheistic deduction "that thing is said to be free which exists solely from the necessity of its own nature." *The Essential Spinoza: Ethics and Related Writings*, ed. Michael Morgan (Indianapolis: Hackett, 2006), 290–91.

[66] HT, *Disciplines of the Spirit*, 29.
[67] Ibid., 121.
[68] Ibid., 30.
[69] HT, "The Sound of the Genuine"; Kierkegaard makes a similar point: "For he who is not himself a unity is never really anything wholly and decisively; he only exists in an external sense—as long as he lives as a numeral within a crowd, a fraction within the earthly conglomeration." Søren Kierkegaard, *Purity of Heart Is to Will One Thing* (New York: Harper & Row, 1956), 45.
[70] Thurman believed that "life contains its own restraints" and that the logic of hatred, e.g., is ultimately self-destructive and unsustainable because it is against life. "A man's horizon may become so completely dominated by the intense character of his hatred that there remains no creative residue in his mind and spirt to give to great ideas, to great concepts. He becomes lopsided. To use a phrase from Zarathustra, he becomes 'a cripple in reverse'" (*Jesus and the Disinherited*, 88).

Whether discussing the internal integration of the personality or the dynamic integration of communities, Thurman thinks that "integration means to unify, to combine, to become whole, to become one."[71]

The struggle for freedom constitutes "a core of discipline and an inner structure." In *Disciplines of the Spirit*, Thurman explores various ways of deepening commitment and restoring hope. In his discussion of prayer and meditation, he says that "the true purpose of all spiritual disciplines is to clear away whatever may block our awareness of that which is God in us."[72] As variations on the theme of commitment, he shows how prayer, or "centering moments" of other types, serve to focus the mind and emotions in ways that "enhance personal communion" and "get rid of whatever may so distract the mind and encumber" the "hunger of the heart." The hunger of the heart is the clue, because "the hunger itself is God," and "prayer is the means by which this clue is pursued."[73]

Like commitment and prayer, suffering is also understood as a spiritual discipline. "Whether one is dealing with sheer physical pain or the more complex aspects of other dimensions of suffering," Thurman notices that pain and suffering necessitate a "turning inward" that "approximates total attention" and a "focusing of the energies of life at a single point."[74] And without trying to explain away or otherwise dismiss the jolting reality of death or pain and suffering, he observed that "there is a fellowship of suffering" and describes how suffering "can be instrumental in shaping community."[75] In *Luminous Darkness*, he writes, "the degree to which [one's] suffering is shared by others marks the potential that such suffering may itself become redemptive."[76] As the culminating chapter of *Disciplines of the Spirit*, he argues that the work of reconciliation is itself a doubly difficult discipline of the spirit because it presupposes each of the preceding phases of the program: "Here again the reconciliation must go on in a man's spirit before he can be at one with the technique of nonviolence which he employs as an instrument for social change."[77]

---

[71] HT, PHWT 5:154.

[72] HT, *Disciplines of the Spirit*, 96.

[73] Ibid., 87, 95. HT, *The Way of the Mystics*, Walking With God: The Howard Thurman Sermon Series, vol. 2, ed. Peter E. Eisenstadt and Walter Earl Fluker (Maryknoll, NY: Orbis Books, 2022), 34, 82.

[74] HT, *Disciplines of the Spirit*, 74.

[75] Ibid., 60–61.

[76] HT, *Luminous Darkness*, 55. Neither Thurman nor King believed that *all* suffering was redemptive. Rufus Burrow puts it this way: "According to King, unearned suffering must be made to be redemptive by sustained and determined nonviolent struggle against it" (Rufus Burrow, *Martin Luther King Jr. and the Theology of Resistance* [Jefferson, NC: McFarland, 2015], 133).

[77] HT, *Disciplines of the Spirit*, 117; see also 104–27.

Thurman often focused on the pernicious because contagious and destructive attitudes distort the personality and thus "render healthy human relations impossible." He explores the inner logic by which the personality is crippled by fear and deception or hatred and violence, but he was also more than eager to discover individual behaviors and social arrangements that nurture growth and optimize potential. He had a "contagion of attitudes"[78] theory that explained how fear and hatred as well as deception can spread as if by contagion and how the power of love could serve as a vaccination or antidote. He believed that hatred, especially, but also fear and deception, could render us "cripples in reverse."[79] In *God and Human Freedom*, a Festschrift in honor of Thurman, Carlyle Felding Stewart III wrote, "Neither individuals nor communities as solemn collectives can experience complete freedom as long as they are prisoners of fear, held hostage in a mosaic of crippling social dogmas which stifle their ability to be."[80] "Ultimately," writes Thurman himself in 1955, "freedom means the ability to actualize potentials."[81]

He argues that "the experience of community, or realized potential, is rooted in life itself because the intuitive human urge for community reflects a characteristic of all life." We can become alienated and diminished in other ways too, of course, both early and late in identity formation. Thurman muses that perhaps it "might not seem too far-fetched to examine a person's need to be loved, to be understood, to be cared for, as the essential building blocks for the actualizing of his potential and the essential stuff of community."[82] Similar to Gandhi, he believes that the power of love—whether construed as ahimsa or agape—provides the clue as well as the vital resources requisite to breaking down barriers that separate us from one another. The restoration of an authentic or nonalienated identity serves to revitalize the individual and generate a reservoir of conatic energy analogous to the power of ahimsa or "soul-force" in Gandhi's philosophy of satyagraha. "At the center of non-violence is a force which is self-acting," Gandhi claimed, "a force more positive than electricity."[83]

Angela Davis also observes that "alienation," whether in the case of Douglass or Covey, "has the effect of sapping whatever physical strength he may have

---

[78] HT, *Strange Freedom*, 301; see also *The Inward Journey: Meditations on a Spiritual Quest* (New York: Harper & Row, 1961), 42.

[79] HT, *Jesus and the Disinherited*, 88; cf. Nietzsche, *Thus Spoke Zarathustra* §42.

[80] Carlyle Felding Steward III, "The Realization of Oneness," in *God and Human Freedom: A Festschrift in Honor of Howard Thurman*, ed. Henry J. Young (Richmond, IN: Friends United Press, 1983), 117.

[81] HT, PHWT 4:117.

[82] HT, SCG, 80, 127.

[83] See Quinton Dixie and Peter Eisenstadt, *Visions of a Better World* (Boston: Beacon Press, 2011), 104.

needed in order to win the battle."[84] The initial phase of the struggle for freedom in India included what Gandhi called the "constructive preparation programme," which aimed at restoring spiritual and physical vitality to the disinherited.[85] Thurman experimented throughout his life with various "constructive" or "preparatory" programs and psychosocial methods by which to restore human dignity and spiritual vitality as well as fostering courage and commitment.

Freedom and Mutual Recognition

> It is a strange freedom to be adrift in the world of men without a sense of anchor anywhere. Always there is the need of mooring, the need for a firm grip on something that is rooted and will not give.... The very spirit of man tends to panic from the desolation of going nameless up and down the streets of other minds where no salutation greets, and no friendly recognition makes secure. It is a strange freedom to be adrift in the world of men.[86]

"The American Dream, it seems to me," wrote Thurman, "is a dream of equality, justice, and freedom."[87] He understood that there were two basic interpretations of the American Dream, one of which constitutes a "cult of inequality."[88] He formulates the disjunction this way: "Either liberty has to do with the total life of man and it is inclusive of all men, or it is a prerogative of a 'cult of inequality.'"[89] The dream of equality, on the other hand, involves "the kind of equality that places a significance upon the infinite estimate that the individual places upon himself and this infinite estimate is constantly being transformed into terms that express social worth."[90] Thurman understood all too well that "it is a strange freedom to be adrift in the world of men without a sense of anchor anywhere," as he put it in 1961, and he all too often felt the demoral-

---

[84] HT, SCG, 83.
[85] HT, 1961. In a 1943 letter to James Farmer, Thurman recalled Gandhi's observation that civil disobedience broke down in India because "the masses of the people were not able to sustain so lofty a creative idea over a time interval of sufficient duration to be practically effective. They were unable so to do, not because they lacked in courage or in unwillingness, but rather in vitality" (PHWT 2:328–29).
[86] As quoted in TH, SF, vii.
[87] HT, PHWT 5:218.
[88] Ibid.
[89] Ibid., 113.
[90] HT, PHWT 4:220. Whether we view humans as equally depraved or equally good, "whether we follow Calvin or Rousseau" (219), as Thurman put it, there is common ground for "democratic dogma and spiritual commitment" (220).

izing "desolation of going nameless up and down the streets of other minds where no salutation greets, and no friendly recognition makes secure." Segregation and its equivalent social vices cripple individuals and entire communities, making us blind to one another.

Late in life, in 1980, his own eyesight failing him, Thurman recalled asking a friend who had gone blind after she was a grown woman about the "greatest disaster that [her] blindness brought [her]." The woman replied, "When I go places where there are people, I have a feeling that nobody knows that I'm here. I can't see any recognition, I can't see … and if nobody knows that I'm here, it's hard for me to know where I am.'" Thurman speculated that "there seems to be a built-in resistance in all human beings against the threat of isolation," which serves as a "major safeguard against the disintegration of the self, for we cannot abide being cut off."[91] He also believed that "the need for belonging, for being cared for," was "instinctive to life itself."[92]

It certainly is a strange if not bizarre freedom that consists in anonymity or unaccountability and irresponsibility. Some have come to conceive of freedom as a license to dominate and a liberty to exploit in a social conglomerate devoid of mutual recognition and human decency. Perhaps less strange is a form of personal and social freedom discovered at the growing edges of a community in which "it is not only reasonable but normal for men to be sharing their values, sharing their lives, sharing the living texture of their togetherness."[93] Thurman seems especially insightful when it comes to a series of "inside-outside dilemmas"[94] that distort the personality and damage the soul. In addition to many other conditions requisite to personal and social freedom, he wished to emphasize the "recognition of the continuing sense of belonging."[95] As a symbol of homeland, especially in the absence of a state religion, the sovereign state "formally defines an outsider and establishes rites and rituals for belonging."[96]

Thurman asserts, "Wherever citizens are denied the freedom of access to the resources that make for a sense of belonging, a sense of being totally dealt with, the environment closes in around them, resulting in the schizophrenic dilemma of being inside and outside at one and the same time. Or worse still, they are subject to the acute trauma of not knowing at any given moment whether they are outsiders or insiders."[97] Such is the terrifying fate of many minorities in America,

---

[91] HT, SCG, 82.
[92] Ibid., 83.
[93] HT, *The Growing Edge*, 57; HT, *SCG*, 88.
[94] Ibid., 84ff.; also PHWT 4:204.
[95] Ibid., 83.
[96] Ibid., 84.
[97] Ibid., 88.

he continues, and "all those ethnic strands that make up the so-called Third World."[98] Thurman also made this point in 1956: "There is an inner need that is a permanent part of our life and my life, for belonging, for feeling and knowing and being assured that we are included, as it were."[99] For Thurman, "the search for community on the part of the Afro-American minority within the larger American community reveals still another facet of the inside-outside dilemma."[100]

He thought that "the value judgment of infinite worth" served as both a "correlative of the conception of freedom" and "an authentic basis of equality."[101] Rather than an abstract idea of freedom deduced from an extended transcendental argument, or posited as a regulative ideal and a presupposition of responsibility, as in Kant, Thurman describes how the denial of freedom distorts the voice of conscience and weakens the bonds of socioethical obligation.[102] He reminds his readers that "the whole point of the attack on the evils of segregation for the individual, as well as the total society, is that the system renders healthy human relations impossible." Like Davis, he was interested in transforming "the idea of freedom into the struggle for liberation." This meant that personal freedom and social freedom both were best understood as a "release from the tyranny of succeeding intervals of events."[103] If the epitome of social unfreedom is loneliness and desolation, or similar forms of alienation, the ideal of social freedom is expressed in dynamic integration in the form of the beloved community.

Thurman argues that dynamic integration cannot be achieved "by any kind of mechanical arrangement of persons or rules or regulations."[104] He suggests that forms of token integration could inadvertently provide "protection to the pattern of segregation."[105] He is also careful to distinguish conformity and togetherness from harmony or uniformity.[106] Beyond the "legal aspect of integra-

---

[98] Ibid.
[99] Ibid., 65; also see *Jesus and the Disinherited*, 24; *Luminous Darkness*, 28.
[100] HT, SCG, 89.
[101] HT, PHWT 4:115.
[102] HT, *Luminous Darkness*, 5: "The common saying in my world was: the white man did not have religion. By implication, we did. That kept me from expecting him to act toward me as I would expect a fellow Christian to act, but curiously enough my religion did not demand of me that I act toward him as a Christian should act. At the risk of being repetitious, he was not regarded as worthy of a Christian response. It was a cruel dilemma; the price paid for a kind of inner balance that would make for some measure of peace of mind was the rigid narrowing or restricting of the Christian ethic. The struggle was to try to achieve a sense of self in a total environment that threatened the self."
[103] HT, SF, 67.
[104] HT, PHWT 5:154.
[105] Ibid.
[106] HT, *Inward Journey*, 110: "We have made an idol of togetherness. It is the watchword

tion," he emphasizes a "second meaning of integration that has to do with the quality of human relations." The social harmony that Thurman has in mind is one that "transcends all diversities and in which diversity finds its richness and significance."

Back in 1966, Thurman wrote, "What is being sought is a way of life that is worth living and a faith in oneself, in others, and the society that can be honestly and intelligently sustained. This is what the beloved community is all about."[107] He continued,

> That which makes any community become the beloved community is created by the quality of the human relations experienced by the people who live within it. The term itself is an abstraction and becomes concrete in a given time and place in the midst of living human beings. It cannot be brought into being by fiat or by order; it is an achievement of the human spirit as men seek to fulfill their high destiny as children of God.[108]

Thurman insists, "If love is not operative, then community is impossible." And in *The Search for Common Ground* he claims that "community cannot for long feed on itself, it can only flourish with the coming of others from beyond, their unknown and undiscovered brothers and sisters."[109]

Conclusion: Seeking and Finding

The philosophical dimension in Thurman's thought often consists more in the seeking than in finding. He brooded over an astonishingly broad spectrum of philosophical problems and strange paradoxes. His thought evolved constantly, incrementally, sometimes by leaps and bounds. When assessing his earlier writings, for example, in *Creative Encounter,* he self-deprecatingly wrote that he discovered "many indications of seeking but perhaps little evidence of finding." But there is no denying that his *Disciplines of the Spirit* and *Search for Common Ground* provided ample evidence of philosophical insight and spiritual discovery. Ultimately, Thurman would say in *Inward Journey* that "seeking and finding are

---

of our times; it is more and more a substitute for God. In the great huddle we are desolate, lonely, and afraid. Our shoulders touch but our hearts cry out for understanding without which there can be no life and no meaning."

[107] HT, "Desegregation, Integration and the Beloved Community," *in Benjamin Elijah Mays: His Life, Contributions, and Legacy,* ed. Samuel D. Cook (1966; repr., Franklin, TN: Providence House, 2009), 205; also, in PHWT 5:155.

[108] HT, "Desegregation," 206; PHWT 5:155–56.

[109] HT, SCG, 104.

so united that failure and frustration, real though they are, are no longer felt to be ultimately real."[110]

There are many strands to Thurman's philosophy of freedom, and there is also the unique way he plaits them together into a whole. What I have sought in him is a tutor and guide. I believe that he would want us to interpret him in "our own idiom," seriously yet creatively, and according to "the grain of our own wood." There remains so much to be learned from him about personal freedom and sociopolitical liberation. Thurman provides an encouraging word that those who seek community are "not going against life but will be sustained and supported by life."[111] He understood that arguments in defense of integration and nonviolence can sometimes seem naïve if not counterrevolutionary. He certainly understood James Baldwin's penetrating point about "integrating into a burning house."[112]

Thurman's spiritual disciplines and centering moments were designed to facilitate "spiritual awareness and insight" into the "underlying unity of all life." He was always on the hunt—throughout his life—for those emancipatory or otherwise liberating experiences of unity and shared identity.[113] Human dignity and self-respect as well as hope and courage were essential and powerful tools in the struggle for freedom. We should read Thurman for a better "understanding of the conditions of oppression and the possibility of abolishing these conditions" and a vital resource for contemporary struggles for freedom qua "liberation from the urgent problems of poverty, economic necessity and indoctrination [as well as] mental health."[114] He encourages us to work together with our "unknown and undiscovered brothers" and sisters struggling—collectively and creatively as well as constantly and courageously at "growing edges of social concern"[115]—to accomplish "the far-flung purpose of God to establish a world community of friendly men living beneath friendly skies."[116]

---

[110] HT, *Inward Journey*, 112.

[111] HT, SCG, 6.

[112] James Baldwin, *The Fire Next Time* (1962; repr., New York: Vantage International, 1993), 94.

[113] Albert J. Raboteau, "In Search of Common Ground: Howard Thurman and Religious Community," *Sociology of Religion* 64, no. 2 (2002): 158.

[114] Davis, "Lectures," 66.

[115] HT, *Luminous Darkness*, 16.

[116] HT, PHWT 4:117.

14

Creating and Cultivating Democratic Spaces

Reflections on Howard Thurman and Democracy

Walter Earl Fluker

At this precarious moment in democratic life and practices—in which we are witnessing the ravages of war, the brutality of state violence, and the horrendous efforts to restrict and confine spaces of dissent and free speech—we are challenged with what Martin Luther King Jr. called "the urgency of now."[1] This essay is a constructive and practical reflection on the ways Howard Thurman envisioned the contemplative life and its implications for creating and sustaining what I shall call "democratic space." In the following I provide a definition of democratic space and demonstrate how Thurman's understanding of preparation, Presence, and practice provide "tools of the spirit" to challenge and transform contested democratic spaces for subjugated bodies of marginalized peoples.[2]

Democratic Space

"Democratic space" refers to the ongoing struggle against *miscounting*, the reconfiguration of space and reordering of time for colonized bodies. This idea is represented in political philosopher Jacques Rancière's notion of *policing* as "the rule that governs the body's appearing, a configuration of *occupations* and properties of the spaces where these *occupations* are distributed." *Politics*, on the other

---

[1] Martin Luther King Jr., "I Have a Dream," speech presented at the March on Washington for Jobs and Freedom, Washington, DC, August 28, 1963, https://www.marshall.edu/onemarshallu/i-have-a-dream/.

[2] Portions of this essay were first delivered as part 1 of my lectures as Visiting Distinguished Professor, McDonald Lecture Series, Candler School of Theology, "Walking with God: Preparation, Presence and Practice," October 23, 2018, https://vimeo.com/298387811.

hand, is "an extremely determined activity antagonistic to *policing*" because it is human activity that turns on equality as its principle or basic presupposition.[3] In this sense, democracy concerns the struggle for the redefinition of the distribution of certain shares or spaces among certain groups whom Rancière calls "that of the part of those who have no part." Here the concern is with the *demos* (common people) who are not accounted for in the configuration of power, those relegated to animal life with sound but who cannot speak. For Thurman, it means "to be ignored, to be passed over as of no account and of no meaning ... to be made into a faceless thing, not a man.... [It is] to act with no accounting, to go nameless up and down the streets of other minds where no salutation greets and no sign is given to mark the place one calls one's own."[4] Gayatri Chakravorty Spivak raised the question in this way: "Can the subaltern *speak*?"[5] Nonetheless, we know from recent movements like the pro-choice movement, Black Lives Matter, and Say Her Name that these bodies dare to speak and to break, shift, and redefine the spaces they have been assigned in "the house that race built."[6] And it is precisely because they dare to speak that they reveal the process of equality, because only a free human can speak.[7] Beyond the facility of speech as a mark of equality and freedom, I am also interested in the human capacity for "affective experiences, occurrences in the world, or aesthetic events"[8] that are not merely thought but are embodied and experienced in the sense of freedom and equality as profoundly imaginative and creative potentialities that point to newness, openness, expectation, fluidity, and expanding boundaries.

---

[3] Jacques Rancière, *Disagreement: Politics and Philosophy*, trans. Julie Rose (Minneapolis: University of Minnesota Press, 1999), ix; Erich Daniel Luna Jacobs, "The Ignorant Philosopher? On Jacques Rancière's Political Ontology," *VIII Congreso Latinoamericano de Ciencia Política*, 2015.

[4] HT, *The Inward Journey: Meditations on the Spiritual Quest* (Richmond: Friends United Press, 1961), 38.

[5] Gayatri Chakravorty Spivak, "Can the Subaltern Speak?," in *Marxism and the Interpretation of Culture*, ed. Cary Nelson and Lawrence Grossberg (London: Macmillan, 1988); see also Rosalind C. Morris, ed., *Can the Subaltern Speak?: Reflections on the History of an Idea* (New York: Columbia University Press, 2010).

[6] Waheema Lubiano, *The House That Race Built: Original Essays by Toni Morrison, Angela Y. Davis, Cornel West, and Others on Black Americans and Politics in America Today* (New York: Vintage, 1998).

[7] Rancière, *Disagreement*, 29–30. See Walter Earl Fluker, "Plenty Good Room: MLK's Vision of the World House and the Ethical Question of Global Citizenship," in *The Great World House in the Twenty-First Century: Reclaiming the Vision of Martin Luther King, Jr.*, ed. Vicki Crawford and Lewis V. Baldwin (Athens: University of Georgia Press, 2018).

[8] Charles E. Scott, "The Betrayal of Democratic Space," *Journal of Speculative Philosophy* 22, no. 4 (2008): 304; Fluker, "Plenty Good Room," 142.

Thurman on the Integrity and Power of Free Speech

In a meditation on his favorite scripture, Psalm 139, "Thou Knowest It All Together" (1960), Thurman speaks to the integrity, power, and sacramentality of speech—the power of the word not only to convey meaning but as a defiant act of resistance, courage, justice, and compassion that counteracts fear and the other hounds of hell: deception and hatred. He argues that the integrity of our speech and actions are meant

> To domesticate the word. To safeguard its character. To purge the violence from its face. To allow no service that defiles, degrades. To make it one with truth, to fill it with the pure intent. This is to make the word the sacrament, the Angelus of God. This is the breath of life that makes man, man. For there is not a word in my tongue, but lo, thou knowest it all together.... There is no miracle greater than the miracle of human speech. Think of it. Out of all the various sounds that one hears in the world, certain sounds have been limited, proscribed, given a certain shape and form, in order to convey meaning. Something that is invisible, something that is soundless, so that when a certain sound meets the ear, this sound conveys to the mind the intent of the person who uses the sound, who makes the noise, so that the integrity of the maker of the sound is at stake in the content which he gives to the words which he uses. Words are the gifts of God to man for communication. There is the quality and a meaning and a history that words—all of them—carry. And it is against the background of the use of a word that the meaning of a word is conveyed to the hearer at the time that the word is spoken.[9]

For Thurman, the integrity and power of the spoken word challenge and disrupt not only discourse and practices that sustain privilege and position, but the veritable *habitus* that guards and hides in silence, the unacknowledged "value gap" that masquerades as normative and moral.[10] He often quoted from Petrarch's "Letters of Old Age":

---

[9] HT, "Thou Knowest It All Together, 1960," Pitts Theological Library, Emory University, Howard Thurman Digital Archive. See also HT, *The Inward Journey*, 144–45.

[10] Pierre Bourdieu, *The Logic of Practice* (1980; repr., Stanford, CA: Stanford University Press, 1990), 91n. See also Eddie S. Glaude's discussion of the "American idea": that spurious, abstract claim that denies the congenital condition of race in American conceptions of democracy, founded on what he calls "the value gap," which is fundamentally the belief that white people are more valuable than others, which I am arguing is a product of this *habitus* that Thurman seeks to disrupt. Eddie S. Glaude, *Democracy in Black: How Race Still Enslaves the American Soul* (New York: Crown, 2016), 29–50.

When a word must be spoken to further a good cause, and those whom it behooves to speak remain silent, anybody ought to raise his voice, and break the silence fraught with evil.... Many a time a few simple words have helped further the welfare of the nation, no matter who uttered them; the voice itself displaying the latent powers, sufficed to move the hearts of men.[11]

Unlike Rancière's definition of politics, Thurman's imaginative theo-political project seeks something akin to *parousia (παρουσία)*—arrival—the coming to itself of embodied presence that denotes expectation, advent, and celebration and extends into political speech as "a perilous traversing of the limits."[12] Thurman, in wedding spirituality and social transformation, provides a way to construct possibilities for new spaces—democratic spaces—new times, and new rhythms for historically marginalized and despised bodies that counteract and counterpose the cultural productions of evil and the incarceration of bodies.[13]

Creating and Cultivating Democratic Space

Creating and cultivating democratic space for Thurman signaled something more than personal fulfillment and nurture of the individual's contemplative life. Instead, it spoke to the very fiber of democratic life and its promise embodied in the interrelated notions of the freedom and equality of dignity and worth. It also required the hard work of *preparation*, cultivating a sense of *Presence*, and engaging in *practices* that assured continued devotion and development of the

---

[11] From J. Lohse, ed., *Thoughts from the Letters of Petrarch* (London: J. M. Dent, 1901), 125. On the Italian humanist Francesco Petrarch (1304–1374), see "Senile," or "Letters of Old Age," book 7, letter 1; see also HT, "Zephaniah: Text, Exegesis, and Exposition," in *The Interpreter's Bible,* vol. 6 (New York: Abingdon, 1956) 1002, reprinted as "Exposition on Zephaniah," in *Walking with God: The Sermon Series of Howard Thurman, Moral Struggle and the Prophets,* vol. 1, ed. Peter Eisenstadt and Walter Earl Fluker (Maryknoll, NY: Orbis Books, 2020), 207–16; HT, *Deep Is the Hunger: Meditations for Apostles of Sensitiveness* (New York: Harper & Brothers, 1951); HT, *Meditations of the Heart* (New York: Harper & Row, 1953); and HT, *The Inward Journey,* 25.

[12] The idea of "arrival" or "coming to oneself" is a fascinating theme in HT that applies to the Divine Presence as well. See HT, "Mysticism and Social Change," July 12, 1978, Pacific School of Religion, in *Walking with God: The Sermon Series of Howard Thurman: The Way of the Mystics,* ed. Peter E. Eisenstadt and Walter Earl Fluker (Maryknoll, NY: Orbis Books, 2021), 121–40; see also Scott, "The Betrayal of Democratic Space," 304; Peter Fenves, "Foreword," in Jean-Luc Nancy, *The Experience of Freedom* (Stanford, CA: Stanford University Press, 1994), xx.

[13] emilie m. townes, *Womanist Ethics and the Cultural Production of Evil* (New York: Palgrave Macmillan, 2007).

inner life and worldly speech, affection, action, and faith in the possibility of democratic space. I would like the reader to imagine these interrelated moments as spiraling movements in what Thurman called "the fluid area of consent."[14]

"The fluid area of consent" refers to an interior dimension that makes available to those concerned about contested democratic spaces the resources to *live into* and *live out* a life characterized by a sense of the vital that extends into the larger orbit of the political world and our struggles for justice. Thurman called these ambassadors of democracy "apostles of sensitiveness" who dare to establish "a beachhead in our society in terms of community," and who serve as "an inspiration to the solitary individual to put his weight on the side of a society in which no man need be afraid."[15] He was insistent that people committed to social change and overcoming socially constructed boundaries make an inward journey to the creative and precarious encounter with the angel with the flaming sword that symbolizes our encounters with truth and the integrity of our actions. There, he argued, one discovers what is literal and irreducible in their being, an authentic and indivisible site of freedom, meaning, and belonging out of which they *speak* and *act* from a core of integrity and wholeness. It is also a source of knowledge, freedom, empathy, love, hope, and imagination that mark one's encounter with the Eternal.[16] The affective products of this creative encounter are also what Thurman called "tools of the spirit." In a moving, intimate meditation on his first experience of viewing the coast of West Africa, he writes,

> From my cabin window I look out on the full moon and the ghosts of my forefathers rise and fall with the undulating waves. Across these same waters, how many years ago they came. What were the inchoate mutterings locked tight within the circle of their hearts? In the deep, heavy darkness of the foul-smelling hole of the ship, where they could not see the sky nor hear the night noises nor feel the warm compassion of the

---

[14] HT, "The Inward Sea," in *Meditations of the Heart* (Richmond, IN: Friends United Press, 1976), 15. This fluid center is "the core of possibility, resilience, and resistance that will not yield even in the severest of circumstances, *le point le verge.*" See Walter Earl Fluker, *The Ground Has Shifted: The Future of the Black Church in Post-Racial America* (New York: New York University Press, 2016), 189; Thomas Merton, *Conjectures of a Guilty Bystander* (New York: Doubleday Religion, 1966), 155.

[15] HT, WHAH, 161.

[16] Walter Earl Fluker, "The Inward Sea: Mapping Interior Landmarks for Leaders," in *Anchored in the Current: The Eternal Wisdom of Howard Thurman in a Changing World*, ed. Gregory C. Ellison (Louisville, KY: Westminster John Knox Press, 2020), 55–70. For the angel with the flaming sword imagery, see George Fox, *Journal of George Fox: Being an Historical Account of the Life, Travels*, ed. Henry J. Cadbury (Richmond, IN: Friends United Press, 2006), 97.

tribe, they held their breath against the agony.... How does the human spirit accommodate itself to desolation? How did they? What *tools of the spirit* were in their hands with which to cut a path through the wilderness of their despair?[17]

Howard Thurman's Black Flesh

Thurman's corpus is filled with stories and reflections that depict his Black body as policed, as chattel, a thing that makes sounds, but cannot speak and feel.[18] He was keenly aware of the tactics used by enslavers "to make them stand in fear" through "disciplinary practices and submission, feelings of inferiority, fear and dependence, incentives, power structures, the cruelty of slaveowners and overseers"—and most importantly for our purposes, the use of religion to render Black bodies as fixed and immobile property.[19] Peter Eisenstadt chronicles three events in Thurman's train travels during the era of segregation that defined his Black body as a "thing," a "that," a "zigaboo," with restricted movement and constantly on guard against fear of violence and death.[20] Contemporary policing practices by vigilantes and state-sponsored violence against Black bodies are continuations of this long-standing "rule that governs the [Black] body's appearing," the ordering and reordering of *Black flesh*.[21] Yet, for Thurman, his experiences as Black flesh that spoke and felt were inseparable from his humanity and his understanding of freedom, equality, and the social mobility of Black bodies.[22]

---

[17] HT, WHAH, 193 (italics added).

[18] HT, "'Relaxation' and Race Conflict," in "Peace Tactics and a Racial Minority," *The World Tomorrow*, December 1928, PHWT 1:18. See also Devere Allen, ed., *Pacificism in the Modern World* (Garden City, NY: Doubleday, 1929).

[19] Kenneth M. Stampp, *The Peculiar Institution: Slavery in the Ante-Bellum South* (New York: Alfred A. Knopf. 1956), chapter 4. For a more detailed discussion on HT and Black skin, see Peter Eisenstadt and Walter Earl Fluker, eds., "Introduction," in HT, *Democracy and the Soul of America* (Maryknoll, NY: Orbis Books, 2022), ix–xxx; see also HT, WHAH, 36.

[20] Peter Eisenstadt, *Against the Hounds of Hell: A Life of Howard Thurman* (Charlottesville: University of Virginia Press, 2022), 160; see also HT, *The Luminous Darkness; A Personal Interpretation of the Anatomy of Segregation and the Ground of Hope* (Richmond, IN: Friends United Press, 2014), 31; PHWT 4:227; and *Jesus and the Disinherited*, 77–78. Thurman writes, "Segregation has a margin of freedom of movement without threat, always available to the powerful but not the weak" (HT, *The Luminous Darkness*, 6); "Artificial limitations are placed upon them, restricting freedom of movement, of employment, and of participation in the common life" (HT, *Jesus and the Disinherited*, 41).

[21] Elizabeth Alexander, *The Trayvon Generation* (New York: Grand Central Publications, 2022), 25–26; Kelly Brown Douglas, *Stand Your Ground: Black Bodies and the Justice of God* (Maryknoll, NY: Orbis Books, 2015).

[22] See HT, "Introduction," in "The Meaning of Loyalty III: The State," May 20, 1951, Fellowship Church, in HT, *Democracy and the Soul of America*. See also Hortense J. Spillers,

Thurman's Black flesh, therefore, is a site of memory, what historians John Blassingame and Mary Frances Berry called "long memory"—long, lingering memories[23] that invite us to revisit places where we remember, retell, and relive the story of African enslavement and trauma: where we read the trees carved on African backs, the undecipherable markings, breaks, fractures, brandings, punctures, missing parts, the hieroglyphics of discardable, fungible flesh, commodity, cargo that built America and the modern world. It is *rememory*[24] of slave patrols; Black bodies laboring in Florida tobacco and sugar plantations, Mississippi cotton fields and Alabama coal mines; and the continuing state-sponsored policing of Black bodies for nine minutes and twenty-nine seconds multiplied by a veritable infinity of not breathing. Thurman's writings are saturated with memories and countermemories of his problematized Black flesh and "the tragic soul-life of African Americans."[25]

"Mama's Baby, Papa's Maybe: An American Grammar Book," *Diacritics* 17, no. 2 (1987): 65–81; Julius B. Fleming Jr., "Shattering Black Flesh: Black Intellectual Writing in the Age of Ferguson," *American Literary History* 28, no. 4 (Winter 2016): 828–34; and M. Shawn Copeland, *Enfleshing Freedom: Body, Race, and Being* (Minneapolis: Fortress Press, 2009).

[23] Mary Frances Berry and John W. Blassingame, *Long Memory: The Black Experience in America* (New York: Oxford University Press, 1982), x. Sterling Stuckey termed this "the lingering memory" of "African tribalism" in "the minds of African slaves." This sense of history and connectedness with the past, according to Stuckey, "enabled [enslaved Africans] to go back to a sense of community in the traditional African settings and to include all Africans in their common experience of oppression in North America." He suggests that slave ships were the first incubators of slave unity across cultural lines, cruelly revealing irreducible links from one ethnic group to the other, fostering resistance thousands of miles before the shores of the new land appeared on the horizon—before there was mention of natural rights in North America. See Stuckey, *Slave Culture: Nationalist Theory and the Foundations of Black America* (New York: Oxford University Press, 1987), 3.

[24] "Toni Morrison's literary idea of *rememory* addresses the analytic relation of *habitus*, memory, and history in the quest for human identity. *Rememory* acts to re-collect, reassemble, and reconfigure individual and collective consciousness into a meaningful and sequential whole through the process of narrativization. The significance of *remembering* is the narrativization of the past, the reclaiming of bodies of disparate and disconnected meaning lodged in the unconscious matrices of the psyche and in the body. It is not only a return to intellectual excavation of historical data, but is also associated with deep emotional energy, which is spiritual and empathic. Remembering personal stories in the context of larger historical narratives offers entrée into forgotten worlds of meaning and allows recovery of dismembered bodies of experience otherwise invisible to consciousness" (Fluker, *The Ground Has Shifted*, 30).

[25] W. E. B. Du Bois, *The Souls of Black Folk* (New York: Bantam Books, 1989), 45–46. Terrence Johnson says, "*Tragic Soul-Life* explores the clash between religious and political discourse in shaping the unasked question of what does it mean to be a problem? A close examination of the Du Boisian question reveals the subtle ways moral beliefs inform political life both historically and in contemporary society" (*Tragic Soul-Life: W. E. B. Du Bois and the Moral Crisis Facing American Democracy* [New York: Oxford University Press, 2012], 9).

It is in this context of memory and rememory that Thurman cites a meeting with his major professor at Rochester Theological Seminary, George Cross, who sympathetically counseled him not to become entangled in the struggle for citizenship rights but rather to give himself "to the timeless issues of the human spirit."[26] Thurman "pondered the meaning of his words, and wondered what kind of response I could make to this man who did not know that a man and his *black skin* must face the 'timeless issues of the human spirit' together."[27] Thurman's response to Cross's question highlights the problematized Black body as a sign, a signification on the timeless issues of the human spirit in his skin that would become over the years a central question for his conception of a mystical encounter that holds transcendence and Black embodiment in creative tension in the construction of democratic space.[28] Therefore, Thurman's understanding of religious experience was not a detached, otherworldly quest that denied particularity; rather particularity—especially individuality, as evidenced in embodied existence—was, for him, a statement about materiality both as a boundary that separates and a fluid arena for affective knowledge, communication, and agency that bring bodies together in the quest for democratic space.[29]

In his preaching, writing, and liturgical experiments, Thurman explored the efficacy of the body as a site for *communitas*, the liminal space produced by the dynamic dialectical interplay of structure and anti-structure.[30] Through the arts, music, dance, poetry, iconography, and silence, he sought to create an egalitarian ecclesial space for interracial, intercultural, and interreligious gatherings that honored the aesthetic dimensions of the body: seeing, feeling, smelling, touching, hearing, and knowing.[31] Therefore, "The deed reveals meaning.

---

[26] HT, WHAH, 60.

[27] Ibid., italics added.

[28] HT shared this story with the author in a conversation in Evanston, Illinois, in April 1978. The impact of Cross's advice, though not fully realized at that moment, became in time a driving principle for decision-making in relation to social action for HT. Luther E. Smith comments on the significance of this occasion and its relation to HT's baptism in *The Mystic as Prophet* (Richmond, IN: Friends United Press, 2007), 24.

[29] To *live in* and *out* of a Black body, to *live as Black flesh*, to be *Black skin*, connotes what Judith Butler identifies as "boundary, fixity, surface, and intensification"—in short, materiality; and "it is through the intensification of feeling that bodies and worlds materialize and take shape, or that the effect of boundary, fixity and surface is produced." See Sara Ahmed, "Collective Feelings: Or, the Impressions Left by Others," *Theory, Culture and Society* 21, no. 2 (April 1, 2004): 29. See also Judith Butler, *Bodies That Matter: On the Discursive Limits of Sex* (New York: Routledge, 1993), 9.

[30] Robert C. Williams, "Worship and Anti-Structure in Thurman's Vision of the Sacred," *Journal of the Interdenominational Center* 14, no. 1–2 (Fall 1986–Spring 1987).

[31] In a sermon preached at the Fellowship Church in 1949, he references the church's commitment to diversity by expanding the boundaries of the self into relationships with

Meaning does not exist as a disembodied force, but becomes evident through relationships"[32]—indeed, bodies matter, because they dare to speak, feel, and act in opposition to fear. As Thurman often stated, "The time and place of a person's life on earth is the time and place of the body, but the meaning and significance of that life is as far-reaching and redemptive as the gifts, the dedication, the response to the demand of the times, the total commitment of one's powers can make it."[33]

His reference to "the total commitment of one's power to make it" is a statement about the social and political location of the body and the moral imperative on the individual's freedom and responsibility to speak and act with integrity. In one of his most enlightening sermons on democracy, he retells the story of the peasant Naboth's refusal to relinquish his vineyard to King Ahab.[34] Thurman reflects on the binding covenantal relationship between the individual and God and the inherent moral obligation to resist political domination even at the risk of death:

> This covenant was the basis, the root, the core of the individual's sense of worth. [Naboth] had a covenant with God. He rated having a covenant with God. This covenant which he had with God was binding upon God as God related to him. This covenant which was the basis of his freedom and the meaning of his life took precedence over any other relationship. If standing within the context of the covenant which he had with God he was required to do anything by any person which did violence to this covenant then he was under moral obligation to defy that power, that force whoever it was.... The covenant with God relates in a moral sense the individual to God and God to the individual.[35]

---

others: "Now, dimension is an aesthetic sense. The experience of unity in the presence of God, of the oneness of God, puts a scent in my nostrils that sends me, in all of the things that I do, trying to express it. In my work, in my relationships with people on the street, I look with new eyes on those with reference to whom, when I was imprisoned in my little narrow self, I had no experience of oneness. The fears that I had, that kept eating away at the basis of social security, are now removed, because I have let down my guards in an effort to move creatively into an understanding of other people and let them move creatively into an understanding of me. And in that moment of shuttling, they become a part of me forever." See also HT, "Prayer for Peace," where he speaks of the "smell of life." HT, SF, 307–8.

[32] Luther E. Smith, "Intimate Mystery: Howard Thurman's Search for Ultimate Meaning," *Ultimate Reality and Meaning: Interdisciplinary Studies in Philosophy of Understanding* 11, no. 2 (June 1988): 97.

[33] HT, WHAH, 208.

[34] HT, "A Faith to Live By: Democracy and the Individual II," sermon, Fellowship Church, October 19, 1952, in HT, *Democracy and the Soul of America*, 83–92. The sermon was delivered within the context of growing tensions in Indochina and the United States' complicity with French colonialism in Asia.

[35] Ibid. Two basic affirmations underscore this covenant between the individual and God as they relate to democracy. One is *the moral inviolability of the individual*, i.e., persons must

Freedom as an indigenous quality of persons is deeply embedded in Thurman's theological vision of creation and moral anthropology. He believed that there was an "unconscious autonomy"[36] engrained in the creation of all human beings. Thus, the realization of this freedom serves as a counternarrative to all spurious and oppressive constructions of social and political domination.[37] His was a challenge to all forms of subjugation of policed bodies whom he identified as "outsiders."[38] Thurman maintained that the dichotomous scenario of "outsiders" living in the midst of "insiders" is perhaps the greatest threat to American democratic values that we are witnessing in contemporary societies around the globe. He believed that a reconfiguration of "the role of minorities in the modern state is crucial not only for the state as a community among world states, but also for the experience of community on the part of minorities themselves."[39]

---

never be used as means to an end. This vertical pole finds its source in the creative intent of God for persons. The horizontal pole of this relationship between individuality and democracy finds its expression in the related principles of equality and freedom, which likewise have their basis in the infinite worth of the individual. Thurman interprets both principles in light of a theocentric perspective that views the creative intent for community as the normative framework for their meaning and authenticity. In respect to the principle of equality, his definition is illuminative of the covenantal motif mentioned above. He contends that "the only ultimate basis for equality is the equality of infinite worth [of the individual]." See also HT, "Judgment and Hope in the Christian Message," in *The Christian Way in Race Relations*, ed. William Stuart Nelson (New York: Harper and Brothers, 1948), 229–35.

[36] HT says, "I didn't have to wait for the revolution. I have never been in search for identity—and I think that [all] I've ever felt and worked on and believed in was founded in a kind of private, almost unconscious autonomy that did not seek vindication in my environment because it was in me." Mary E. Goodwin, "Racial Roots and Religion: An Interview with Howard Thurman," *Christian Century*, May 9, 1973, 534.

[37] Walter Earl Fluker, "The Politics of Conversion and the Civilization of Friday," in *The Courage to Hope: From Black Suffering to Human Redemption*, ed. Quinton Dixie and Cornel West (Boston: Beacon Press, 1999); Willie James Jennings, *The Christian Imagination: Theology and the Origins of Race* (New Haven, CT: Yale University Press, 2010), 60; Charles H. Long, "Howard Thurman and the Meaning of Religion in America," in *The Human Search: Howard Thurman and the Quest for Freedom*, Proceedings of the Second Annual Thurman Convocation, Martin Luther King Jr. Memorial Studies in Religion, Culture and Social Development, vol. 1, ed. Mozella G. Mitchell (New York: Peter Lang, 1992), 141.

[38] While HT's notion of democracy references historical documents like the Declaration of Independence, the Constitution of the United States, and the Emancipation Proclamation, one cannot assume that democratic space for Thurman was the same as it was for the American founding fathers or European intellectuals and *philosophes*. Benjamin Isakhan, "Eurocentrism and the History of Democracy," *Politische Vierteljahresschrift* 51 (2016): 56–70.

[39] HT, SCG, 87–88; see also HT's conversation with Gandhi in WHAH, 132; and HT, "With Our Negro Guests," in PHWT 1:332–39; HT, "Black Pentecost III, Footprints of the Disinherited," taped message, May 31, 1972, Howard Thurman Virtual Listening Room, HTC; also in HT, *Democracy and the Soul of America*, 102–113; HT, "A 'Native Son' Speaks,"

Democratic space, for Thurman, demonstrates both the claiming of the right and the moral duty to dissent—to disagree based on the radical freedom and the inherent dignity and worth of the individual. This argument represents a long and neglected philosophical tradition.[40] Thurman's theo-political project, therefore, is both an imaginative conjuring of sequestered space and a moral demand for the reconfiguration of time and memory that rests in a return to and re-narration of creation and the reclaiming of the body as sacred space. For Thurman, the return to and re-narration of creation is not an idyllic journey into puritanical innocence; it is a perilous pilgrimage into the interiority of religious experience and the exteriority of democratic landscapes witnessed in bodily existence and resistance, or what he called in a 1945 essay "the inner life and world-mindedness."[41] He believed that the clue to one's public and civil engagement is found in the inner world of experience, in nature and embodied existence.[42] The cultivation of the inner life is the basis for the development of a genuine sense of self and authentic bodily existence in the world. Therefore, it was not sufficient simply to focus on the inner life without being aware of and engaged in the complex social, political, and economic arrangements that order and structure the individual's embodied existence and personal and social mobility.

It should be clear that, for Thurman, walking with God in *Black flesh*, negotiating space and movement, is dangerous and costly. In his last extant letter to Martin Luther King Jr., dated May 13, 1966, Thurman expresses his regret for the time that had elapsed since he and King last spoke. He ends the short note with a rather foreboding quote from the American naturalist and essayist Loren Eiseley: "Those as [us] hunts treasure must go alone, at night, and when they find it they

---

in PHWT 2:246–52; HT, "Good News for the Underprivileged," *Religion in Life* 4, no. 3 (Summer 1935): 409; HT, *The Growing Edge* (Richmond, IN: Friends United Press, 1974), 174–80; HT, SCG, 88–104; HT, *Deep River and The Negro Spiritual Speaks of Life and Death* (Richmond, IN: Friends United Press, 1975), 39–40, 63–65; HT, *The Creative Encounter: An Interpretation of Religion and the Social Witness* (Richmond, IN: Friends United Press, 1972), 130; and HT, *Deep Is the Hunger: Meditations for Apostles of Sensitiveness* (Richmond, IN: Friends United Press, 1978), 2.

[40] Bernard R. Boxill, "The Roots of Civil Disobedience in Republicanism and Slavery," in *To Shape a New World: Essays on the Political Philosophy of Martin Luther King, Jr.*, ed. Tommie Shelby and Brandon M. Terry (Cambridge, MA: Belknap Press of Harvard University Press, 2018), 58–77. In the same volume, see Robert Gooding-Williams's "The Du Bois–Washington Debate and the Idea of Dignity," 19–34. Especially important in this discussion is the theme of dignity.

[41] The "sense of self" is rooted in the nature of the self. HT makes a distinction between the inner and outer dimensions of the self. For him, the individual is both a child of nature and a child of spirit. The outer dimension of the self is part of the external world of nature. HT, *The Creative Encounter*, 19; HT, *Disciplines*, 57; HT, SCG, 21.

[42] See HT, "The Inner Life and World-Mindedness," PHWT 3:110.

have to leave a little of their blood behind them."⁴³ To dare to experience the freedom of the body without fear is to enter dangerous territory without a map; to "perilously traverse the limit"; to trespass embodied and structural boundaries set by racial, ethnic, cultural, gender, sexual, and religious norms; to cross into forbidden territory of unjust laws and legal prohibitions; and to remember, retell, and relive stories of "a part of those who have no part." It is a confrontation with evil that lurks in the shadows, in silence and in open gaze, within us and around us, mocking us and demanding that we see our complicity with fear and horror—begging us to return to a fluid center where we rediscover what our voices, hands, and feet are for and to inquire with Thurman, "How does the human spirit accommodate itself to desolation? How did his ancestors? What *tools of the spirit* were in their hands with which to cut a path through the wilderness of their despair?" "What methods, strategies, practices of the spirit are available to us to cut away this ghastly conundrum of evil, disguise and repeated lies of a fascist masquerade?"⁴⁴ How do we—Christians and others with whom we are willing to journey alongside—prepare to encounter Presence and to practice in and through embodied acts of justice and compassion in contested democratic space? What tools of the spirit are in our hands that can help us carve out a fresh path for people who are quickly losing hope?

Tools of the Spirit: Preparation, Presence, and Practice

Preparation

In 1963 Thurman published a small book entitled *Disciplines of the Spirit*. It grew out of a two-semester course, "Spiritual Resources and Disciplines," he taught at Boston University from 1953 to 1962. Among his many students were some who became celebrated pioneers in religious studies, interreligious faith, and social activism. These include Houston Smith,⁴⁵ Rabbi Zalman

---

⁴³ HT, "To Martin Luther King, Jr.," May 13, 1966, PHWT 5:140. Loren Eiseley (1907–1977) was an anthropologist and historian of science, best known for his popular collections of essays on natural science and nature. See Loren C. Eiseley, *The Mind as Nature* (New York: Harper, 1962), 59–60.

⁴⁴ HT, "The Fascist Masquerade," in *The Christian Way in Race Relations*, ed. William Stuart Nelson (New York: Harper and Brothers, 1948), in PHWT 3:145–62.

⁴⁵ Huston Smith (1919–2016) was a leading scholar in religious studies and a long-time colleague of Thurman. See PHWT, xxxii, xlvii, n82, 119, 294n3. Smith served as the Thomas J. Watson Professor of Religion and Distinguished Adjunct Professor of Philosophy, Emeritus, Syracuse University. His many books include *Forgotten Truth: The Common Vision of the World's Religions, Beyond the Post-Modern Mind*, and *Why Religion Matters: The Fate of the Human Spirit in an Age of Disbelief*, as well as the classic *The World's Religions*. See World

Schachter-Shalomi,[46] and Walter Pahnke (1931–1971).[47] Thurman identified five regular spiritual practices—"tools of the spirit" (commitment, growth, prayer, suffering, and reconciliation)—designed to "allow students to clear away whatever may block our awareness of that which is God in us."[48]

Fundamental to preparation for the work of creating democratic space is the act of commitment. Commitment involves volition, which may be a radical self-conscious yielding on the part of the individual, or a systematic, disciplined effort over a period of time.[49] The result of the commitment of the agent is a new, integrated basis for moral action—a new value content and center of loyalty that inform one's speech and actions in the world.[50] The person's loyalty to God, which proceeds from the personal assurance of being loved by God, forms the ground of the moral life, but that which is discovered in private must be witnessed to in the world. Thurman comments on the nature of the individual's commitment and its relationship to moral action: "His experience is personal, private but in no sense exclusive. All of the vision of God and holiness which he experiences, he must achieve in the context of the social situation by which day-to-day life is defined. What is disclosed in his religious experience he must define in community. That which God shareth with him, he must inspire his fellows to seek for themselves. He is dedicated therefore to the removing of all barriers which block or frustrate this possibility in the world."[51]

Preparation, for Thurman, also involved a readying of the mind and spirit, which he sometimes calls prayer or meditation. Prayer is a discipline by which the individual prepares or "readies" her spirit for the creative encounter within the fluid center. Especially in the experience of meditation, the individual quiets the stirring of the mind so that the Presence residing within may come to Itself. In meditation, he claimed, "the self moves toward God" and "God touches the spirit and the will and a wholly new character in terms of dimension enters the experience."[52] The individual is both participant and observer in the encounter, which means that she enters the experience with her own facticity or "residue of God-meaning," the patterns and contents of one's bodily affections, emotions, beliefs, value judgments, strengths, and weaknesses—the totality of the individual's

---

Wisdom, "Huston Smith's Life and Work," http://www.worldwisdom.com/public/authors/Huston-Smith.aspx, accessed June 29, 2022.

[46] See HT, PHWT 4:241n1.
[47] See HT, PHWT 4:196n1.
[48] HT, PHWT 4:xxix.
[49] HT, *Creative Encounter*, 67–71, 121.
[50] Ibid., 81.
[51] Ibid., 124.
[52] Ibid., 37–38.

experience in and with Presence. The emphasis is on that which *recedes* from the experience of the creative encounter, not on that which *precedes*; in other words, this experience marks the recession of essence from experience (existence), not existence preceding essence. This is an important feature of his understanding of religious experience, which has significant implications for the freedom of the individual.[53]

Presence

Two samples from Thurman's private journal provide insight into this encounter with Presence. One is from September 1963 when he embarks upon what he called "the wider ministry," an extended two-year sabbatical before his formal retirement from Boston University,[54] in which he makes the following entry while on board a ship to London. In the throes of pressing personal concerns, retirement, fears regarding his visa application to Nigeria, and anxieties born of his struggle with finitude, he enters consultation with Presence:

> After lunch I walked for 25 minutes—then I went to the Catholic chapel. I was not conscious of praying but I was overcome by a full sense of the Presence of God. [My?] manifestations were all the same—a warm sensation all through my body with a sense of moisture in my eyes. My mind was dormant. I was open and quiet while wave after wave of warmth flowed over me washing and cleansing in a renewing and refreshing manner. Three priests came in to pray. They went about in a direct and business like manner—with dispatch it was done and they went out leaving the little chapel to a young woman and me.[55]

After arriving in London and waiting for matter of the visa to be resolved, he makes another entry:

> The first night after I retired, I discovered that I was disintegrating in my spirit. I began to despair—to be visited constantly by a desire to [panic?] into depression. So in my time before going to sleep I prayed. It was very simple—I placed again my life in God's hands. I [savored?] in great and intimate detail the 139th Psalm. There was no drama but a quiet settling down of my spirit in God's great abiding. I did a strange thing. I asked for a sign—some simple kind of assurance. Then with moist eyes I went to sleep.[56]

---

[53] Ibid., 26–27.
[54] See HT, "The Africa Journal," PHWT 5:35–102.
[55] Ibid., 38–39.
[56] Ibid., 41.

It is important to note that, for Thurman, *Presence* is *felt experience*—bodily affectation and surfaced emotionality—warmth, moisture, a "quiet settling down" of the spirit and sleep. It is in the Presence of God that one recognizes the integrity of one's body and the personal assurance of one's inherent dignity and worth as a child of God. It is also the space where one understands one's relation to others and the larger creation of which she is a part as new landscapes of possibility and configuration emerge. In the Presence, one discovers love as an affective political practice of the *erotic*—to quote Keri Day, "as a religious and/or spiritual good, [that] enables the transformation of self and society away from the alienating proclivities of neoliberal culture."[57] For Day, the "erotic is about self-expression and connection rather than repression and disconnection from one's deepest feelings of love and togetherness."[58] Whatever impedes the actualization of togetherness (community) at either the personal or social levels must be confronted. Thurman believed that the way to the transformation of society is through self-conscious redemptive acts of suffering rooted in love and that meaningful experiences of love shared among individuals would accomplish that end.[59] This was the central ethical imperative that recedes and proceeds from religious experience, to love and to be reconciled and provide the modus operandi for creating and sustaining democratic space.[60] To those who are "concerned about social change," Thurman warns, creating and sustaining democratic space is not about finding "better schemes, better utopian dreams" but opening their innermost selves to a transformation wrought by "an increasing exposure" to "the mind of God and the literal truth which it inspires."[61] The emphasis is on expanding horizons based upon love, equality, and freedom that are not bound by externally imposed prerogatives and sanctions.[62]

Thurman's formal understanding of Presence is indebted to his association with the Society of Friends' teachings on the Inner Light. This principle, sometimes referred to as the "seed" or "the root," maintains that within everyone there is an element of God, a divine intelligence and energy that discern good

---

[57] Keri Day, *Religious Resistance to Neoliberalism: Womanist and Black Feminist Perspectives* (New York: Palgrave Macmillan, 2016), 77.

[58] Ibid.

[59] "Experiences of meaning which people share are more compelling than the barriers that separate them," HT writes. "If such experiences can be multiplied over a time interval of sufficient duration, then any barrier between men [sic], whatever kind, can be undermined" (HT, *Disciplines*, 120).

[60] Ibid., 122.

[61] For earlier examples of similar arguments, see HT, "The Sources of Power for Christian Action," and "Christian, Who Calls Me Christian?," in PHWT 2:93–101, 106–13.

[62] One of his favorite poems often used as an illustration of this point was Stephen Crane, "I Saw a Man Pursuing the Horizon."

and evil and open the committed soul to the consciousness of its indwelling.[63] Thurman often refers to this principle as "principal," as "the tutor," one's own "working paper" or the "unseen model" by which one structures the facts of his or her experience.[64] For this reason, he counseled, "The person concerned about social change must not only understand the materials with which he has to do, the things which he is trying to manipulate, to reorder, to refashion but again and again he must expose the roots of his mind to the literal truth that is the tutor of the facts, the orderer and reorderer of the facts of his experience."[65]

This must be done so that, in the quest for justice, one's vision of the good society never conforms to some external pattern, but is "modeled and shaped in accordance to the innermost transformation that is going on in his spirit."[66] Therefore, it was Thurman's insistence that those who were engaged in the work of creating and expanding democratic spaces continually examine the sources of their motivation and the ways in which the circling series of social and political processes they seek to change are related to their own spiritual pilgrimage. Always, the primary questions are, "Who are you, really? What are you trying to do with your life? What kind of person are you trying to become?"[67] It was his conviction that the individual in his or her actions "is trying to snare into the body of his facts, his conviction of those facts." He cautioned, however, that faith thusly understood always runs the risk of becoming idolatrous, as in patriotic visions of "the American way."[68] Therefore, in the Presence of God, one must

---

[63] See Brian Drayton and William P. Taber Jr., *A Language for the Inner Landscape: Spiritual Wisdom from the Quaker Movement* (Philadelphia: Tract Association of Friends, 2015). Douglas V. Steere, the famed Quaker theologian and one of HT's lifelong interlocutors, writes, "It is, then, in this principle and in the dominion of this principle over all, that we have our true being. It is in this principle that we receive our inner education." Delivered at Arch Street Meeting House, Philadelphia, Quaker pamphlets (Wallington, PA: Pendle Hill, 1937).

[64] See HT, *Jesus and the Disinherited*, 110–12, for HT's understanding of the working paper; see also HT, "Your Life's Working Paper," April 1949, HTC.

[65] HT, "He Looked for a City," Sermon, Marsh Chapel, Boston University, January 2, 1955, PHWT 4:105–8.

[66] Ibid.

[67] See Thurman, *Disciplines of the Spirit*, 26–37, where he discusses three primary questions related to the discipline of commitment.

[68] HT, "He Looked for a City," January 2, 1955, 105. This is a remarkable observation and the note that I sought to strike in my first book: *They Looked for a City: A Comparative Analysis of the Ideal of Community in Thought of Howard Thurman and Martin Luther King, Jr.* (Lanham, MD: University Press of America, 1989). HT had given a similar sermon with an identical title, six years earlier to the day: HT, "He Looked for a City," January 2, 1949, at the Fellowship Church. For more on this general theme, see Walter Earl Fluker, "Dangerous Memories and Redemptive Possibilities: Howard Thurman and Black Leadership in the South," in *Black Leaders and Ideologies in the South: Resistance and Non-Violence*, edited by Preston King and Walter Earl Fluker (New York: Taylor & Francis, 2004), 147–176.

always examine the motivational content of action that involves a tutoring of the will (intentionality), by the unseen model that for him was the truth resident within the individual.

Again, as a matter of preparation for the arrival of Presence, here the issues of *identity*, *purpose*, and *method* are combined in relation to the sociopolitical context in which the individual finds oneself. This deep sense of the abiding Presence within is also the pilgrim's ground of hope. The individual who seeks a better world, a better society, "may fail, he may be upset in his timetable, his heart may be broken but he does not give up because within him is the city which hath foundations whose builder and maker is God."[69] This is a persistent theme in Thurman's examination of the spirituals. In *The Negro Spiritual Speaks of Life and Death*, he suggests that in the midst of bondage and subhuman existence, these old Black and unknown bards sought "a city that hath foundations where the builder and maker is God."[70] Make no mistake that, for Thurman, this "quest for the city that hath foundations" is not vague and otherworldly; rather it is a signification on the controlled and limited democratic spaces constructed for oppressed and marginalized bodies. Referencing chapter 11 of the Epistle to the Hebrews, Thurman comments on the pilgrimage of Abraham and Sarah, who discover that the city that they sought was never far away, but already within them. And for those who would follow their example, "he may fail, he may be upset in his timetable, his heart may be broken, but he does not give up because within him is the city."[71]

Reimagining Practices

Creating and sustaining democratic spaces demands the inculcation of practices that are rooted in our personal quests for freedom and equality, which means returning again and again to the fluid area of our consent in a spiraling dance of the inner life and world-mindedness. We have to be about preparing, meeting Presence, and practicing love, openness, and diversity—experimenting with new ecclesial and nonecclesial models that embrace and appreciate difference. With the killing of Black youth, the rise in legal antiabortion campaigns, restraints on voting rights, the contested confirmation of the first Black female Supreme Court justice, the policing of fem, trans, queer, Black, and Brown bodies, and the erection of legal, cultural, and physical barriers against immigrants—especially from countries that our former president called holes for defecation—the need for a reimagined vision of democracy is urgent and necessary.

---

[69] HT, "He Looked for a City" (1955), 107.
[70] HT, *Deep River and The Negro Spiritual Speaks of Life and Death*, 56.
[71] HT, "He Looked for a City" (1955), 107.

What might Thurman's creative construction of democratic space for subjugated bodies mean for our times? As a new generation of activists and freedom fighters engage the long and complex history of contested democratic spaces in the United States and around the globe, religious scholars and social justice activists must take a long look at the ways in which this new moment calls us, like Thurman, to remember, retell, and relive our stories.

The acts of remembering, retelling, and reliving stories of enslavement, oppression, and liberation involve calling forth creative hermeneutical strategies and processes that allow us to return to memory and history and reconstruct these defining narratives in respect to futures that can only be imagined. Our imagined futures are necessary because of the ambiguities and contingencies of the present. And they are possible because of the gift of spirit and transcendence that allows us to stand with Thurman on the high tower and overlook the complex and jagged contours of history, patiently and painfully waiting for the moving finger of God to join us in reimagining, revising, and reconstructing new visions in the contexts of the present. We must inquire within our own contemporary contexts and seek responses that proceed from "the sound of the genuine" within us. This challenge that Thurman lays before us involves reimagining his work and legacy at this critical impasse in democratic life and practices to forge new tools of the spirit that enable us to imagine new possibilities for democratic spaces and seek practices to ensure that our speech and actions are always rooted in the vitality of life and spirit.

Taking our cue from Thurman's own creative and imaginative play with language and signs, I suggest considering the threefold movement of *congregating*, *conjuring*, and *conspiring* in *common(s)* that I explored in *The Ground Has Shifted*.[72] *Congregating* (*congregare*)—gathering, binding, and coming together—involves repenting by rethinking, regretting, running away *from*, and running *to* new imagined futures by acknowledging and receiving the voices and visions of the new movements of the Spirit in our midst. Thurman's primary concern, which marks his distinctive contribution to the present impasse, was the place of religious experience and the role of moral imagination in funding ethical insight for public discourse and practice. In this respect, he was engaged in *conjuring*—the imaginative art of taking the materials at hand, that which experience gives us, and imaginatively refashioning them into creative tools. His intellectual and aesthetic experiments were a type of "spiritual bricolage," the process of inclusion, exclusion, and reconfiguration of experience and language through an internal locus that becomes incarnate in public speech and action. His innovative prac-

---

[72] Fluker, *The Ground Has Shifted*, 169–96.

tices of inclusion and diversity are invitations to *conspire* with him, to literally breathe together, to plot and to do together as one; to covenant with God as Presence against the facile, undemocratic imaginings of the past and literally breathe and run together toward common goals and purposes that inspire and guide leaders, scholars, activists, and others to aspire into new commons.

Commons is a rereading of Thurman's common ground that can be reconfigured and translated into *common loyalties and commitments to justice and peace*. These common(s) may well expire over time, and new strategies for that moment will of necessity be constructed. The challenges to Black and other colonized bodies in the United States and throughout the many diasporas of which we are a part are so multitudinous that we could resign to fatedness and despair, as many of our religious and political leaders have done in this era of "Make America Great Again." Or we can choose to congregate in this new moment and begin again (for some, continue) the work of conjuring new narratives and strategies for the struggle by building on the gifts and tools of the past that have been handed down to us from so many of our prophets and seers, like Thurman, whose lives bear witness to the Broken Body whose dangerous memory leads us to *crossing(s)*.

I refer to *crossing(s)* as quests for appropriate ways of speaking to movements, pluralities, and temporalities associated with marginalized bodies and the birthing of consciousness at different turns in individual and collective runs to the future. *Crossing(s)* point to the yoke of infinity and time, in-between spaces where congregating, conjuring, and conspiring in commons take place; it is also where the living and dead speak, and Presence is enfleshed in defiant acts of integrity, freedom, and equality of worth. *Crossing(s)* are dangerous democratic spaces where we become aware of the intersections between transcendence and immanence, hope and melancholy, eternity and time—spaces where liminality intrudes, breaks in, and leaves a crack—a revelation of God's presence in the world—an aperture of light, a tiny opening through which we peer at new possibilities for the world and ourselves. For Thurman, *crossing(s)* emerge at a "Deep River," the dynamic, changing quality of life and existence. Therefore, his conception of common ground reemerges as a narrative that is mutable and portable with a temporary-fixed character that is always becoming other, differentiated, stretching, better, flowing toward *More*. "Nothing is fixed, forever and forever and forever, it is not fixed; the earth is always shifting, the light is always changing, the sea does not cease to grind the rock," James Baldwin wrote.[73] It

---

[73] James Baldwin, "Nothing Personal," in *The Price of the Ticket: Collected Nonfiction 1948–1985* (New York: St. Martin's Press, 1985), 393.

is not fixed for Thurman because the River is always changing, moving toward something More. Our home is over Jordan, not the fictive enterprise of conquest and annihilation of the other in death and dying for the sake of land and territory; or for recognition and respect from clandestine puppeteers who hide behind the curtains of social fictions and manipulate the mindscape. Home has to do with remembering, retelling, and reliving our many stories in the quest for a sense of wholeness within ourselves (identity), with others and with creation.

> See over there! The path to the *River*—no, the path that crosses the River—or is it the River crossing the path, who knows? One must be careful, however, at *crossing(s)*, for while they bring information, knowledge and possibility, they are also fraught with dangers, perils, and crucifixions, for we do not quite know who or what goes there and where to set our feet on shifting grounds![74]

We cannot accomplish this courageous task of *congregating, conjuring, and conspiring* in *commons* with Thurman until we are willing to enter *crossing(s)* that meet us at every interchange, every act of resistance and solidarity. Yet the *crossing(s)* that we must enter as we negotiate transcendence represent the source of hope as we commit ourselves to reimagining strange new futures of democratic spaces.

In Toni Morrison's *Beloved*, Baby Suggs's sermon in the Clearing is an example of *crossing(s)*—this powerful space of *congregating, conjuring,* and *conspiring in commons* where running, resistance, and revelation meet. Baby Suggs called the women to her. "'Cry,' she told them. 'For the living and the dead. Just cry.'"

> And without covering their eyes the women let loose. It started that way: laughing children, dancing men, crying women and then it got mixed up. Women stopped crying and danced; men sat down and cried; children danced, women laughed, children cried until, exhausted and riven, all and each lay about the Clearing damp and gasping for breath.... This is flesh I'm talking about here.[75]

This is flesh that Thurman is talking about here, where (Black) subjectivity conspires with language and the body as a conjurer of hope in the creation of democratic spaces. For Thurman, hope joined to dangerous memories is a

---

[74] Fluker, *The Ground Has Shifted*, 141.
[75] Toni Morrison, *Beloved* (New York: Vintage International, 2004), 102–4. See also Carl Plasa, ed., *Toni Morrison: Beloved, Columbia Critical Study Guides* (New York: Columbia University Press, 1998), chapter 4, "This Is Flesh I'm Talking About: Language, Subjectivity and the Body."

signifier on impossibility. As political praxis, this hope is incarnate in defiant speech—first-order, embodied language: the speech of the Black living dead, which proceeds from conjured in-between spaces of death and possibility.

Conclusion

Before his death in 1981, Thurman had concerns about whether the creation and sustainability of democratic spaces in the United States were possible given its unreconciled history of racial inequality and violence. In a speech at the University of the Redlands in 1976, he said that "America was in search of its soul";[76] he warned his listeners, "Now, school is out. School is out and it's been out for some time."[77] His eerily astute observations of the spiritual and moral climate of America over forty years ago has striking resonance for the crisis of democratic life that is being debated at all levels of our society, throughout Europe and around the globe.

The jury was out in 1976 (and still is) on whether America has the moral capacity to expand its boundaries to include others, those present, and those who were coming, but he believed if a new birth of freedom were to emerge it would come from a new cadre of leaders who were spiritually disciplined, intellectually astute, and morally anchored. He called these new leaders "apostles of sensitiveness," new ambassadors of courage and hope who were situated in "a time of bivouac on a promontory overlooking the entire landscape of American society."[78]

Thurman hoped for another creative moment for America when these new ambassadors would come forth bearing the dream of community.[79] For him, the eschatological hope for America and the world was bound to the struggle

---

[76] Delivered in the year of the bicentennial celebration of the United States and during the infamous 1975–1976 Boston busing crisis, the lecture underscored HT's concern with racism as an obstacle to Americans' realization of democracy at home and in the world. HT, "America in Search of a Soul," the Robbins Lecture Series, University of the Redlands, Redlands, California, January 20, 1976, in SF, 265–72; and HT, *Democracy and the Soul of America*. HT provided pastoral counsel to one of the families featured in J. Anthony Lukas's definitive account of this painful episode, *Common Ground* (New York: Vintage, 1986), as he had to so many others—Black and white—struggling with racial injustice, and this may partly explain his use of such terms as "schools" and "neighborhoods" as spiritual metaphors. HT, "The Commitment," March 1949, in PHWT 3:309. See also Peter R. Eisenstadt, "'Neighborliness Is Nonspatial': Howard Thurman and the Search for Integration and Common Ground," *Journal of Urban History* 46 (2017): 1206–21.

[77] HT, "America in Search of a Soul," in SF, 269.

[78] HT, SCG, 103.

[79] Ibid., 104.

of oppressed peoples everywhere and the expanding of boundaries, walls, and restrictions of any kind on the freedom and equality of the individual. For those who dared enter the dangerous, no-trespassing zones of race, gender, class, religion, sexuality, territorialism, and physical and mental ability—and all barriers that separated brothers and sisters from one another—he extended to them an invitation to challenge contested democratic spaces because he believed that "community cannot feed for long on itself; it can only flourish where always the boundaries are giving way to the coming of others from beyond them—unknown and undiscovered [sisters and] brothers."[80]

---

[80] Ibid.

Acknowledgments and Editorial Note

Most of the papers in this volume are products of a conference, "The Unfinished Search for Common Ground: The Life and Work of Howard Thurman," at Candler School of Theology, Emory University, April 8–9, 2022. The title "The Unfinished Search for Common Ground," which was the defining theme of his life and ministry, is also taken from Thurman's 1971 book, *The Search for Common Ground*. Born at the turn of the twentieth century in Daytona Beach, Florida, in 1899, during the dehumanizing onslaughts of Jim Crow and segregation, Thurman committed himself to transforming parochial and dogmatic pockets of organized religion into a community transcending barriers of racism, classism, sexism, denominationalism, and religious exclusivism. He died on April 10, 1981, but his legacy lives on in the lives of many, especially those who gathered in person and virtually to join his "unfinished search for common ground."

The editor thanks the authors whose essays are presented in this volume who trusted me with their precious reflections. These essays are the distilled products of their critical analyses and proposals for reimagining Thurman's life and work for this time. The sections and chapters are aligned with the three conference themes. A special thanks is extended to Damellys Sacriste, the Candler Foundry, coordinator of events, grants, and courses, for her scheduling and management of these busy scholars. I am grateful to Robert Ellsberg for his continuing support reflected in this volume and others published by Orbis Books. One of the rare delights of this work is to meet new colleagues who quickly become friends. Jon M. Sweeney, editor-at-large for Orbis Books, certainly deserves this designation. His technical expertise and broad experience are demonstrated here, as well as his very kind and generous spirit.

Four of the essays here were not presented at the conference. A special thanks to Or N. Rose, David Gowler, and Kipton Jensen for their contributions. The editor also expresses his gratitude to Brill Publishers[1] and

---

[1] A revised reprint with permission to publish from Brill Publishers "Sit and Listen; Go and Do: The Parables of the Good Samaritan and Prodigal Son in Howard Thurman's Life and Thought," in *Anatomies of the Gospels and Beyond the Gospels: Essays in Honor of R. Alan*

Westminster John Knox Press[2] for allowing the use of previously published and revised material. In addition, I would like to thank W. James Abbington Jr. for his essay, "Reimagining Howard Thurman's Use of the Negro Spirituals and Hymnody" which was not presented at the conference, but constitutes the background of liturgical performance by Professors Khaliah Williams and Abbington, who led the gathered community in dance and musical celebration of Thurman's experiments in liturgy and common ground.

Some of the texts in this volume are taken from transcriptions of audiotapes; the transcriptions were made under the auspices of the Howard Thurman Educational Trust in the 1970s. When possible, the editor has checked the accuracy of the transcriptions against the original tapes. The editor has silently corrected obvious mistakes and resolvable confusions in the transcriptions and essays. Whenever possible, the editor has included complete quotations from Thurman. In other instances, where full quotes were cumbersome and interfered with the readability and coherence of the author's argument, the editor has assigned a reference in the notes section of the essay.

Throughout his career Thurman used masculine pronouns to refer to persons or people in general, and the editor has not changed his wording. In this regard and others, the editorial procedures used in preparing this volume closely follow the editorial statement in Walter Earl Fluker, ed., *The Papers of Howard Washington Thurman: The Wider Ministry*, vol. 5 (Columbia: University of South Carolina Press, 2019), lvii–lxi.

Culpepper. E. J. Brill Biblical Interpretation Series 164, ed. Elizabeth Struthers Malbon, Mikeal C. Parsons, and Paul N. Anderson (Leiden: E. J. Brill, 2018), 434–51.

[2] See Gregory Ellison's essay in the present volume, "The Unfinished Search from Head to Heart: Howard Thurman's Crossroad Pedagogy," revised and reprinted from Gregory C. Ellison II, *Fearless Dialogues: A New Movement for Justice* (Louisville, KY: Westminster John Knox Press, 2017), 123–29.

About the Contributors

W. James Abbington Jr. is associate professor of church music and worship at Candler School of Theology, Emory University. His research interests include music and worship in the Christian church, African American sacred folk music, organ, choral music, and ethnomusicology. He is also executive editor of the *African American Church Music Series* by GIA Publications, and he has produced numerous recordings under GIA. One of the nation's most respected choir directors, musicians, and authors, Abbington is a popular speaker, performer, and conductor at universities, conferences, symposiums, and churches around the world. From 2000 to 2010, he served as codirector of music for the Hampton University Ministers' and Musicians' Conference, and as national director of music for both the Progressive National Baptist Convention and the NAACP. In 2010, Hampton's Choir Directors and Organists Guild honored Abbington by naming their Church Music Academy after him, and in 2015 he became the second African American to be named a Fellow of the Hymn Society in the United States and Canada.

Amanda Brown is an American intellectual and cultural historian and the author of *The Fellowship Church: Howard Thurman and the Twentieth-Century Religious Left*, the first historical monograph about the Church for the Fellowship of All Peoples. Brown examines nonviolent social movement building tactics that have contemporary relevance, positions Howard Thurman as a pragmatist, establishes his place within modern American intellectual history, and highlights minority agency within the modern American Christian left. She received her PhD in history, a master of arts in American studies from Lehigh University, and has taught at several colleges and universities, including Lehigh University, Monmouth University, and Ocean County College.

Peter Eisenstadt is an affiliate scholar in the history department at Clemson University. He received his doctorate in history from New York University and is the author of *Against the Hounds of Hell: A Life of Howard Thurman*, and the associate editor of the five volumes of the *Papers of Howard Washington Thurman*. With Walter Earl Fluker, he is coeditor of the multivolume *Walking with God:*

The Sermon Series of Howard Thurman, and coauthor with Quinton Dixie of *Visions of a Better World: Howard Thurman's Pilgrimage to India and the Origins of African American Nonviolence.* He was managing editor of the *Encyclopedia of New York City,* editor in chief of the *Encyclopedia of New York State,* and coeditor of the forthcoming *Lincoln's Unfinished Work.* His 2010 book, *Rochdale Village: Robert Moses, 6,000 Families, and New York City's Great Experiment in Integrated Housing,* was awarded the New York Society Library Prize for the best book on New York City history.

Gregory C. Ellison II is associate professor of pastoral care and counseling at Candler School of Theology, Emory University. He is author of *Cut Dead but Still Alive: Caring for African American Young Men* and *Fearless Dialogues: A New Movement for Justice,* and editor of *Anchored in the Current: Discovering Howard Thurman as Guide, Educator, Activist, and Prophet.* He is an ordained Baptist minister who has served on the ministerial staffs at Methodist and Presbyterian churches. Ellison received the master of divinity from Princeton Theological Seminary and PhD in pastoral theology from Emory University. In 2013, he and a team of colleagues founded Fearless Dialogues™, a grassroots initiative committed to creating unique spaces for unlikely partners to engage in hard, heartfelt conversations about taboo subjects. They have gathered over sixty thousand leaders from churches, schools, and Fortune 200 companies for hard, heartfelt conversations domestically and abroad.

Walter Earl Fluker joined the Candler School of Theology faculty as Dean's Professor of Spirituality, Ethics, and Leadership upon his retirement in 2020 from Boston University, where he is Martin Luther King Jr. Professor Emeritus of Ethical Leadership and editor of the Howard Thurman Papers Project. He has served in a number of academic, ministerial, and administrative roles across his career, including pastor of historic St. John's Congregational Church in Springfield, Massachusetts; assistant professor of Christian ethics, Vanderbilt Divinity School and Graduate Department of Religion; dean of Black church studies and Martin Luther King Jr. Professor of Theology at Colgate-Rochester Divinity School; and founding executive director of the Andrew Young Center for Global Leadership and Coca-Cola Professor of Leadership Studies at Morehouse College. Fluker is an internationally regarded consultant, speaker, lecturer, and workshop leader. Select publications include *The Ground Has Shifted: The Future of the Black Church in Post-Racial America* (recipient, Honorable Mention, Theology and Religious Studies PROSE Award); *Ethical Leadership: The Quest for Character, Civility and Community*; the multivolume series, *The Papers of*

Howard Washington Thurman (ed.); and with Peter Eisenstadt, coeditor of the multivolume *Walking with God: The Sermon Series of Howard Thurman* and *Educating Ethical Leaders for the Twenty-First Century*.

David B. Gowler is the Pierce Professor of Religion, Oxford College of Emory University, where he also directs the Pierce Program in Religion and is Senior Faculty Fellow at the Center for Ethics. He received a master's degree in divinity in New Testament from Cambridge University and holds a PhD. He taught at Berry College and was assistant dean for academic affairs, chair of the Religion Department, and professor of religion at Chowan University. Gowler is the author of several books including *What Are They Saying about the Historical Jesus?*, *James through the Centuries*, and *The Parables after Jesus: Their Imaginative Receptions across Two Millennia*. His most recent book is a coedited volume with Kipton Jensen: *Howard Thurman, Sermons on the Parables*. His current writing project is a revised and expanded edition of his *What Are They Saying about the Parables?*

Paul Harvey is Distinguished Professor of History at the University of Colorado, Colorado Springs. Most recently he is the author of *Howard Thurman and the Disinherited* and *Martin Luther King: A Religious Life*. Harvey received the PhD from University of California–Berkeley, and researches, writes, and teaches in the field of American history from the sixteenth century to the present. Harvey is also the author of *Christianity and Race in the American South* and *Bounds of Their Habitation: Religion and Race in American History*. His recent coauthored book, *The Color of Christ: The Son of God and the Saga of Race in America*, was named a Top 25 Outstanding Academic Title by *Choice* magazine.

Anthony Sean Neal is a Beverly B. and Gordon W. Gulmon Humanities Professor at Mississippi State University. He is currently an associate professor of philosophy in the Department of Philosophy and Religion, and a faculty fellow in the Shackouls Honors College, an affiliate with the Department of African American Studies. Neal has also been selected as a Visiting Research Fellow for the Warburg Institute, a unit of the School for Advanced Studies at the University of London. He received his doctorate in humanities from Clark Atlanta University, and his master's in divinity from Mercer University. He is the author of two books: *Common Ground: A Comparison of the Idea of Consciousness in the Writings of Howard Thurman and Huey Newton* and *Howard Thurman's Philosophical Mysticism: Love against Fragmentation*. He serves on the editorial board of *The Acorn: Philosophical Studies in Pacifism and Nonviolence*. His current book project is *A Freedom Gaze: Philosophical Grounding for The Modern Era of the African American Freedom Movement*.

Geshe Lobsang Tenzin Negi is cofounder and director of the Emory-Tibet Partnership, a multidimensional initiative established in 1998 to bring together the foremost contributions of the Western scholastic tradition and the Tibetan Buddhist sciences of mind and healing. A professor of practice in Emory University's Department of Religion, Negi is also the founder and spiritual director of Drepung Loseling Monastery in Atlanta, Georgia. He serves as codirector of both the Emory-Tibet Science Initiative and the Emory Collaborative for Contemplative Studies. Negi has developed Cognitively-Based Compassion Training (CBCT), a compassion meditation program that is utilized in a number of research studies, including an NIH-funded study examining the efficacy of compassion meditation on the experience of depression. A former monk, born in a small Himalayan kingdom adjoining Tibet, Negi began his monastic training at the Institute of Buddhist Dialectics and continued his education at Drepung Loseling Monastery in South India, where he received his Geshe Lharampa degree—the highest academic degree granted in the Tibetan Buddhist tradition.

Or N. Rose is the founding director of the Betty Ann Greenbaum Miller Center for Interreligious Learning & Leadership of Hebrew College. Rabbi Rose has also taught for the Bronfman Youth Fellowships, the Wexner Graduate Fellowship, the Hebrew College Me'ah community education program, and in a variety of other academic, religious, and civic contexts throughout North America and in Israel. He is also copublisher of the *Journal of Interreligious Studies* and the author or editor of many scholarly and popular works on Jewish spirituality, interreligious engagement, and social justice, including *Rabbi Zalman Schachter-Shalomi: Essential Teachings*, coedited with Netanel Miles-Yépez; and *Words to Live By*. He is the creator of the weekly scriptural commentary series *70 Faces of Torah,* and curator of the web-based project *PsalmSeason*.

Luther E. Smith Jr. is Professor Emeritus of Church and Community, Candler School of Theology at Emory University, where he served on the faculty for thirty-five years. He writes and speaks on issues of church and society, congregational renewal, interfaith cooperation, Christian spirituality, and the thought of Howard Thurman. He is the author of *Howard Thurman: The Mystic as Prophet* and *Intimacy and Mission: Intentional Community as Crucible for Radical Discipleship*, and editor of *Howard Thurman: Essential Writings*. He is the senior advisory editor for the five-volume *The Papers of Howard Washington Thurman*. In recognition of his scholarship, teaching, and community service, he has received awards and honors from Morehouse College, the Black Religious Scholars Group, Candler School of Theology, and Phillips School of Theology.

He is a founder of the Interfaith Children's Movement (Georgia) that educates, mobilizes, and networks faith communities in being advocates for all children. He currently serves as coordinator for the Pan-Methodist Campaign for Children in Poverty that mobilizes the churches and theological schools of six Methodist denominations to be active in service to and advocacy for children in poverty.

Shively T. J. Smith serves as assistant professor of New Testament at Boston University School of Theology. She earned her PhD in New Testament at Emory University and is the author of *Strangers to Family: Diaspora and First Peter's Invention of God's Household*, and the forthcoming *Exploring 2 Peter: Bridge to Christian Social Justice*. Smith is currently working on two new projects, one on Howard Thurman and the Bible and the other on nineteenth-century African American women writers and the Bible. She has appeared on the History Channel documentary *Jesus, His Life*, presented at the National Museum of African American History and Culture, and participated in panel discussions on C-SPAN and the White House Historical Association Happy Hour: "Conversations between a First Lady and a University Dean: An Untold Story," featuring correspondence between Howard and Sue Bailey Thurman and Eleanor Roosevelt. Smith is also an ordained itinerant elder in the African Methodist Episcopal Church where she proudly serves as member and resident scholar at the historic Metropolitan AME Church (Washington, DC).

Barbara Brown Taylor is a *New York Times* bestselling author and Episcopal priest who spent fifteen years in parish ministry before joining the faculty of Piedmont University as the Butman Professor of Religion & Philosophy in 1998. During her tenure at Piedmont, she also taught at Columbia Theological Seminary, Candler School of Theology, Oblate School of Theology, and the Arrendale State Prison for Women in Alto, Georgia. A graduate of Emory University and Yale Divinity School, she was named one of the twelve "most effective" preachers in the English-speaking world by Baylor University in 1996. Among her many books are *Learning to Walk in the Dark*, *An Altar in the World*, *Leaving Church*, *Holy Envy*, and *Always a Guest: Speaking of Faith far from Home*.

Index

Against the Hounds of Hell (Eisenstadt), 154
Ambrose, Nancy, 147–48
An American Dilemma (Myrdal), 146
The American Dream, 194
apostles of sensitiveness, 75, 117, 118, 122, 164
   as ambassadors of democracy, 203
   apostles of sensitiveness at work today, 76–79
   describing and defining, 69, 74, 114–15
   eccentricity of, 79, 112
   leadership of, 91, 121, 123, 219
   meeting people where they are, 115, 120
   nature as a path to becoming an apostle, 113
   racial minorities as uniquely qualified, 70
   Schachter-Shalomi as an apostle of sensitiveness, 133
   sermon by Thurman on, 75–76, 115–16
   Thurman as an apostle of sensitiveness, 166
Augustine, Saint, 103, 173, 182, 189

Baldwin, James, 42, 143, 198, 217
Bell, Derrick, 153–54, 155
Beloved (Morrison), 218
Bennett, Lerone, Jr., 154
Berry, Mary Frances, 205
Bessey, Sarah, 78
Béthune, Pierre-François de, 134
Beyond Motivation (Dalai Lama), 118–19
Black Boy (Wright), 142
Black Flesh (Thurman), 204–5, 209
Black liberation philosophy, 180, 181
Black Lives Matter movement, 41, 200
Black Skin, White Masks (Fanon), 183
Blake, Dorsey, 110
Blassingame, John, 205
bodhisattvas, 112

   at the growing, leading edge, 119, 123
   as meeting people where they are, 120–21
   suffering, deliberately engaging with, 115, 116, 118
Boston University (BU), 5, 150, 157, 166, 210, 212. *See also* Marsh Chapel
Bridges, Hal, 83
Brown, Michael, 41
Bucko, Adam, 76
Buddhism, 58, 112, 117
   the Buddha, 113, 121–22
   Buddha crown, 115–16
   buddhahood, 116, 120
   Buddhist-Christian interfaith dialogue, 114
   Buddhist monks, 44, 78
   Tibetan Buddhism, 79, 119
Burleigh, Harry T., 104

Carlyle, Thomas, 171
Cayton, Horace, 142, 143
Center for Spiritual Imagination, 76–77
Chakravorty Spivak, Gayatri, 200
Chandler, Marvin, 7
Chandrakirti, 116
Chicago Defender (periodical), 146
Christian Century (periodical), 166
Chu, Jeff, 78
Church for the Fellowship of All People, 5, 72, 78, 85, 91, 93, 187
   in *Footprints of a Dream,* 30, 101
   former pastors of, 7, 110
   interracial vision of, 63, 143, 164
   pamphlets produced by, 81, 88–89
   sermons given at, 33, 69, 149–50, 158
   Thurman as co-founder, 72, 87, 96, 108–9, 157
   worship style of, 73, 95, 97
   Zeitgeist, in tune with, 90

Collins, George (Shorty), 4
Commerse, Elesa, 47, 48
common ground, 12, 14, 27, 32, 38, 71, 112
  alternative expressions of, 89
  bodhisattvas as seeking, 117, 121–23
  bodily experience, prioritizing, 78
  Christian teachings as a path towards, 51
  continuing search of Thurman for, 1–2, 5, 11, 50, 94, 159–64, 169–70
  liturgy, role in common ground, 94, 96
  loyalty to God as final stance regarding, 13
  Negro spirituals as expressing a yearning for, 101
  new common ground on the horizon, 156
  parables as providing insights on, 52, 54
  reimagining the search for, 3–4, 16–17, 217
  rigor in the search for, 34, 159
  "stuff of life" as compromising, 35–36
  Thurman's prophetic vision for, 8–9, 21–24, 26, 27, 28–29, 37
  See also *The Search for Common Ground*
Common Ground (journal), 144
compassion, 22, 24, 28, 116, 121, 135, 210
  apostles of sensitiveness as addressing, 120, 123
  compassionate motivation, 112–13, 118–19
  empathy as the foundation of compassion, 115, 117
  parable illustrating compassion, 54, 56
  prayers expressing compassion, 122–23
  speech as an act of compassion, 201
  wisdom, complementary nature with, 112
Congress of Racial Equality (CORE), 162, 167
Covey, Edward, 183, 193
COVID-19 pandemic, 74, 92, 155
The Creative Encounter (Thurman), 26–27, 34, 197
critical race theory, 153–54
Cross, George, 206

Dalai Lama, 113, 114, 116, 117, 118–19, 121, 124
dance and the church, 33, 72, 78, 94, 108, 206, 222
Davidson, Sara, 128
Davis, Angela, 196
  on the alienated self, 191, 193–94
  liberation, on the role of resistance in, 187–88
  philosophy of freedom, 180, 182–84
  on slavery and freedom, 185, 186
Dawson, William L., 105
Day, Keri, 213
December Project (Davidson), 128
Deep Is the Hunger (Thurman), 45, 114
Deep River and The Negro Spiritual Speaks of Life and Death (Thurman), 102, 185, 215
  "A Balm in Gilead," reflecting on, 95, 105
  freedom, exploring the meaning of, 182
  "The Negro Speaks of Rivers," examining, 100–101
  "On Viewing the Coast of Africa" section, 184
  river analogies found in, 103–4
Democracy in Black (Glaude), 172
"Democracy is for the Unafraid" (Himes), 144
democratic spaces, 5, 206, 209
  contested democratic spaces, 210, 220
  creating and cultivating democratic space, 202–4, 211, 214
  crossings and, 217, 218
  describing and defining, 199–200
  new possibilities for, reimagining, 16, 216
  religious experience and, 2, 213
  sustainability of democratic space, 215, 219
discernment, 23, 28, 37, 49, 110, 168, 184
  of apostles of sensitiveness, 69
  compassionate motivation complemented by, 112–13, 118–19
  Inner Light as a guide, 213–14
  mentors during the time of, 40
  working paper as a tool of, 47–48
Disciplines of the Spirit (Thurman), 21, 45, 165, 173, 182, 197

INDEX 231

nonviolence, exploring in, 165
reconciliation, on the work of, 192
"Spiritual Resources and Disciplines" course, growing out of, 210–11
Dollard, John, 144, 145
Dorrien, Gary, 83
Douglass, Frederick, 152, 183, 187, 193
DuBois, W. E. B., 160

eccentric apostles, 70, 71, 76, 112, 115, 121
Eiseley, Loren, 209–10
Eisenstadt, Peter, 121–22, 133, 158, 204
Eleanor Clubs, 143
Elijah (Mendelssohn), 106
Ellison, Gregory C., II, 77
Ellison, Gregory C., Sr., 43, 45
Emerson, Ralph Waldo, 143, 181
Emotional Intelligence (Goleman), 118
ethics, 51, 82, 113, 118–19, 121, 122
Evans, Rachel Held, 78
Evolving Faith conference, 78

Face to Face (television program), 61
Faith for Living (Mumford), 145
Fanon, Franz, 183
Farmer, James, 72–73, 162, 167
fascism, 13, 29, 145, 146, 147, 210
"The Fascist Masquerade" (Thurman), 152–52, 159
fear, 110, 147, 149, 176, 186, 193, 204
  Black fear, 141–44, 148, 150, 151, 153
  bodies in opposition to fear, 207, 210
  of the dispossessed, 161, 175–76, 178
  FDR on eradication of fear, 145–46
  as a hound of hell, 140, 155, 161, 163, 201
  as a private emotion and social reality, 139–40
  radical nonviolence as an antidote to fear, 150, 152–53, 155–56, 165, 170
Federation of Indigenous Chiefs of Saskatchewan, 35
Fellowship Church. *See* Church for the Fellowship of All Peoples
Fellowship of Reconciliation, 148
Fisk, Alfred, 72, 96, 143

Fluker, Walter Earl, 45, 95, 99, 121–22, 158, 189
Francis of Assisi, Saint, 122–23
freedom, 2, 12, 35, 92, 153, 173, 187
  actualization of alternatives and potentials in, 75, 193
  American Dream, as part of, 194
  consent and individual freedom, 174
  in democratic space, 213
  the disinherited as struggling for, 155, 183
  fear, freedom from, 146, 155
  growing edge, freedom found at, 181, 195
  identity and freedom, 188–94
  as an indigenous quality of persons, 208
  Martin Luther King on, 162, 166
  mutual recognition and, 194–97
  in Negro spirituals, 102, 155, 186
  personal freedom, 180, 183, 185, 189, 195, 196, 198
  possibility of freedom, exploring, 174–76
  the struggle for others to be free, 176–78
  unfreedom, 182, 183, 184, 185, 188, 196
  the value of freedom, 178–79

Gadamer, Hans-Georg, 34
Gandhi, Mahatma, 107, 161, 170, 171
  American Gandhi, Thurman cast as, 167, 168
  constructive preparation programme and, 194
  Gandhian nonviolence, 86, 150–52, 165, 193
"The Glad Surprise" (Thurman), 36
Glaude, Eddie, 171–72
God and Human Freedom (Young, ed.), 193
Goleman, Daniel, 118
The Good Heart (Dalai Lama), 114
Good Samaritan parable, 52, 53–54, 60–64, 65
The Ground Has Shifted (Fluker), 216

Hagedorn, Hermann, 4, 29
Handel, George F., 108
Harding, Vincent, 154, 155
Hasidic Jews, 124, 131, 132–33
Haverford College, 100, 149

Hegel, Friedrich, 172, 183
"Hegel and Recognition" (Fanon), 183
Heraclitus, 102, 103
Himes, Chester, 144
Hope, John, 148
hospitality, 125, 126–33, 133–35
Howard Thurman (Yates), 15
Howard Thurman Educational Trust, 2, 7, 72
Howard University, 5, 33, 70, 72, 96, 108
Hughes, Langston, 100, 102
"The Hunter" (Schreiner), 4
hymnody, 94–95, 106, 108, 109, 111. *See also* spirituals

Inner Light concept, 213–14
Interdenominational Theological Center (ITC), 6
interreligious dialogue, 12, 114
interreligious hospitality, 133–35
The Inward Journey (Thurman), 44, 189, 197–98
"The Inward Sea" (Thurman), 31

Jackson, Jesse, 158
James, William, 144
Jefferson, Thomas, 172–73
Jesus and the Disinherited (Thurman), 23, 30, 45, 158, 175, 182
  Black fear, exploring, 146–47
  "The Fascist Masquerade," reading in conjunction with, 151–52
  first-century context for Jesus, providing, 50–51
  Martin Luther King, as an influence on, 162
  nonviolence, addressing, 122, 150
  the oppressed, on Jesus as representing, 161
  slavery, grappling with Christian support for, 175
  spiritual reflection, as a work of, 146–47
  on the three hounds of hell, 140–41
  white necessity, on the abandonment of, 155
Jesus Christ, 52, 77, 111, 121, 122, 130
  community, focus on the building of, 182, 190
  as a dangerous figure, 26–27
  first-century context for, 50–51
  Good Samaritan parable and, 60, 62–63, 64, 65
  in Negro spirituals, 102, 106–8
  the oppressed in American society, representing, 161
  Prodigal Son parable and, 54–56, 58–60, 65
  the religion of Jesus, 157, 163, 187
  On the Rocks, portrayal in, 139
  voice of the genuine in Jesus, 188
Jim Crow segregation, 29, 87, 147, 162
Johnson, James Weldon, 55–56, 59
Jones, Rufus, 100, 149, 168

Katznelson, Ira, 145
Keen, Sam, 7
King, Martin Luther, Jr., 42, 86, 151, 157, 165
  correspondence with Thurman, 209–10
  domesticating the message of, 22
  as mentored by Thurman, 117, 157, 162, 166–68
  the urgency of now, calling attention to, 199

Lawson, James, 170
"Lectures on Liberation" (Davis), 180, 187
"Letters of Old Age" (Petrarch), 201–2
Lincoln, Abraham, 100, 172
"Lines from an Unknown Soldier" (Hagedorn), 29
The Living Wisdom of Howard Thurman (audio recording), 32
Lloyd, William Freeman, 106
The Luminous Darkness (Thurman), 175, 189–90, 192
Luna, Pat, 77

Mahayana Buddhism, 115
mantras, 48–49
Marsh Chapel, 46, 190
  Good Friday service, 95, 105–8

INDEX

inclusive worship experiences, featuring, 132
Thurman as dean, 33, 63, 70, 72, 97–98, 109, 125, 128–33, 134–35
Marx, Karl, 183, 187
Mays, Benjamin, 88, 142, 143, 150
McCarthy, Joseph, 150
McFague, Sallie, 36–37
meditation, 158, 191, 192
   Eastern meditation, 79, 82
   meditation spaces, setting up, 87, 126
   as a preliminary practice, 84, 211
   sermons, meditation before, 52, 58, 73, 97
   worship services, meditation as part of, 105, 110
Meditations of the Heart (Thurman), 31
Metaphorical Theology (McFague), 37
Mirabehn (Madeleine Slade), 171
Mitchell, Mozella, 99, 180
moral imagination, 10–11, 11–14, 17, 216
Morrison, Toni, 218
Mount Zion Baptist Church, 96
Mumford, Lewis, 145
Murray, Pauli, 167
Myrdal, Gunnar, 146
mysticism, 5, 73, 88, 90, 124, 182, 206
   affirmation mysticism, 83
   Christian mystics, 149, 169
   interfaith practice as initiating mystical experience, 87
   Quaker mystics, Thurman training with, 170
   spiritual trees of reflection and, 113
   Thurman as a mystic, 57–58, 83–84, 86, 157, 159, 161, 168, 181
   twentieth-century interest in, 82
"My Times Are in Thy Hands" (hymn), 106

Naboth (biblical figure), 207
Narrative (Douglass), 183
Native Son (Wright), 142
"*A 'Native Son' Speaks*" (Thurman), 141–42
Negi, Lobsang Tenzin, 79
"The Negro in the City" (Thurman), 141
"The Negro Speaks of Rivers" (poem), 100–101

Negro spirituals. *See* spirituals
Nietzsche, Friedrich, 171
nonviolence, 27, 159, 161, 166, 168, 170, 198
   the danger moment problem and, 153
   Fellowship Church, nonviolent activism of, 87
   as a fundamental philosophical principle, 165
   Gandhian nonviolence, 86, 150–51, 167
   orderly recklessness of, 155–56
   racial justice based on the principles of, 162
   radical nonviolence, 14, 150, 151, 152, 155
   social change, as an instrument for, 192
   spiritual commitment, requiring, 158

On the Rocks (Shaw), 139

Panchen Lama, 117, 120
Papers of Howard Washington Thurman (PHWT), 141
pastoral work of Howard Thurman
   crossroad pedagogy of Thurman, 40–41
   Good Friday service at Boston University, 95, 105–8
   Good Samaritan parable, expounding on, 52, 53–54, 60–64, 65
   as a liturgist, 94, 95, 96, 98
   Prodigal Son parable as foundational to, 52, 53–54, 54–60, 65
   the sacred in worship, vision of, 98–99
   silence, use of, 33, 97, 105, 110, 113, 176, 206
   verbal aesthetic, 33–35, 35–38
   See also Church for the Fellowship of All People
Pelikan, Jaroslav, 109
Petrach, Francesco, 201
Pittsburgh Courier (periodical), 142
Pollard, Alton, 88
post-evangelicals, 77–78
practice as a spiritual tool, 199, 201–2, 210, 211, 215–19

prayer, 27, 42, 84, 97, 131, 159, 191
  compassion for humanity, expressing in prayer, 122–23
  hunger of the heart pursued through prayer, 192
  in *Meditations of the Heart,* 31
  nonviolence and prayer, 158
  prayer space, making accommodating, 126–30
  segregation, praying for cessation of, 164
  sermons, prayerful meditation before, 52, 58, 73
  Shaharit morning prayers, 126–27
  as a spiritual tool, 8, 211
  Thurman experiences with prayer, 21, 30, 131, 212
preparation as a spiritual tool, 199, 202, 210–12, 215
Presence, 199, 202, 210, 211, 212–15, 217
Principles of Psychology, 144
Proctor Institute for Child Advocacy, 78
"Prodigal Son" (poem), 55–56, 59
Prodigal Son parable, 52, 54–60, 65, 188

Quakerism, 159, 168, 170, 213

Rancière, Jacques, 199–200, 202
Rankin Chapel, 5, 33, 70, 72–73, 96, 108–9
Resist Harm initiative, 77
Rohr, Richard, 76, 78
Roosevelt, Eleanor, 88, 143
Roosevelt, Franklin Delano, 145, 146
Rosenwein, Barbara, 147
Ruach Hadodesh (Spirit of Holiness), 129, 130

samsara (conditioned world of suffering), 113
Sanders, Cheryl J., 107
Schachter-Shalomi, Zalman, 124–25, 126–27, 128–33, 134–35, 210–11
Schreiner, Olive, 4
The Search for Common Ground (Thurman), 30, 38, 73, 83–84
  community, on the notion of, 177, 197
  freedom, exploring the topic of, 182

as last theological work of Thurman, 21, 166
self-absorption, 112–13, 118
sermons of Howard Thurman, 32, 33, 52, 60, 69, 154, 161
  "Apostles of Sensitiveness," 75–76, 115–16
  "Community of Fear," 150
  democracy, sermons on, 149–50, 207
  Fellowship Church, last sermon at, 158–59
  "Freedom," 182
  "Growing Edge," 80
  King, Thurman quoted in sermons of, 162
  "Lost Sheep and Lost Coin," 56
  "Love of God," 59
  "Meaning of Loyalty III," 13–14
  "Prodigal Son," 56, 58
  "Quest for Peace and Responsibility," 24–25
  reading, opening sermons with, 139
  "Religion of Jesus," 190
  spirituals, series of sermons on, 101
  "Your Life's Working Paper—Commitment," 46
shamans, 99
Shantideva of Nalanda, 122, 123
Shaw, George Bernard, 139
"Silent Night, Holy Night" (hymn), 106, 108
sin, 54, 64, 106, 169
Smith, Luther, 3, 41, 44, 190
Society of Friends. *See* Quakerism
social concerns of Howard Thurman
  ancillary struggles of the oppressed, identifying, 175–76
  atomic bombings, on Americans' responsibility for, 24–26
  on the basic community, 177
  Black bodies, reflections on, 204–10
  Black fear, addressing, 140–41, 143, 146–52
  on the darkness of the times, 145
  democracy, extended consideration of, 149–50
  democratic space, cultivating, 202–4

Index

free speech, on the integrity and power of, 201–2
friendly world, on the creation of, 60, 94, 113
on harmony, 8, 11, 13, 22, 82, 180, 188, 197
islands of goodwill, desire to build, 81, 88, 89, 93
local level, on social change starting at, 81, 89
on meeting people where they are, 75, 115, 120
peaceful community, on the human longing to create, 83–84
on racism, 23, 24, 27, 74, 82, 85, 157, 169
religious experience, on its relationship with social change, 82, 84–86
speech and speeches, 22, 199, 202
   America in search of its soul, Thurman speech on, 219
   "Deep River," Thurman speech on, 102
   democratic space and, 16, 203, 211, 216
   equality and freedom, speech as a mark of, 200
   FDR's freedom-from-fear speech, 146
   integrity and power of free speech, 201–2
   public speech, 12, 33
   speech acts of Thurman, 32, 34
   Zelenskyy speech before UN Security Council, 77
Spellman College, 100, 149
spirituals, 149, 186, 215
   "Balm in Gilead," 95, 101, 104–5
   "Deep River," 95, 100–104, 184–85
   hymnody and, 108, 109, 111
   as making something out of nothing, 154–55
   protest music, as more than, 160–61
   "Were You There?," 95, 106, 107
   worship, use of spirituals in, 94–95, 104
Stewart, Carlyle Felding, III, 193
Student Nonviolent Coordinating Committee (SNCC), 170
suffering, 107, 121, 161, 191, 213

apostles of sensitiveness as responding to, 74, 115
bodhisattvas as deliberately engaging with, 116, 118
Buddhist contemplation of, 113, 117, 122
Fellowship Church as a respite from, 88
as a spiritual discipline, 8, 192, 211
tong-len practice and, 119–20

Taylor, Barbara Brown, 85, 92, 112, 115, 121
Tennyson, Alfred, 102
Tesfamariam, Rahiel, 42
Thoreau, Henry David, 191
Thurman, Anne Spencer, 7
Thurman, Howard
   Bigger Thomas character, comparing to, 141–42
   common ground, search for, 1–2, 5, 11, 50, 94, 159–64, 169–70
   contemplations on living, 171, 173
   dreams, on saddling them before riding, 15–16
   eccentricity, as marked by, 70–74, 85
   Fellowship Church, as co-founder, 72, 87, 96, 108–9, 157
   the fringes, operating from, 85, 86
   Ingersoll Lectures, 37, 100
   Marsh Chapel, as dean of, 33, 63, 70, 72, 97–98, 109, 125, 128–33, 134–35
   Martin Luther King as mentored by, 117, 157, 162, 166–68
   on the moral imagination, 10–11, 11–14, 216
   as a mystic, 57–58, 83–84, 86, 157, 159, 161, 168, 181
   nature, importance to, 21, 33, 71, 83, 113, 148, 159, 168, 209
   Negro spirituals, writings on, 100–105, 184–88
   new, potential audience for, 90
   the now, on the spiritual disciplines of, 165–70
   oak tree, friendship with, 5, 6, 26, 71, 113
   oral presentations of, 30–32, 38–39

Thurman, Howard *(continued)*
  as a philosopher of freedom, 180, 181–84, 188–90, 198
  prayer and, 21, 30, 131, 212
  prophetic vision of common ground, 8–9, 21–24, 26, 27, 28–29, 37
  Rankin Chapel, as dean of, 5, 33, 70, 72–73, 96, 108
  on spirituals and making something out of nothing, 154–55
  tools of the spirit, recognizing, 210–19
  unfinished search of, 1–2, 4–7, 11–14, 50, 94
  on unity, 21, 22, 33, 35, 87, 95, 98, 148, 181, 191, 198
  on wholeness, 22, 82, 83, 99, 177, 180, 181–82, 188, 190–91, 203
  "working paper" theme in writings, 45–46, 47, 49
  See also pastoral work of Howard Thurman; sermons of Howard Thurman; social concerns of Howard Thurman
Thurman, Sue Bailey, 7, 166
tong-len practice, 119–20
tools of the spirit, 16, 184, 199, 203–4, 210–19
Toward a True Kinship of Faiths (Dalai Lama), 114
Toynbee, Arnold, 16
Tozer, A. W., 109
trees, 5, 6, 26, 71, 112, 113
Truman, Harry, 25
Turner, Nat, 187

"Ulysses" (poem), 102
"The Unfinished Search for Common Ground" (conference), 69
United Methodist Church, 77

Varieties of Religious Experience (James), 82
Victory over Fear (Dollard), 145–46

Waal, Frans de, 117
Ward, Bob, 64
"We Are Climbing Jacob's Ladder" (spiritual), 101, 149
"We Shall Overcome" (anthem), 151
West, Cornel, 42, 189
"What Child Is This?" (hymn), 106, 108
"What Do I Want, Really?" (Thurman), 42–43
Wild Goose Festival, 77–78
Williams, Robert C., 98–99
Wilson, Starsky, 42
With Head and Heart (Thurman), 154, 187
"working paper" concept, 45–47, 47–49
worship, 33, 38, 97
  Christian worship space, modifying, 127–28, 130, 132, 134
  at Fellowship Church, 73, 87–88, 96–97, 158
  Negro spirituals, use in worship, 101, 104
  religious experiences arising from, 21, 84
  the sacred in worship, Thurman's vision of, 98–99
  Thurman as a worship leader, 60, 72, 94–95, 98, 106, 108–11
  at Wild Goose Festival, 77–78
"Worship and Anti-Structure in Thurman's Vision of the Sacred" (Williams), 98–99
Wright, Richard, 142, 143, 146

Yates, Elizabeth, 15, 55

Zelenskyy, Volodymyr, 77
Zimmerman, Joyce, 110